French Dramatists
of the
Nineteenth Century

French Dramatists
of the
Nineteenth Century

by

Brander Matthews

Third Edition, Enlarged

BENJAMIN BLOM New York/London

First published 1901
Reissued 1968 by Benjamin Blom, Inc.
Bronx, N.Y. 10452
and 56 Doughty Street, London W.C. 1

Library of Congress Catalog Card No. 68-20239

Printed in the United States of America

TO

EDMUND CLARENCE STEDMAN.

κρέσσον μελπομένω τεῦ ἀκουέμεν ἢ μέλι λείχεν.
THEOC. viii. 83.

PREFACE.

IT is not yet sixty years since the Romanticists and the Classicists first met in battle-array; and it is but little more than fifty years since Hernani sounded his trumpet, and the hollow walls of Classicism fell with a final crash. This half-century is a period of no slight importance in the history of the drama: it is one of the two epochs when the plays of France have been conspicuously and incomparably superior to the plays of any other country; the earlier epoch was when the French stage saw in rapid succession the newest works of Corneille, of Molière, and of Racine. Although, with our ownership of Shakspere constantly in mind, we may not be willing to allow that the French have reached the highest pinnacle of the drama, we can see clearly enough that it is in the drama that they have mounted highest. If we seek to know why this is, why they have done better work in the drama than in any other department of literature, it is easy (although

perhaps not altogether sufficient) to answer that it is
because the dramatic is the form best suited for the
expression of certain qualities in which the French
excel the men of other races. Chief among these
national characteristics are a lively wit, a love of effect
for its own sake, a gift for writing beautiful prose,
and a passion for order and symmetry and clearness. These are precious qualities to the dramatist;
and, just as they did their share toward the beauty of
the comedy and the tragedy which amused and moved
the people of Paris and the court of the king in the
age of Louis XIV., so they now help to make the
present drama of France what it is. The plays of
Corneille, of Molière and of Racine, have been written
about superabundantly; while, so far as I know, the
story of the more modern French drama has nowhere
been told. Now and again one may chance on the
portrait of an individual, but a picture of the whole
period is not to be found anywhere. For this reason,
I have sought in the following pages to give an outline
of the course of the drama in France from the first
quarter of this century to the present time. In the
attempt to embrace the whole I have been forced to
neglect some of the parts, and to pass with but casual
attention over more than one dramatist of note, — Casimir Delavigne, for example, Alfred de Musset (who,
in spite of his genius and of the latter-day success of
certain of his comedies, was a dramatist only second-

arily, and, so to speak, by accident), François Ponsard, and Mme. de Girardin, among the dead; M. Jules San-deau, M. Ernest Legouvé, M. Édouard Pailleron, and M. Edmond Gondinet, among the living.

In an earlier and less complete condition, most of the chapters which make up the book have already appeared here and there in various reviews and magazines. Before taking its appointed place in these pages, each chapter has been carefully revised, often enlarged, and in all cases "brought down to date." Space has been found for more minute criticism and for more ample quotation than was possible in the scant quarters of a serial. It will be noted that the French titles of plays have been turned into English whenever a translation appeared possible and profitable; and the use of French has been conscientiously avoided, save where no English equivalent could be found for a technical term, and in an occasional specimen quotation of the verse of Victor Hugo or Émile Augier, to which no translation would do justice.

I take pleasure in expressing my thanks here to a friend, who, in spite of our constant disagreement as to the relative value of M. Augier and M. Dumas, has lent me the aid of his literary skill and of his knowledge of the modern French drama, as he did before, when the 'Theatres of Paris' was passing through the press.

B. M.

NEW YORK, October, 1881.

NOTE TO THIRD EDITION.

To the second edition of this book, published in 1891, there was added a chapter covering the years of the ninth decade; and the present edition is now enlarged by a final chapter considering the condition of the French drama at the end of the nineteenth century.

COLUMBIA UNIVERSITY, February, 1901.

CONTENTS.

FRENCH DRAMATISTS

19th CENTURY.

CHAPTER I.

THE ROMANTIC MOVEMENT.

"THERE is in every thing a maturity which must be waited for," said Chamfort; "happy the man who arrives at the moment of this maturity!" Toward the end of the first quarter of this century it was evident, to any one who had eyes to see, that a moment of maturity in the history of the French drama was soon coming. The time was ripe for a new growth. Elsewhere in literature and in art, there was the murmur of new life; in prose fiction and in poetry, there had been a new birth; even on the stage there were beginning to be signs of the coming of new blood. And nowhere else was there as much need of a renascence as in the theatre, where all was chill and lifeless.

During the imperial rule of Napoléon the position of the Parisian theatres had been peculiar. They were under the direct control of the General Government, represented at the fall of the empire by M. de Rémusat. They were limited in number; and the style of play each could perform was rigidly prescribed by the imperial decree. To one theatre the production of *opéras-comiques* was permitted, and nothing else; to another, *vaudevilles;* to a third, melodramas; while to the Théâtre Français was reserved the exclusive right to perform the pieces of the classic repertory. The comedies and tragedies of Corneille, Molière, Racine, Regnard, Marivaux, Voltaire, and Beaumarchais, could be seen on the stage of the Théâtre Français, and nowhere else. This lack of liberty brought about the usual result of restriction, — a dearth of novelty and a desolating monotony. The imperial interference was, in part at least, responsible for the low condition into which French dramatic literature was sinking in the first ten years of the Bourbon restoration. At the Théâtre Français comedy was almost childish, and tragedy was in its dotage: there was neither action nor animation; all was dull, dreary, and commonplace. Now and again, in a minor theatre, there was an attempt at something less constrained: *opéra-comique* was beginning its lively career; the national *vaudeville* had been renewed by Eugène Scribe, who had stamped it forever with his own image and superscription; and Pixérécourt and Victor Ducange had made themselves masters of melodrama imported from Germany, and were using it to wring all hearts.

But the official theatre and the official critics chose to ignore, even the existence of *vaudeville* and melodrama, or at best, to regard them as wholly inferior forms of art, if indeed they were not altogether beyond the pale of art. The attitude of the French critics toward such unliterary plays as *vaudevilles* and melodramas was not unlike that of a cultivated New-Yorker toward the old Bowery Theatre, or that of a cultivated

Londoner toward the similar Transpontine houses. Such places might serve to amuse the vulgar throng; but the plays acted therein were too far removed from literature to call for criticism, or even consideration. The new comedies and tragedies brought out from time to time by the Comédie-Française received all the more consideration and criticism: they were judged according to a code of Draconian severity; and if they broke one jot or tittle of the dramatic law, if they were found wanting in one iota of dramatic decorum, condign and exemplary punishment was at once visited upon the hapless author. In general, however, authors and critics were quite comfortably agreed on what was fit and proper and in accordance with the dignity of the drama. To be dignified was the chief end of the dramatist, and both tragedy and comedy were constantly taking lessons in deportment. Never to infringe upon the rules laid down by Boileau, and discussed by numberless commentators, was an equal duty. Slowly and surely the desire to do nothing outside of the rules, or in any way indecorous, was choking all life out of the drama. As Mr. Saintsbury aptly puts it, "Each piece was expected to resemble something else, and originality was regarded as a mark of bad taste and insufficient culture." The French drama of the first quarter of this century is the empty echo of a hollow past. Its aim was to equal Voltaire. Voltaire had admiringly copied Racine; Racine had sought to reproduce in French the tragedy of the Greeks as he saw it, chiefly through the medium of the Latin adaptations; and thus there was imitation of an imitation, and no end. "French tragedy," said Goethe, "is a parody of itself." If the great critic thought this of the tragedy of Voltaire, what must he have thought of the tragedy of Voltaire's feeble followers?

The trademark of a tragedy, according to the rules, was the blind obedience paid to the "unities." The French critics pretended to derive from Aristotle a law that a dramatic poem should show *one* action happening in *one* place in the space of *one* day: these were the unities of action, place, and time. As to the unity of action, there need be no dispute: any work of art must have a single distinct motive and mainspring. But both the unity of time, which compelled the hurried massing of all the straggling incidents of a tale into the course of twenty-four hours; and the unity of place, which forbade all change of scene, — these were absurdities. In 1629 a Frenchman, Mairet, had brought out at Rouen an imitation of the Italian Trissino's 'Sofonisba,' in which the three unities appeared for the first time. Corneille early gave in his adhesion to the principle, but found it hard to reconcile his practice. Although the Italians and French supposed that they were imitating the ancients, it is a fact that the unities of time and place were not erected among the Greek tragedians into a principle, nor does Aristotle lay them down as laws.[1] He says nothing at all as to the unity of place; and in speaking of the unity of time he probably meant merely to declare the habitual practice among the best dramatists. It is safe to say that not Æschylus, Sophocles, nor Euripides ever gave a thought to either the unity of time or the unity of place. By accident, and because of the physical condi-

[1] For an elaborate discussion of the subject, with abundant citation of authorities, see the 'Dramatic Unities in the Present Day,' by Edwin Simpson. London. Trübner, 1874.

tions of the Greek theatre, they had to condense their story as well as they could, and to be sparing of change of scene. That they did not hesitate to shift the place of action when it suited their purpose, there can be no doubt. The 'Hecuba' of Euripides is an instance, and others are not wanting.

The simplicity, the directness, and, above all, the unconsciousness to which the Greek drama owed so much of its poetry and its power, were qualities wholly foreign to the French court of Louis XIV., and they were neither appreciated there, nor in the main even understood. The severity and stately dignity of the Greek drama, in great part the result of the circumstances under which it was acted, were foreign to the turbulent and fiery tragedy of Corneille, produced under wholly different conditions and in a wholly altered state of society, with far more complex emotions. The Greek actor, raised in lofty buskins, and speaking through a resonant mask, that he might be seen and heard by the vast multitude seated before him in the open amphitheatre, was thus hampered from all violent action, and achieved perforce a certain stateliness. But the French actor, in the rich and elaborate costume of his own time, declaimed his verses in a small hall, before a select audience, many of whom had seats upon the stage, crowding the performers into a narrow lane between these rows of spectators, and into a narrow space between these spectators and the footlights. To attempt to reproduce, under these conditions, the massive dignity of the Greek stage, was to attempt the impossible. Of a certainty, the result would be literary merely, and not lifelike. It is not to be denied that the regularity and concentration and nudity imposed on the dramatist by the observance of the three unities may at times have helped the writer of genius, who is but the stronger for the difficulties he struggles with : the feeble, however, were made more feeble still ; and even a writer of genius, like Corneille, chafed against rigid restrictions he was not flexible enough to get around. It is pitiful to see how the virile and vigorous Corneille, in his three discourses on dramatic composition, humbles himself before the shadow of Aristotle and the ancients, and begs to be allowed to stretch the "single day" to, say, thirty hours, and to take as the "single place" a whole town, in different parts of which the action may go on. How the bonds hampered the poet is summed up concisely in the judgment which the Academy, at Richelieu's order, passed on Corneille's best play, the 'Cid,' to the effect that the poet, in endeavoring to observe the rules of art, had chosen rather to sin against those of nature.

Racine's calmer genius worked without revolt under the rules which pinioned Corneille : he found his account in them. To him his characters were of first importance, and what they felt and thought and said ; whereas Corneille was concerned chiefly with the action, and with what his people did, — what they might have to say was of less interest. When action was proscribed, and little was done, and every thing was talked about, Corneille chafed against the tightening bonds ; but Racine seemed to dance best in fetters. And as Racine came after Corneille, and became the foremost tragic writer of the magnificent court of Louis XIV., the courtly graces with which he had endowed tragedy were afterward inseparable from it.

So the frank and free-spoken drama of Corneille gave way before the fine-lady muse of Racine, — not any weaker, it may be, but more polished and mannered. The twist once given, French tragic drama turned more and more away from nature, and became more and more artificial and barren. Later came Voltaire, who was never tired of finding fault with Corneille, and had nothing but praise for Racine. He gave in to the pseudo-unities of time and place, although with characteristic ingenuity he evaded them, while pretending to be bound by them. Voltaire even refined on his predecessor. He had a horror of the colloquial : he screwed dramatic diction two or three turns higher, and still farther from nature. For his fastidious taste, even Greek tragedy was too simple and too familiar. He never by any chance allowed to pass any of those homely words which reach the heart so readily : these were banished, and a dignified periphrasis took their place.

Voltaire, after all, was a man of genius, however false his doctrines ; and the full feebleness of which French tragedy was capable, when it was made according to his precepts, was evident only after his death and in the works of his followers, — men of moderate talent, able to copy correctly the faults of their elders and betters. In their hands the tragic drama lost what little life it had left, and the red heels of Racine lengthened into unmistakable stilts. There were not wanting those who now and then inveighed against long monologues, and the two false unities, and the device of confidants ; but the admirers of "dignity" and "correctness" made a firm front against these barbarians. As time went on, tragedy went from bad to worse.   Even in the hot days of the Revolution, even in the carnage of '93, the Théâtre Français continued to bring forth vapid and innocuous classical tragedies.   With the return of order and the subsequent worship of Republican Greece and Rome, the so-called classic drama got the benefit of the craze for antiquity.   When Napoleon was first consul, and after he was firmly seated on the throne, every thing was still more pseudo-classic.   In tragedy, as in sculpture and in painting, subjects were chosen almost exclusively from Greek and Roman history and legend. Napoleon was anxious to have a great dramatist to illustrate his reign.   He fostered tragedy as well as he knew how: but the conditions were not favorable; the moment of maturity had not yet come; and somehow or other the great dramatist refused to be made to order.

The fall of Napoleon and the restoration of the Bourbons made no change in literary fashions.   The returning exiles found the tragic drama as they had left it.   In 1792, the year before the Terror, the good Ducis had produced his 'Othello,' in which a *bandeau* is the token of guilt, and the Moor stabs his wife, instead of smothering her; for the sight, or even the mention, of so low and common a thing as a handkerchief or a pillow would have been fatal to the proper elevation of tragedy.   In 1815, when the Bourbons sat again on the throne of their fathers, there was the same painful effort after "dignity" and "correctness."   Holding that action or even violent emotion was unseemly, every thing was told, and nothing was done.   As Victor Hugo put it in the preface to his 'Cromwell,' published in 1827, "Instead of scenes, we have narrations; instead of pictures, descriptions. Grave personages, placed like a Greek chorus between us and the drama, come and tell us what is taking place in the temple, in the palace, in the public place, until we are tempted to call out to them, 'Truly? Then why do you not take us there? It must be amusing, it must be well worth seeing.'" Still worse, not only was real emotion proscribed, but also the simple, homely, heartfelt words in which real emotion is wont to show itself. The language of tragedy had to be literary, and without any phrase plucked from the roots of humanity, and racy of the soil. The words such as Shakspere was wont to use without stint, simply and nobly, were shunned for a roundabout pomposity. The simple and direct word, to obtain which without baldness is the highest poetry, was always avoided. In its stead were strained and stilted verses, in which an infantine idea was swaddled in long robes of verbiage. By a process of selection and purification the vocabulary had become extremely impoverished. No welcome was extended to new words, and good old words were constantly getting thrust aside because they lacked "dignity." There was a steady attempt to reach the grand style by the use of big words, and to attain elevation by standing on tip-toe. Laced in a tight corset thus, poor tragedy could scarcely breathe, and was, indeed, well-nigh at its last breath. Yet it died hard. Talma, whom Carlyle notes as incomparably the finest actor he ever saw, asked for Shakspere, and got Ducis, and left the stage without having played one part really worthy of him. All over the tragic drama was the abomination of desolation.

By the end of the first quarter of this century, how-

ever, the moment of maturity approached, and the time
began to be ripe for revolt against the rigid restraints
and monotonous mannerism of the Classicists.   During
the forcible-feeble reign of the Bourbons, a new generation, born in the thick of the Napoleonic combats and
conquests, had grown to manhood.   It was restless
and militant, and it had a congenital impatience of
inherited authority.   A change came over the spirit
of the scene : instead of a slumber like unto death, there
were signs of a general awakening.   In all departments of art there were wars, and rumors of wars.
The effect of Mme. de Staël's precepts on the one
hand, and of Chateaubriand's practice on the other,
was beginning to be felt.   Byron and Scott, and our
own Cooper, were getting themselves read in France
as no foreign authors ever had been read there.   A
knowledge of Goethe and of Schiller was spreading
slowly.   Weber's 'Freischütz,' sadly mutilated, it is
true, was sung with success.   In art, pictorial and
plastic, in architecture, in music as well as in poetry,
both lyric and dramatic, there was turmoil and ebul-
lition.   From Byron, in a measure, came a spiritual
unrest and a mild misanthropic pessimism ; and from
Germany came a certain tendency to vehement exaggeration.   Like the movement headed by Wordsworth,
the movement headed by Hugo was "a great movement of feeling, not a great movement of mind."

The publication of Victor Hugo's 'Odes et Ballades'
was the signal for a general revolt against the established forms ; and it began to be evident that an artistic
revolution impended, although where the first rising
might be expected was doubtful.   But in 1827 the best
actors of England — Kean, Young, Charles Kemble, and

Macready — crossed the Channel, and revealed the English drama to the Parisians. No greater contrast could well be imagined than the tumultuous action of Shakspere, and the decorous declamation of French classic tragedy. One enthusiastic admirer of the English performances said to Charles Kemble, "Othello! voilà, voilà la passion, la tragédie. Que j'aime cette pièce! il y a tant de *remue-ménage!*" [1] In December, 1827, a few weeks after the English actors had left Paris, Victor Hugo published his 'Cromwell,' a historical drama in five acts, accompanied by a preface, which was at once a protest against the prevailing taste, a plan of reform, and a declaration of war. Obviously the theatre was to be the battle-ground of the factions: nowhere else could they fight hand to hand and face to face; nowhere else would there be so stubborn a resistance to the new gospel.

In every group there is an individuality, acting as a pivot, around which the others gravitate, just as a system of planets revolves around the sun. Among the impatient romanticists this central individuality was Victor Hugo. He was the happy man, who, to use Chamfort's phrase cited at the beginning of this chapter, "arrived at the moment of maturity." More multifarious and of higher genius than any of his companions-in-arms, Hugo was well fitted to be a chief. He was void of fear, and he believed in himself. His friends and followers believed in him and in the righteousness of their common cause, and they made ready for battle. The political debates and disturbances which

---

[1] "There, there's passion for you, and tragedy! How I love that play! There is so much of a rumpus in it." — Mrs. KEMBLE's 'Recollections of a Girlhood.' New York: Holt, 1879. p. 115.

led to the final fall of the Bourbons, in 1830, were scarcely more acrimonious than the contemporaneous romantic attacks on the Classicism which, like the exiled family, had learnt nothing, and forgotten nothing. "Something of the intensity of the *odium theologicum* (if, indeed, the *æstheticum* be not in these days the more bitter of the two) entered into the conflict," wrote Lowell of the war of critics, which began when Wordsworth proclaimed himself the prophet of a new poetic dispensation. And Hugo's disciples were like Wordsworth's, in that "the verses of the master had for them the virtue of religious canticles, stimulant of zeal, and not amenable to the ordinary tests of cold-blooded criticism."

Second only to Hugo, if, indeed, second even to him, came Alexandre Dumas, whose 'Henri III.' was to shock the staid frequenters of the Théâtre Français, and to achieve an indisputable and unexpected success a full year before Hugo's 'Hernani' was acted. Next came Alfred de Vigny, whose 'More de Vénise' also won a triumph at the Théâtre Français before the final fight over the first acted play of Hugo. Besides these three leaders, there were Charles Nodier (much the oldest of them all), Gerard de Nerval, Théophile Gautier, Auguste Maquet, Joseph Bouchardy, and many another as ardent for the cause as the chief himself.

Ranged in battle-array over against the irregular band of Romanticists were the serried ranks of the Classicists, — men full of years and honors, and all so carefully forgotten now of the public that their names can be recalled only with an effort, even by the professed student of the stage of that time. Between the combatants, a little off at one side, and perhaps a trifle nearer to the Romanticists than to the Classicists, was a tiny group of conservatives, who stood halting between the old and the new. In his entertaining account of this phase in the history of French dramatic literature, Alphonse Royer considers this group of conservatives as Classicists, holding that those who were not for the Romanticists were against them. Consequently he divides the Classicists into two sets, the pure Classicists and the mitigated Classicists; designating by this latter name those whom I have called the conservatives. The pure Classicists were the no-surrender and die-in-the-last-ditch party, who brooked no compromise with the Romanticists, and who always voted the straight ticket. The mitigated Classicists, or conservatives, were the more amiable persons, who confessed some of the failings and abuses of the existing state of things, but believed in "reform within the party."

The little knot of the mitigated, who thus sought safety in the middle path, had for its chief Casimir Delavigne, remembered now as the author of 'Louis XI.' The only other authors of any permanent value belonging to this group were Lebrun, whose 'Marie Stuart' is still remembered; and Soumet, whose tragedy, 'Norma,' is familiar to all as the book of Bellini's opera. Great was the dismay among the pure Classicists when Casimir Delavigne quit the camp, and set up for himself as the chief of a new sect, conciliatory and conservative, — when, in 1829, he chose the Porte St. Martin Theatre, instead of the Théâtre Français, to produce his 'Marino Falièro,' based on Byron, as his 'Louis XI.' had been made out of Scott's 'Quentin Durward.' In like manner his later drama, the 'Enfants d'Edouard,' was taken from Shakspere. And this frequency of imitation was characteristic of the timid talents of Delavigne. His plays lacked boldness, and his verse lacked relief. His was an amiable talent : but during the hot battle between the Romanticists and the Classicists was no time for a merely amiable talent; and Delavigne had to submit to be thrust on one side, and remembered rather for the share he might have taken in the combat than for any positive quality in the work he actually did.

The interest in the fight of the factions centres almost altogether around the two chiefs, Victor Hugo and Alexandre Dumas ; and the course of the combat can best be told in considering their separate dramas. It suffices now to note that the English actors left Paris in the fall of 1827, and that Victor Hugo published his profession of faith in the preface to 'Cromwell' before the end of the year. Less than fifteen months afterward Alexandre Dumas brought out his first acted play, 'Henri III.,' at the Théâtre Français. In another year, at the same theatre, came 'Hernani,' the first acted play of Victor Hugo. Within eighteen months 'Antony' and 'Marion Delorme' followed, and victory was assured. The Romanticists, like Jove's thunderbolts, were but a handful, yet they annihilated the Titans who had overawed their predecessors.

CHAPTER II.

In the year 1778 there was acted in Paris, at the Théâtre Français, 'Irène,' the last tragedy of Voltaire, whose first play, 'Œdipe,' had been brought out at the same theatre in 1718, — sixty years before. On March 31, at the sixth performance of 'Irène,' the presence of the aged author called forth the greatest enthusiasm. To the yet living Voltaire, it was, as it were, à foretaste of literary immortality, and he was much affected by the demonstrations. "You smother me with roses," he said, "and kill me with pleasure."

In our day we have seen but one sight like unto this. On Feb. 25, 1880, at the same Théâtre Français where Voltaire was honored, was celebrated the fiftieth anniversary of the first performance of 'Hernani,' a play by Victor Hugo. In the half-century it had been acted over three hundred times in that theatre. The house was full and enthusiastic ; and the list of those present at this semi-centennial performance holds nearly all the notable names of modern France. After the acting of 'Hernani,' the curtain drew up again, and discovered that incomparable company of actors, the Comédie-Française, grouped around a bust of Victor Hugo in the centre of the stage. Then from the ranks of the performers, each of whom was dressed in the costume of the character he had acted in one of the poet's plays, came forward the chief actress of tragedy, and recited in the most musical of voices, and amid the plaudits of the audience, the poem written for the occasion by one of the foremost of younger French poets, — a poem which proclaimed that Victor Hugo would have long life before he had immortality, and which declared that his drama and Glory had celebrated their golden wedding.

Voltaire has been dead only a century, and already the dust lies thick on his dramatic works. A hundred years is a long life for any thing in literature. What may befall Victor Hugo's dramas in a hundred years, it were vain to prophesy. Shakspere has been dead two centuries and a half, and his plays are as young as the day they were born. Victor Hugo does not lack partisans who declare him to be of the race and lineage of Shakspere. Mr. Algernon Charles Swinburne, for instance, is an English poet and critic who cannot mention M. Hugo's name without dithyrambic rhapsodies; and the late Théophile Gautier was a French poet and critic, who, when almost on his death-bed, told a friend, that, if he had the ill-fortune to find a single line of Hugo's poor, he would not dare to confess it, to himself, all alone, in the cellar, without a light.

Gautier, at least, had the excuse that Hugo had been his leader in a fierce fight, and that it ill becomes a soldier to doubt the captain who brought the battle to an end. It is needless to tell again, and at length, the tale of the battle between the Romanticists and the Classicists. It is enough to remember that the theatre was the chief battle-ground. Now, for an assault on the stage, Hugo was the best possible leader. He was a born playwright. Although only twenty-five years old when he put forth 'Cromwell,' in 1827, he had already published two novels and two volumes of poetry. Novelist and poet then, he has revealed himself since as critic, orator, historian, and satirist ; but in every disguise he shows his strong native bent toward the theatre. His poems are often but the lyric setting of a dramatic motive : his novels are but plays told in narrative, instead of put on the stage. All the elements of the play are to be found in the novel : situations, scenery, effects, even to the exit-speeches, — all are there. No reader of the 'History of a Crime' need be reminded how dramatic, not to say theatrical, he can make history. As an orator, also, his stage-training stands him in good stead : his oration becomes a play with only one part, and he uses as best he may the scenery which chances to surround him. In 1851, for example, pleading in court against the death-penalty, he pointed to the crucifix over the judge's head, and appealed to "that victim of capital punishment." It is in his novels, however, that his dramatic instinct is most plainly seen. His methods are those of a melodramatist. He plans and paints his scenery himself, and far better than the material brush of the scenic artist could do it ; and he delights in the violent contrasts always effective on the stage, in the cut-and-thrust repartee of the theatre, and in the sharply outlined characters whose complexity is only apparent.

Abundant proof of the dramatic tendencies of his youth are to be found in the curious book, 'Victor Hugo ; raconté par un Témoin de sa Vie,' which is at least semi-autobiographical : it is an open secret that the Witness of his Life was his wife. In this we are told that he wrote a tragedy, 'Irtamène,' at the age of fourteen and an *opéra-comique,* 'À Quelque Chose Hasard est Bon,' before he was sixteen. Between the two, at fifteen, he had written a more elaborate tragedy, 'Athalie.' The witness of his life tells us that it was "perfectly regular, in five acts, with unities of time and place, dream, confidants," etc. At nineteen he planned a play, 'Amy Robsart,' taken, for the most part, from 'Kenilworth.' Seven years later he gave it to his brother-in-law, Paul Foucher, not thinking it fit that after the publication of 'Cromwell,' he should borrow a subject. The play was acted anonymously, and hissed. Hugo at once came forward, and claimed his share of the failure. None of these early dramatic attempts of Hugo has been published; but the witness of his life prints in full another play, 'Inez de Castro,' written at the age of sixteen, apparently just after the composition of the *opéra-comique*, and three years before the adaptation from Scott.

'Inez de Castro' is a remarkable production for a boy of sixteen, and it has never received the attention it deserves from critics of Hugo's literary career. We can detect in this youthful sketch the germ of his later dramatic work. Here, in fact, is Victor Hugo the playwright, in the chrysalis. 'Inez de Castro' is a melodrama in three acts and two interludes. These latter are spectacular merely, and call for no comment. But the three acts of melodrama repay study. The story of the play need not be told here at length: it has a juvenile want of profundity, and it shows a juvenile love of the marvellous and astounding. But the effects are not altogether external, and there is a willingness to grapple with weighty subjects, not a little characteristic. Here are the firstlings of Hugo's theatrical genius, and we can see here in embryo some of his later qualities. The scene is laid in Spain, where the poet had passed part of his wandering childhood; and there is a lavish use of local color. That the young poet had already broken with the unity of place is shown by the frequent change of scene. There is the commingling of the comic and the serious, which, nine years later, in the 'Cromwell' preface, he declared to be essential to a proper dramatic presentation of life. The humor is not grim and grotesque, as it became in some of his later plays, but frankly mirthful. There is the use of the prattle of little children to relieve the strain of tense emotion, — an effect repeated half a century later in 'Ninety-three.' There are intriguing officials, recalling those in 'Ruy Blas;' and there is a liberal use of spies and poison, recalling 'Lucrèce Borgia' and 'Angelo.' There are lyric interludes and antitheses, and violent contrasts, and a seeking of startling effects by the sudden diclosure of solemn situations. There is one scene in the tomb of the king, which perhaps suggested the act of 'Hernani' in the tomb of Charlemagne; and there is another in a vast hall, hung with black draperies, and containing a throne and a scaffold, around which are grouped guards in black and red, and executioners in the black robes of penitents, with torches in their hands. This scene seemingly has served as raw material for one in 'Marie Tudor,' and also, it may be, for the famous supper-scene in 'Lucrèce Borgia.' And, last of all, there is a ghost, which, I am glad to say, Victor Hugo has made no attempt to utilize in any of his later works.

After Victor Hugo had begun to be recognized as the chief of a new sect, his liking for the stage prompted him to plan a play which should exemplify what the drama of the future ought to be. He sketched out

'Cromwell,' intending it for Ta'ma, who heartily approved of the new principles. Unfortunately, the great actor died, worn out with giving form to the emptiness of the plays he had to act. Bereft of the one actor who could do justice to his hero, Hugo gave up the thought of the stage, and elaborated the play, until it is well-nigh as long as Mr. Swinburne's interminable 'Bothwell.' However, the original acting-play remains visible, though embedded in a mass of superabundant matter. Although the scenes are unduly prolonged, and the characters developed at needless length, careful cutting would make its performance a possibility. It is to be judged frankly as a play for the stage, and not as that half-breed monstrosity, a "play for the closet." Of course, it marks an immense advance on the 'Inez de Castro' of nine years before; but it is far inferior to the 'Hernani' of three years later. The restrictions of actual stage representation are wholesome to Hugo's exuberant genius.

As a historical drama, 'Cromwell' is not quite so accurate as its author pretends; but it presents vividly the superficial aspects of a man and a time still waiting for a dramatist who can see their great capabilities. The plot, the incidents of which are not as closely serried as in Hugo's later plays, turns on the Protector's intrigues for the crown he afterward refused. There is the familiar use of moments of surprise and suspense, and of stage-effects appealing to the eye and the ear. In the first act Richard Cromwell drops into the midst of the conspirators against his father, — surprise: he accuses them of treachery in drinking without him, — suspense; suddenly a trumpet sounds, and a crier orders open the doors of the tavern where all are sitting, — suspense again ; when the doors are flung wide, we see the populace and a company of soldiers, and the crier on horseback, who reads a proclamation of a general fast, and commands the closing of all taverns, — surprise again. A somewhat similar scene of succeeding suspense and surprise is to be found in the fourth act. The setting off of the Roundheads against the Cavaliers is rather French in its conception of character, but none the less effective. There is real humor in the contrast of Carr, the typical Puritan, with Lord Rochester, the ideal courtier ; and the improbable, not to say impossible, disguise of Rochester as Cromwell's chaplain is fertile in scenes of pure comedy. The fun, light and airy and graceful in Rochester, gets a little forced and farcical in Dame Guggligoy : the effort is obvious, and the hand rather heavy.

The opening line of 'Cromwell' was a protest against the stiff, stilted, and unnatural decorum which forbade the use of the simple word for a simple thing, prescribing in its place a sort of roundabout hinting at it : this is the first line of Hugo's first published play, — a date only.

"Demain, vingt-cinq juin, mil six cent cinquante-sept." To see the curtain rise on a tavern, and to hear a date as the first phrase of a five-act historical drama in verse, was enough to shock even the most liberal Classicist. The second act began, in like manner, with a question as to the time of day, and the simple answer, "Noon." In the preface to the play, — a preface which was as a declaration of independence, — the attempt to get away from effete conventionalities was set up as a principle. In this iconoclasm, Hugo broke the shackles of the tragic stage   He disavowed the unities of time and p ace; he proclaimed the supreme importance on the stage of action; he demanded a return to nature in poetic diction; and he rejected the rigid couplets of contemporary poets, to plead, not for prose, but for a freer use of verse; for, as he says, "an idea steeped in verse becomes at once more cutting and more glittering: it is iron turned to steel." A poet who can handle such verse need not fear the simplest and humblest phrases, for to him nothing would be trivial. "Genius is like the stamp, which prints the royal image on the coins of copper as well as on coins of gold." Above all, the poet must not be afraid to mingle the grotesque with the terrible: he must, indeed, choose rather the characteristic than the abstractly beautiful. In this principle, especially the juxtaposition of tragedy and comedy (which he supported in this preface by citation of the Greeks, Dante, Shakspere, Molière, and Goethe), we may see the mainspring of his next plays.

As Dryden has told us, "They who would combat general authority with particular opinion must first establish themselves a reputation of understanding better than other men." Now 'Cromwell' was unactable. Its preface irritated many, but converted few. It remained for Hugo to prove his superior understanding of the stage by his own works acted on the stage. In the spring of 1829, eighteen months after the publication of 'Cromwell,' Hugo was asked to write a play for the Comédie-Française. He had two subjects in his head. He chose to write first 'Marion Delorme,' — a task which took him from June 1 to June 24, the fourth act having been finished in one day's steady labor. Accepted by the theatre, the play was interdicted by the censors. Hugo at once turned to his second sub-

ject, and in three weeks he had completed 'Hernani.'
It is a coincidence that Voltaire wrote 'Zaïre,' much
his best tragedy, in just the same space of time that
Hugo took to write 'Hernani,' his most popular play.
In explanation of this wondrous improvisation, — for
'Hernani' is a play in five acts of full length, — one
may venture to suggest that the plot had been slowly
matured in the author's head, the situations had linked
themselves together in order, and that, when the poet
sat him down to his desk, he had but to clothe his con-
ceptions with verse.   To him this was a task of no difficulty, for Hugo has superabundantly the gift of metrical
speech : his vocabulary is surpassingly rich, and he has
lyric melody at his beck and call.   And of a truth his
Muse responded nobly to the appeal.   In no other play
of Hugo's is the verse finer or firmer.   The lumbering
and jingling rhymed Alexandrine is not the best metre
for dramatic poetry ; it is not even a good metre ; but
it is here handled by a master of verse.   Though no
carelessness betrays the improvising, the verse retains
the rush and impetus of its making.   The whole work
is full of the freshness and vigor of youth.   One can
almost hear the rising sap, and see the spreading foliage
of spring.

Although the French cannot be accused of taking
their pleasure sadly, the first performance of an important play at the national theatre is a solemnity.   The
production of 'Hernani' at the Théâtre Français on
the evening of Feb. 25, 1830, was a national event.
It was the first pitched battle between the Classicists
and the Romanticists.   The pit was filled with bands
of young artists of all kinds, who had volunteered in
place of the salaried applauders of the theatre, and who

were admitted on the presentation of a special ticket, — the word *hierro* (Spanish for iron) stamped in a bold handwriting on a little slip of red paper. Chief among these young enthusiasts was Théophile Gautier, resplendent in a flaming crimson waistcoat. With the first line the conflict broke out. The hisses of the old school were met by the plaudits of the new. Phrases which now pass without notice were then jeered and hooted. Extra-hazardous expressions were cheered before they were fairly out of the actors' mouths. When the curtain fell, the victory lay with the young author. But the end was not yet. The fight was renewed with the same bitterness at every performance; speeches roughly received one night were rapturously applauded the next; a scene lost by the Romanticists to-day was taken by assault to-morrow; until at last there was not one single line in the whole five acts which, at one time or another, had not been hissed. The theatre was crowded night after night. The excitement was not confined to the capital, and provincial towns echoed the animated discussions of Paris. At Toulouse a quarrel about 'Hernani' led to a duel, in which a young man was killed.

It was the position of the play as a manifesto, and not its merits, remarkable as they were, which called forth such demonstrations. Yet it needs no wide acquaintance with the works then holding the stage in France to understand that a play as fresh and as full of force as 'Hernani' must needs make a strong impression. The rapid rush of its action carries the spectator off his feet; the lyric fervor of its language is intoxicating; and it is only a sober second-thought which lets us see the weak points of the piece. If this is its effect now, when the play has no longer the charm of novelty, when, indeed, its startling innovations have been worn threadbare in the service of second-rate and often clumsy followers, we may guess what its effect was then on the ardent generation of 1830, surfeited with the sickly inanities of the self-styled classic school. Whatever we may now think of Doña Sol and her three lovers, the young artists of half a century ago took them for types of a dramatic renascence, — a new birth of the stage. What we do now think of them is, that all four characters — although full of movement, and rich in color — are hollow, and without real life. They live, move, and have their being, in a world that never was : in brief, they are operatic impossibilities, ruled by an inexorable fate and the firm hand of the author, who has decided on ending a picturesque play with a pathetic situation.

The plot may be recalled briefly. Ruy Gomez intends to marry his niece, Doña Sol, who, however, loves a mysterious bandit, Hernani, — own brother to my lord Byron's 'Giaour.' The King of Spain also loves Doña Sol, and bears her away with him. Hernani owes his life to Ruy Gomez, to whom he gives his hunting-horn, agreeing to take that life himself whenever he hears the horn ; and then Ruy Gomez and Hernani, for revenge, join in a conspiracy against the king. But Don Carlos, the King of Spain, is elected Roman Emperor, and he surprises the conspirators. Changed by his higher office, he pardons. Hernani is restored to all his rank and titles, and Doña Sol is wedded to him. In the midst of the marriage-feast comes the sound of the horn. Ruy Gomez is implacable : Hernani has sworn to die ; and his poison serves also for his bride. 'Castilian Honor,' the sub-title of the play, seems a very queer thing when we consider this story in cold blood. For the plot not to look ludicrous, one must be almost as hasty and hot-headed as the hero himself. And the incidents are as like each other as the whole play is unlike life. As Mr. W. H. Pollock has aptly remarked, every act ends with somebody sparing the life of somebody else, save the last, in which all the chief characters, except Charles V., die together. The catastrophe, although it is the logical sum total of the situations, would be revolting, if it were not so extravagant. The lugubrious tooting of the horn it was, doubtless, that Goethe had in mind when he called 'Hernani' "an absurd composition."

But to detect these demerits takes afterthought. While the play is acting before us, we are under the spell : we are moved, thrilled, excited. The pleasure it gives is not of the highest kind intellectually, if, indeed, it may be termed intellectual at all ; but as to the amount of pleasure it gives, there can be no question. The quality of its power may be doubted, never the quantity. It is a very interesting play, — melodramatic in its motive, poetic in its language, and picturesque at all times.

The same phrase describes fairly enough 'Marion Delorme' and 'Le Roi s'amuse,' which followed 'Hernani' upon the stage. 'Marion Delorme,' forbidden by the Bourbon censors, waited a few months, till the revolution of 1830 overturned the Bourbon throne; and then, in a few months more, on Aug. 11, 1831, it was brought out at the Porte St. Martin Theatre. It was received with the same outburst of contending prejudices and preferences which had been let loose upon 'Hernani.' To my mind it is a better play than its predecessor on the boards. To the full as moving and as picturesque, it bears study better. For one thing, it mingles humor and passion far more skilfully. It may perhaps be called the only one of Hugo's plays which fulfils the conditions of the new drama as laid down by the author in the preface to 'Cromwell.' And from this freer use of humor results a great superiority in the presentation of character. In no other play of Hugo's are the characters as natural as in 'Marion Delorme.' They are not mere profile masks set in motion to face each other in a given situation. Louis XIII. and Saverny are real flesh and blood. The king indeed is a royally well conceived character; Hugo brings before us by a few light and humorous touches the feeble, melancholy, pious, moral, fearful, restive, and helpless monarch, chafing under the iron curb of his red ruler, and yet inert in self-assertion. True to history or not, the portrait is true to itself, which is of greater importance in dramatic as in other art. The scene between Louis and his solemn jester, who seeks to gain his end by playing on the king's failings, is in the true comedy vein, and would greatly surprise those, who, familiar only with Hugo's later works, pretend that he does not know what humor is.

Saverny is a figure filled in with a few easy strokes of an airy fancy: he is the embodiment of light-hearted grace and true-hearted honor. He is a young fellow who wears feathers in his cap, it is true: but he bears down in his heart the motto of his order, "*Noblesse oblige;*" and he acts up to it when time serves. His is a poetic portrait of a characteristic Frenchman, with the national quality of style, and a capability for lofty sacrifice.   There is true comedy, again, in his attitude, when his friend, the Marquis de Brichanteau, tries to console Saverny's uncle for his supposed death, by pointing out his faults, and dwelling on them at length, until at last Saverny revolts.   There is, perhaps, a slightly too epigrammatic emphasis in the final self-possession of Saverny, which lets him coolly point out three mistakes in the spelling of his own death-warrant.   Emphasis and epigram, however, are kept more subordinate in 'Marion Delorme' than in any other of Hugo's plays.   Marion Delorme the heroine, and Didier the hero, are simpler figures, and more like those to be found in the 'Hernani.'   Didier is another brother of the Giaour, — mysterious, melancholic, misanthropic. Like Hernani, he is a wanderer on the face of the earth, and has great capacity for suffering.   Marion Delorme is a poetic portrait, no doubt highly flattered, of the fair and fragile beauty who has come down to us from history, leaving her character behind her.

Although, as in all of Hugo's plays, the plot is of prime importance, I have said nothing of it here, because it is both hard and unfair to give in a scant sentence or two a sample of the situation for which the playwright has cunningly prepared by all that precedes it.   In the skill with which the plot is conducted, in the force and effect of its situations, 'Marion Delorme' does not yield to its fellows.   In no other play of Hugo's is there any thing to compare with the skill with which the action of the drama is dominated by the red figure, and stiffened by the steel will of the unseen cardinal, the Richelieu, who, before Prince Bismarck, proved his belief in the efficacy of blood and iron.

It was possibly to 'Hamlet' that Hugo owed the troop
of strolling players among whom Marion Delorme hides;
and he may have been indebted for the self-sale by
which she tries to procure Didier's escape either to
the fiction of 'Faublas,' or to the fact in the relations of Josephine Barras and Napoléon; just as it
may have been a recollection of an incident in the
'School for Scandal' which suggested the far more
dramatic picture-scene of 'Hernani.' To conclude this
list of hypothetic borrowings, there are in 'Cromwell'
four clowns almost too Shaksperian in the most objectionable sense of that much-abused word. When he
began to write for the stage, Hugo seemed to be
greatly taken with the king's jester, — a figure at once
mediæval and grotesque, and therefore doubly capti-
vating. After the four in 'Cromwell,'— let us imagine,
if haply we can, the Protector with four fools, — we
have the doleful and black-robed jester in 'Marion
Delorme.'

In the next piece, the 'Roi s'amuse,' the protagonist
is the court-fool, Triboulet, the jester of Francis I. of
France. This play was brought out at the Théâtre
Français, in Paris, one evening in November, 1832.
Before the first night audience it failed, and it had no
chance of recovery, for the next morning the government forbade the performance of the play on the ground
that it libelled Francis I. So the 'Roi s'amuse' has
had but one performance; and yet the plot of no play
of Hugo's is so well known out of France, for it served
Verdi as the libretto of 'Rigoletto.' Space fails to
consider it here in detail. In form and spirit it does
not differ from 'Hernani' or 'Marion Delorme,' although it rises to a higher reach of passion than they.

If any one wishes to see how a strong story can be watered into symmetrical sentimentality, he may read the 'Roi s'amuse,' and then take up the 'Fool's Revenge,' a drama in three acts, by Mr. Tom Taylor. The essential tragedy of the motive is weakened to a triumph of virtue, and conversion of the vice. The desperation and death, which are the vitals of the French play, are in the English anodyned for the sake of the conventional happy ending.

Now we come to a curious change of manner. The 'Roi s'amuse,' 'Marion Delorme,' and 'Hernani' are all written in a rich and ample verse, full of fire and color: the three plays which followed — 'Lucrèce Borgia,' 'Marie Tudor,' and 'Angelo' — are in prose; and the effect of the change of medium is most surprising. Of course verse is not always poetry, and prose may aim as high and be as lofty as verse; but in Hugo's case the giving-up of verse seems like a giving-up of poetry. The elevation, the glow, and the grace of, say, 'Hernani,' are all lacking in 'Lucrèce Borgia' and its two companions in prose. There is no falling-off in the ingenuity of invention, or in the constructive skill of the author; but the plays in prose seem somehow on a much lower level than those in verse; and this is in spite of Hugo's use of a metre hopelessly unfit for the quick work of the stage. Before Mr. Matthew Arnold, Stendhal [1] had dwelt on the insufficience of the Alexandrine for high poetry. The jigginess of the metre and the alternating pairs of male and female rhymes are fatal to continued elevation of thought. Shak-

---

[1] "Les vers italiens et anglais permettent de tout dire; le vers Alexandrin seul, fait pour une cour dédaigneuse, en a tous les ridicules." — 'Racine et Shakspere,' p. 36, note.

speare and Dante could not have been sublime in
Alexandrines. Yet the metre has a certain fitness
to the French intellect, to the French love of order
and balance; and, moreover, it is the recognized and
regular metre of the higher theatre: so a French
dramatist must needs make the best of it. Victor
Hugo is a master in versification; it has no mysteries
for him: and in his hands, even the stubborn Alexandrine is bent to his bidding. Archbishop Trench calls
Calderon " nearly as lyric as dramatic." Victor Hugo
is even more lyric than dramatic. The most poetic lines
in his plays have a lyric lilt and swing. A friend of
mine who has a most acute insight into rhythmic
intricacies has suggested to me a subtle likeness
between the verse of 'Hernani,' particularly, and of
the 'Lays of Ancient Rome;' and just as the quotation
of a single stanza would do injustice to Macaulay,
whose merit lies mainly in the movement of his verse,
so it is almost impossible to pick out for quotation any
passage of the far finer and higher verse of Hugo
which will be fairly representative. A pretty couplet
is that of the king, Don Carlos, in 'Hernani,' when
he, having been elected emperor, pardons his rival,
gives him Doña Sol to wife, and finally bestows the
accolade:—

> . . . "je te fais chevalier.
> Mais tu l'as, le plus doux et le plus beau collier,
> Celui que je n'ai pas, qui manque au rang suprême,
> Les deux bras d'une femme aimée et qui vous aime!
> Ah, tu vas être heureux;—moi, je suis empereur."
>
> ('Hernani,' act iv. sc. 4.)

And lovely are the last lines of the same play, after
Hernani and Doña Sol have taken the fatal poison.

Hernani falls back; and Don Ruy Gomez, lifting his head, declares him dead; but Doña Sol will not have it so:—

> ... "Mort! non pas! ... nous dormons.
> Il dort! c'est mon époux, vois-tu, nous nous aimons,
> Nous sommes couchés là.   C'est notre nuit de noce.
> Ne le réveillez pas, seigneur duc de Mendoce ...
> Il est las. ... Mon amour, tiens-toi vers moi tourné,
> Plus près ... plus près encore ..."

('Hernani,' act v. sc. 6.)

And then she, too, falls back dead.   Fine lines again are those of Didier at the end of 'Marion Delorme,' when the bell tolls the hour of his execution, and he turns to the by-standers:—

> "Vous qui venez ici pour nous voir au passage.
> Si l'on parle de nous, rendez-nous témoignage
> Que tous deux sans pâlir nous avons écouté
> Cette heure qui pour nous sonnait l'éternité!"

('Marion Delorme,' act v. sc. 7.)

Perhaps as beautiful a monologue as any in the language is the touching speech of the jester, Triboulet, over the body of the daughter he has killed, thinking to slay the king:—

> ... "Je croi
> Qu'elle respire encore! elle a besoin de moi!
> Allez vite chercher du secours à la ville.
> Laissez-la dans mes bras, je serai bien tranquille.
> Non! elle n'est pas morte! oh! Dieu ne voudrait pas.
> Car enfin il le sait, je n'ai qu'elle ici-bas.
> Tout le monde vous hait quand vous êtes difforme,
> Ou vous fuit, de vos maux personne ne s'informe;
> Elle m'aime, elle!—elle est ma joie et mon appui.
> Quand on rit de son père, elle pleure avec lui.
> Si belle et morte! oh, non!—Donnez-moi quelque chose
> Pour essuyer son front.—Sa lèvre est encor rose.

Oh! si vous l'aviez vue, oh! je la vois encor
Quand elle avait deux ans avec ses cheveux d'or!
Elle était blonde alors!—O ma pauvre opprimée!
Ma Blanche! mon bonheur! ma fille bien-aimée!—
Lorsqu'elle était enfant, je la tenais ainsi.
Elle dormait sur moi, tout comme la voici!
Quand elle réveillait, si vous saviez quel ange!
Je ne lui semblais pas quelque chose d'étrange,
Elle me souriait avec ses yeux divins,
Et moi je lui baisais ses deux petites mains!
Pauvre agneau!—Morte! oh non! elle dort et repose.
Tout à l'heure, messieurs, c'était bien autre chose,
Elle s'est cependant réveillée.—Oh! j'attend.
Vous l'allez voir rouvrir ses yeux dans un instant!
Vous voyez maintenant, messieurs, que je raisonne,
Je suis tranquille et doux, je n'offense personne;
Puisque je ne fais rien de ce qu'on me défend,
On peut bien me laisser regarder mon enfant.
J'ai déjà réchauffé ses mains entre les miennes;
Voyez, touchez les donc un peu! . . .

UNE FEMME.

Le chirurgien.

TRIBOULET.

Tenez, regardez-la, je n'empecherai rien.
Elle est évanouie, est-ce pas?

LE CHIRURGIEN.

Elle est morte." [1]
(' Le Roi s'amuse,' act v. sc. 5.)

When Hugo drops verse, he gives up a great advantage. His plays in verse may pass for poetic dramas; but his plays in prose are of a truth prosaic. A garment of verse veils 'Hernani' and 'Marion Delorme;' but

---

[1] A metrical translation of this passage into English will be found in the note to this chapter.

'Lucrèce Borgia' and 'Marie Tudor' are naked melodrama, without any semblance of poetry. 'Lucrèce
Borgia,' written in the summer of 1832, immediately
after the 'Roi s'amuse,' and acted in 1833, is strangely
like 'Inez de Castro,' its predecessor in prose. It is
simply a melodrama, owing its merit mainly to its simplicity. We have an adroit and cunning handling of a
single fertile theme. There is none of the involute
turgidity of the ordinary melodramatic playwright; but
for all its simplicity the play is a melodrama, even in
the etymological sense, which requires the admixture
of music. With all her accumulated vices, Lucrèce
Borgia herself has no grandeur, no touch of the wand
which transfigures the wicked woman of Webster or
Ford. It is not imaginative, it is not poetic, and it is
immensely clever. In spite of the magnitude of her
crimes, and the force with which she is depicted, she
remains commonplace. She arouses the latent instinct
of caricature. When, in the first act, she tries special
pleading for herself, and lays the blame and the burden
of her sins on her family, — "It is the example of my
family which has misled me," — one involuntarily recalls
the fair Greek heroine of the 'Belle Hélène,' who com-
plains of "the fatality which weighs upon me!"

Coincident with the change from verse to prose is a
sudden falling-off in the humor which lightened the
sombre situations of the metrical plays. The romantic
formula which prescribed the mingling of comedy and
tragedy to make the model drama is disregarded already
in 'Lucrèce Borgia;' in Gubetta the humor we found
frank and free in the Saverny of 'Marion Delorme'
is getting grim and saturnine. It is less frequent and
more forced, as though the author was beginning to

make fun with difficulty. In 'Marie Tudor,' written and acted in the same year (1833), the humor has wholly disappeared, and we may therefore detect a growing extravagance of speech and structure. The 'Marie Tudor' of M. Hugo is the 'Queen Mary' of Mr. Tennyson; and the poets themselves are scarcely more unlike than the pictures they present us of the miserable monarch who went down to history as Bloody Mary. Tennyson could probably give chapter and verse for every part of his play. Hugo has no warrant for dozens of his extraordinary assertions and assumptions as to the manners and customs of the English. Tennyson is patriotic, and always seeks the subjects of his plays in the national history which he has reverently studied. Hugo has laid the scene in France of only two of his plays: he prefers foreign countries, which offer more frequent opportunities for sharp contrasts and strange mysteries. Spain, Italy, England, even Germany, can be taken by storm with less fear of the consequences. But in 'Marie Tudor' the joke is really carried a little too far. The play is absurd where it is not ridiculous. It is a caricature of history, a wanton misreading of records, and, worse yet, a passing-over of the truly dramatic side of the reign, to invent vulgar impossibilities. The play is in every way inferior to its predecessors. It has action, and it is shaped solely with an eye to effect before the footlights; but even as a specimen of journeyman play-making it is cheap. There is no touch or trace of poetry anywhere. The unfortunate queen is transformed into a sanguinary and lascivious virago, a Madame Angot of a monarch, scolding like a fishwife, and threatening like a fury.

The third play in prose, 'Angelo,' written and acted

in 1835, though inferior to 'Lucrèce Borgia,' is superior
to 'Marie Tudor,' because it does not make history to
suit itself, and because its story is simpler and more
pathetic.   The contrast of the chaste patrician lady
with Tisbe, the lawless woman of the people, is capable
of development into affecting situations.   The two parts
were originally acted by Mlle. Mars and Mme. Dorval.
Tisbe was afterward acted by Rachel, and in America
an adaptation by John Brougham was played by Charlotte Cushman.   Outside of these two parts there is
little in the piece.   Homodei is not very like a man of
God, though he is represented as the personification
of ubiquitous omniscience.   It is one of Hugo's first
attempts at embodying an abstraction, or rather at
clothing a really commonplace character with marvellous attributes.   He looms up as something far more
wonderful than he appears when seen close to.   There
is an effort to pack a quart into a pint, to the resulting
fracture of the vessel.   'Angelo' has no more humor
than 'Marie Tudor:' so the extravagance has a chance
to grow.   There is a perceptible increase in the affecta-
tions of plot and dialogue, and an equally perceptible
increase in Hugo's fondness for mystic devices.   In all
his plays there are sliding panels, and secret passages,
and hidden staircases in plenty; spies and hireling
bravos and black mutes are to be found in them; subtle
Italian poisons, and sudden antidotes thereunto, and
strange narcotics, at an instant's notice are ready at
hand: in short, there is no lack of tools for the most
Radcliffean mysteries and mystifications.   Of poison
especially, is there no miserly use.   Hernani poisons
himself, and so does his bride; Ruy Blas takes poison;
Angelo thinks to poison his wife; and Lucrèce Borgia

poisons a whole supper-party. In fact, to read Hugo's plays straight through is almost as good as a course in toxicology. The dagger is abused as freely as the bowl. To call the death-roll of all the *dramatis personæ* who die by the sword or the axe would be as tedious as unprofitable.

In 1838, three years after 'Angelo,' came 'Ruy Blas,' in many ways Hugo's finest play. It is a happy return to verse and the earlier manner. The plot — suggested possibly by the story of Angelica Kaufmann, and slightly similar to Lord Lytton's 'Lady of Lyons' — is at once simple and strong. Verse again throws its ample folds over the characters, and cloaks their lack of the complexity of life. And again we have the wholesome and lightsome humor which kept the metrical dramas from the exaggerations and extravagances of the prose plays. It is as though the exuberant genius of Victor Hugo needed the strait-jacket of the couplet. There is true comedy in the conception of Don César de Bazan; and very ingenious and comic is the scene in the fourth act, when he drops into the house occupied by Ruy Blas (who has assumed the name of Don César), and is astonished at the adventures which befall him, and does in every thing the exact reverse of what would be done by Ruy Blas, for whom the adventures were intended. It is only in this scene, and in one or two in 'Marion Delorme,' that we can see any thing in Hugo's work approaching to large and liberal humor. Wit he has in abundance, and to spare; grim humor, ironic playfulness, grotesque fancy, are not wanting: but real comic force, the enjoyment of fun for its own sake, the *vis comica* of Molière, for example, or of Shakspere, or Aristophanes, is nowhere to be found.

I have already dwelt on the utter absence of any kind of comedy from the prose plays. If it were not for 'Ruy Blas,' which seems to come out of its proper chronological order, since it is closely akin to its fellow metrical dramas, and not to the prose plays which preceded it, — if it were not for 'Ruy Blas,' we might trace the gradual decay of Hugo's feeling for the comic. After 'Ruy Blas,' after 1838, neither in play nor in any other of the multifarious efforts of Victor Hugo, can I recall any attempt at comedy, or even any consciousness of its existence. It is as though, born with a full sense of humor, in the course of time he had allowed his vanity to spring up and choke it; for, oddly enough, as his humor died, his vanity grew apace. It is an aggressive vain-glory, and may best be seen in his prefaces. In that to 'Cromwell' he is defiant, and not on the defensive; in those to later plays we can see the undue humility which is the chief sign of towering vanity. Just after 'Hernani,' Châteaubriand, who was gifted with no slight self-esteem, hailed Victor Hugo as his fit successor. And Hugo has inherited, not only some of the literary methods and some of the authority of Châteaubriand, but a full share of his intellectual arrogance.

It was this intellectual arrogance which prompted him to withdraw from the stage after the popular failure of his next play. The 'Burgraves,' written in October, 1842, and acted in March, 1843, is an attempt to set on the stage something of the epic grandeur of mediæval history. It sought to make dramatic use of the legend of the mighty and undying Barbarossa. As a poem, it is one of Hugo's noblest; as a play, it is his poorest. We have a powerful picture of Teutonic decadence and of imperial majesty; but in aiming high Hugo naturally missed the heart of the play-goer. There is nothing human for the play-goer to take hold of, and carry away with him. The plot, with but little of the melodramatic machinery Hugo directs so effectively, is uninteresting, and in its termination undramatic. The characters, grandly conceived as they are, seem like colossal statues, larger than life, and not flesh and blood. No real passion was to be expected from such stony figures, perfect as may be their cold and chiselled workmanship. The 'Burgraves' is the most ambitious of Hugo's dramas, and the least successful in performance. Its career on the stage was short. About this time, too, a re-action had set in against the Romanticists, and Ponsard's 'Lucrèce' was hailed as a return to common sense. Victor Hugo took umbrage, and declared that it was unbecoming to his dignity to submit himself to the hisses of a chance audience. Although he had two plays nearly ready for acting, he has never again presented himself as a dramatist. One of these plays, the 'Jumeaux,' was about finished in 1838; and since then he has written 'Torquemada,' a drama of the Spanish Inquisition, a most promising subject for his peculiar powers; neither of which is to be acted until after Hugo's death. A recent biographer refers to still other pieces of the poet, among them a fairy-play called the 'Forêt Mouillée,' in which trees and flowers speak.

In this enumeration of Hugo's plays I have omitted only one, — the libretto of an opera, 'Esmeralda,' produced at the Opéra of Paris in November, 1836. It was a lyric dramatization of his romance 'Notre Dame de Paris,' made for Mlle. Bertin, the daughter of a friend, after he had refused to do it for Meyerbeer.

Dramatizations of the same story and of the 'Misera-
bles' have been acted; and an adaptation of 'Ninety-
Three' is announced for the winter of 1881–1882.
If his own libretto chanced upon an incompetent composer, certain of his dramas are better known to the
world at large as opera-books than in their original
and more literary form as French plays. 'Hernani'
and the 'Roi s'amuse' served Verdi as the books of
'Ernani' and 'Rigoletto.' 'Ruy Blas' has been turned
into a libretto several times. Balfe's 'Armorer of
Nantes' is based on 'Marie Tudor.' Mercadante's
'Giuramento' is a setting of 'Angelo.' 'Lucrèce Borgia,' the final act of which is full of contending emotions and scenic contrasts culminating in the thrilling
commingling of the bacchanalian lyrics of the supper-
party with the dirge for the dying chanted by the
approaching priests — a situation which almost sets
itself to music — has been turned to excellent account
in the 'Lucrezia Borgia' of Donizetti. These trans-
formations were not always to the poet's taste, as was
shown by the savage way in which he warned off the
librettist in a note to one of his later plays.

All Victor Hugo's plays are the work of his youth
(he was not forty when the 'Burgraves' was acted), and
they are thus free from the measureless emphasis
which is the besetting sin of his later work. And
unfortunately Hugo has not obeyed Goethe's behest,
to beware of taking "the faults of our youth into our
old age; for old age brings with it its own defects."
This is just what Hugo has done. No author of his
years and fame has ever changed so little since he first
came forward. There has been extension, of course;
but there has not been growth. So, although Hugo

stopped short his dramatic production, we may doubt
whether the future would have had any surprise in
store for us. We may fairly enough discount what
manner of play he would have given us had he written
more for the stage. We should have found the "lively
feeling of situation and the power to express them,"
which Goethe tells us "make the poet;" but now and
then the situation would have been overcharged, and
the expression extravagant. We should have had plays
in the highest degree ingenious in device, thrilling in
incident, and, if they chanced to be in verse, full of
lyric melody. But these are not the chief attributes
of a great dramatic poet. Indeed, excess of ingenuity
is fatal to true grandeur, as Hugo himself seems to
have felt; for in his one attempt at a lofty theme, the
'Burgraves,' he instinctively cast aside cleverness, and
strove for a noble simplicity. In the two chief qualities
of a great dramatic poet, — in the power of creating
character true to nature, and in unfailing elevation of
thought, — in both of these Victor Hugo is deficient.

If one seek proof that Hugo is not a great dramatic
poet of the race and lineage of Shakspere, but rather
a supremely clever playwright, an artificer of dramas,
not because the drama was in him and must out, but
because the stage offered the best market and the
most laurels, one has only to consider 'Marie Tudor,'
or 'Angelo.' No great dramatic poet, no one who was
truly a dramatic poet, could have written such stuff.
In spite of all their cleverness, they are unworthy of a
poet who has any sense of life. That these plays are
so inferior to the metrical dramas goes to show that
Hugo needs the restraint of verse, and that he is at
his best when working under the limitations of the

Alexandrine, — limitations, which, as I have said, are fatal to dramatic poetry of the highest rank. Putting this and that together, I find that Hugo's plays are melodramas, written by a poet, and not poetic plays written by a dramatic poet. In Molière's plays, as in Shakspere's, the man is superior to the event; but in Hugo's, as in Calderon's and in Corneille's, the situation dominates the characters. Unlike Calderon's and Corneille's, Hugo's plays are not poetic in conception, however poetic they may be in verbal clothing. Neither the plots nor the personages are poetic in conception. The plot is melodramatic, but the best of melodramas because of its simplicity and strength, and because it is the work of a man of heavier mental endowment than often takes to melodrama. Nor are the characters more poetic than the situations: they are not saturated with the spirit of poesy, and lifted up by the breath of the muse. Most of Hugo's people, especially the tragic, are drawn in outline in monochrome: they are impersonations of a single impulse. Miss Baillie wrote a series of Plays for the Passions : Hugo gives a passion apiece to each of his people, and lets them fight it out. Put one of Hugo's villains, the Don Salluste of 'Ruy Blas,' say, — a sharp silhouette, all black, — and set it by the side of Iago, and note the rounded and life-like complexity of Shakspere's traitor. Or compare Hugo's characters with Molière's, and see how thin their substance seems, how petty their natures, in spite of all their swelling speech. They have not the muscle and the marrow, they have not the light and the air, of Molière's poetically conceived creatures.

Melodramatic as situations and characters are, however, the best of Hugo's plays are still poetic, in appearance at least. This is because Victor Hugo is a great poet, although not a great dramatic poet. It is because his plays, while they are melodramas in structure, are the work of an artist in words. The melodramatist, when he has once constructed the play, calls on the poet to write it; for in Hugo are two men, — a melodramatist doubled by a lyric poet. The joints of the plot are hidden, and the hollowness of the characters is cloaked, by the ample folds of a poetic diction of unrivalled richness. It is the splendor of this lyric speech which blinds us at first to the lack of inner and vital poetry in the structure it decks so royally. Although, therefore, his plays are immensely effective in performance, and his characters wear at times the externals of poetic conception, Victor Hugo is not that rare thing, a great dramatic poet, — a thing so rare, indeed, that the world as yet has seen but a scant half-score.

There is no need to say here that Victor Hugo's glory does not depend on his dramas, nor, indeed, upon his work in any single department of literature. His genius has, turn by turn, tried almost every kind of writing, and on whatsoever it tried it has left its mark. He is a master-singer of lyrics and a master-maker of satires. The song is as pure as the spring at the hillside, and the satire is as scorching as the steel when it flows from the crucible. He is mighty in romance, and moving in history; giving us in 'Notre Dame de Paris' historical romance, and in the 'History of a Crime' romantic history. Even in criticism and philosophy he has done his stint of labor. But his best work is not merely literary. Literature is too small to hold him, and the finest of him is outside of it. The best part of him has got out of literature into life. What he has done in politics and philanthropy is on record, and he who runs may read if he will. The politics may at times have been a little erratic, and the philanthropy may have seemed sentimental and opinionated; yet these defects are but dust in the balance when weighed against the nobler qualities of the man. In times of doubt and compromise it is worth much to see one who holds fast to what he believes, and who stands forth for it in lofty and resolute fashion. During the darkest and dirtiest days of the Second Empire a beacon-light of liberty and hope and faith flashed to France from a rocky isle off the coast where dwelt one exile from the city he loved, one man at least who refused to bow the head or bend the knee before the man of December and Sédan. Beyond and above Hugo's great genius is his great heart. He is the poet of the proletarian and of the people; he is the poet of the poor and the weak and the suffering; he is the poet of the over-worked woman and of the little child; he is the friend of the down-trodden and the outcast; and his is the truly Christian charity which droppeth like the gentle dew from heaven.

Mr. Swinburne concludes the ode he wrote in 1865, 'To Victor Hugo in Exile,' with two stanzas, to be fitly quoted here, before we take leave of the foremost figure among all European men of letters : —

> "Yea, one thing more than this,
> We know that one thing is, —
> The splendor of a spirit without blame,
> That not the laboring years
> Blind-born, nor any fears,

Nor men, nor any gods, can tire or tame;
    But purer power with fiery breath
Fills, and exalts above the gulfs of death.

    Praised above men be thou,
    Whose laurel-laden brow,
Made for the morning, droops not in the night;
    Praised and beloved, that none
    Of all thy great things done
Flies higher than thy most equal spirit's flight;
    Praised, that nor doubt nor hope could bend
Earth's loftiest head, found upright to the end."

CHAPTER III.

On the 11th of February, 1829, a full year before any piece of Hugo's was played, there was produced at the Théâtre Français a five-act drama, full of fire and action, called 'Henri III. et sa Cour,' and written by Alexandre Dumas, a young quadroon, who owed to his fine handwriting a place as clerk under the Duke of Orléans, and who had promised himself some day to live by his pen instead of his penmanship.

Like Victor Hugo, Alexandre Dumas was the son of a revolutionary general. His father, the Count Mathieu Dumas, was the son of the Marquis Davy de la Pailleterie. In his characteristically voluminous memoirs, Dumas tells us how he spent his early youth in the country, running wild and laying up stores of strength. He seems to have grown up as void of learning as he was of fear. His mother tried to get him to read Corneille and Racine: he confesses that he was prodigiously bored by them. But one day there came along a company of apprentice actors from the conservatory, and gave the 'Hamlet' of the good and simple-minded Ducis, with Hamlet acted in imitation of Talma. It made so great an impression on Dumas, that when he wrote his memoirs, thirty-two years afterward, he could recall distinctly every detail of the performance. He sent to Paris for the 'Hamlet' of Ducis, and in three days he had the part by heart. He was

46

then not sixteen years old. Two or three years later, he ran up to Paris, and saw Talma as Sylla, and was introduced to him as a young man who aspired to be a dramatist. Talma greeted him so kindly that he was emboldened to ask the great actor to lay hands on him in consecration, as it were, and to bring him luck in his vocation. "So be it," said Talma, laying his hand on the youth's head; "Alexandre Dumas, I baptize you poet, in the name of Shakspere, of Corneille, and of Schiller."

When he was twenty years of age, he and his mother came up to Paris, and he got himself a clerkship under the Duke of Orléans. Then he took up in earnest the hard trade of a professional playmaker. In the first four years of his life in Paris, he succeeded in getting acted three vaudevilles of no special value, and each written in collaboration with one or two of his comrades, hopeful and struggling youngsters like himself. He made also a tragedy of 'Fiesque,' imitated from Schiller; but he had not been able to place it. Then, in 1827, arrived the English actors; and he saw in succession the masterpieces of the English drama. (He had English enough to follow Shakspere, as he had German enough to paraphrase Schiller.) He records the immense impression made on him by this first sight of real passions moving men of flesh and blood. Just before the English performances ended, leaving Dumas with new lights, and having opened beyond him new ranges of vision, the Salon set forth its annual show of pictures and sculptures; and here Dumas saw two bas-reliefs, the energy and firmness of which struck him. One was a scene from the 'Abbot,' and the other represented the death of Monaldeschi. Dumas did not

know who Monaldeschi was : so he borrowed a biographical dictionary, and there made the acquaintance of
Christine of Sweden and of her physician-lover ; and
he began at once to work their story into a five-act
tragedy in verse. When it was done, by good luck he
got audience of Baron Taylor, the manager of the
Théâtre Français, who invited him to read it before
the committee of comedians which had the accepting of
new plays. Very comic indeed, and very characteristic
of the changing condition of the drama just then, was
the declaration of the committee, that it did not know
whether the play was classic or romantic. "What matter?" asked the author : "is it good, or bad ?" And
the committee did not know that either. Finally, however, it accepted the piece on condition that it was
approved by one of the regular dramatists of the house.
So Dumas was forced to leave the play for a week with
Picard, the author of the 'Petite Ville,' imitated by
Kotzebue. When he went for his answer, Picard
asked him if he had any other means of existence than
literature ; and when Dumas answered that he had a
fifteen-hundred-franc clerkship under the Duke of Orléans, the withered old dramatist handed back the
manuscript of 'Christine,' saying, "Go to your desk,
young man ! Go to your desk !"

In spite of this chilling criticism, the Comédie-Française accepted 'Christine,' and put it in rehearsal. But
delays arose, and disagreements with Samson, according to one account, and with Mlle. Mars, according to
another ; and in a little while Dumas was convinced
that 'Christine' would never be acted at the Théâtre
Français. He was right ; and his first drama, like
Hugo's, was brought out after his second. It was, per-

haps, well for Dumas that this was so, for it is a great
advantage to begin by hitting the bull's eye ; and
'Christine' would never have made so striking a success as 'Henri III.' After he was established as a
dramatist, Dumas remodelled 'Christine ;' and from
a quasi-classic tragedy it became a frankly romantic
"trilogy in five acts, with prologue and epilogue,"
with changes of scene to justify the new sub-title
'Stockholm, Fontainebleau, and Rome,' and with the
introduction even of a wholly new and important character, — Paula. As the original version is no longer
before us, criticism is impossible. No doubt it was
tamer in movement, and duller in color, than the play
as we have it. No doubt it was a somewhat timid
attempt at Romanticism : even in the revised version
it is not one of Dumas's best. The verse in which it is
written is verse : it is not poetry. Dumas, although
not exactly constrained in writing Alexandrines, never
handles them with the assured ease of a master. Although he bends the metre to obey him, the result is
good journeyman verse-making, nothing more ; and
there is never the burst of lyric fervor which often
makes Hugo's lines sing themselves into the memory.

Dumas threw off the shackles of metre when he
began to write his second drama, 'Henri III.' In
style, too, as well as in speech, it was ampler, and more
frankly romantic, than his first. Since 'Christine' had
been originally outlined, Hugo had published the preface to 'Cromwell,' the revolt of the Romanticists had
gained great headway, and then the time for faltering
between the two schools had passed forever. 'Henri
III.' showed no hesitation. It was a bold, not to say
brutal picture of an epoch of history : it was the first

French play in which history was set squarely on the stage much as Scott had shown it in his novels. And, truth to tell, Scott had his share in the drama, directly as well as indirectly. Dumas had found one suggestion in Anquetil, and another in the 'Mémoires de l'Estoile.' By combining and developing these hints from the records, he had made the main plot of his play; utilizing for one of its chief situations a scene from Scott's 'Abbot,'—probably the one represented in the other of the two bas-reliefs. Dumas also drew on his abandoned version of Schiller's 'Fiesco.' He has told us that he had studied Schiller and Goethe and Calderon and Lope de Vega, seeking to spy out the secret of their skill; and what wonder was it that a few fragments of the foreign authors should get themselves somehow worked into his model? Made, in a measure, of reminiscences, 'Henri III.' hangs together wonderfully well, and has a unity of its own. Some of the brick and some of the mortar are borrowed without leave; but the finished house is Dumas's property beyond all question.

Alphonse Royer, who was present at the first performance, has recorded that he never again saw such a sight, and that from the third act on the audience was wild with excitement. The changing scenes and startling situations were followed with breathless interest. The touches of local color, the use of the language, and even of the oaths of the time, the ease and grace of the sketch of the king's court, with the *mignons* playing cup-and-ball, the life and vigor of the whole drama, charmed and delighted an audience tired with the dignified inanity of the Classicists. The very violence of the action gave a shock of pleasure to the

willing spectators. It is to be said, too, that the partisans of the Classicists, not afraid of the first play
of an unknown writer, had not assembled to give it
battle, as they did a year later when 'Hernani' was
brought out; and so 'Henri III.' took them by surprise,
and gained the victory before they could rally. A
profitable victory it was for the author. Before writing 'Henri III.' he was a clerk at fifteen hundred francs
a year, — a little less than six dollars a week. 'Henri
III.' had been written in about eight weeks; and, in
addition to what he received from the Théâtre Français
for the right of performance, he sold the copyright for
six thousand francs. By two months' labor of his pen
he had gained far more than he could have made in
four years by his penmanship.

Taking all things into consideration, I am inclined to
call 'Henri III.' Dumas's best drama. Looking down
the long list of his plays, it is not easy to pick out
another as simple, as strong, as direct, and as dignified.
It has a compressed energy, and a certain elevation
of manner, not found together in any of his other
plays. Whether the best of his dramas or not, it is
emphatically a very remarkable play to have been written by a young man of twenty-six. It is especially
remarkable when we recall that it sprang up from the
dust of the Classicist tragedies, and that it was the
first flower of Romanticism on the stage. There are
many things one might single out for praise. For one,
the intuition by which Dumas grasped the cardinal
principle of historical fiction, deducing it, perhaps,
from the example set by Scott in his novels. This
principle prescribes that the chief characters in which
the interest of the spectator or the reader is to be

excited shall be either wholly the invention of the author; or, if suggested by actual personages, the originals must be known so slightly that the author may mould or modify them as he please. A transcription of historic fact may then serve as the scaffolding of the story, and real characters may be reproduced to give it solidity and pomp. In other words, history may be stretched for the warp; but fiction must supply the woof. This is what Dumas generally did in his novels, and it is what he did admirably in 'Henri III. We see the crafty, courageous, and effeminate Henri III. himself, the resolute, masculine, intriguing Catherine de Medicis, and the stern and rigorous Duke of Guise; and these serve to set off the high and noble heroine, and the melancholy and devoted hero, who, although bearing historic names, are in fact truly projections of the dramatist's imagination.

The story of 'Henri III.' has a purity and a sobriety lacking to most of Dumas's other plays; yet it yields to none of them in effect, in freedom, or in force. Slighting the purely historical incidents, the plot may be told briefly. The weak-kneed but quick-witted king, Henri III., is under the rule of his mother, Catherine de Medicis, who fears the ascendency gained over him by St. Mégrim, and dreads the growing power in the state of the Duke of Guise. She craftily sets one against the other by fostering the love of St. Mégrim for Catherine of Cleves, wife of the duke; and she contrives an interview between them at an astrologer's, — an interview innocent enough, even if the speedy coming of the duke had not put to flight the duchess, who leaves behind her a handkerchief, which her husband finds. In the next act the Duke of Guise and

St. Mégrim bandy words before the king, who makes St. Mégrim a duke too, that he may fight Guise as his peer ; and the combat is fixed for the morrow. But the wily Guise has no desire to die in a duel : so, in the third act, we see him in full mail armor standing over his wife, grasping her arm with his iron gauntlet, and by physical pain forcing her to write a letter to St. Mégrim, bidding him to her palace that night. In the following act St. Mégrim gets the note ; and the king, anxious about the issue of the single combat the next morning, lends St. Mégrim his own special talisman against death by fire or steel. In the last act St. Mégrim comes to the apartment of the duchess to keep his appointment. While Catherine of Cleves is trying to tell him hastily how she has vainly sought to give warning of the trap in which he is caught, the outer door of the palace clangs to, and the tread of armed men is heard on the stairs. Helpless and unarmed before the danger which draws nearer and nearer, St. Mégrim knows no way to turn, when suddenly a bundle of rope falls at his feet, thrown through the window by the duchess's page, who has overheard enough to suspect. Catherine thrusts her arm through the rings of the door, in place of the missing staple, to give St. Mégrim time to let himself down to the ground. When the door opens, the duke strides in, and goes straight to the window. St. Mégrim has fallen among thieves, for Guise's men are below. He is wounded and bleeding, but not dead. "Perhaps he has a talisman against fire and steel," says the Duke of Guise : "here, strangle me him with this." And he drops down to his hirelings the handkerchief of his wife which he picked up at the beginning of the play.

This telling of the tale is bare and barren indeed: it hides the good points while exposing the weak. That the story is of thinner texture at times than one could wish is sufficiently obvious. French and English wits have readily found spots to gird at. In a French parody of the play the moral was summed up in four lines, which made fair fun of the handkerchief expedient:—

> "Messieurs et mesdames, cette pièce est morale
> Elle prouve aujourd'hui sans faire de scandale,
> Que chez un amant, lorsqu'on va le soir,
> On peut oublier tout . . . excepté son mouchoir!"

Lord Leveson Gower's English adaptation, called 'Catherine of Cleves,' gave the author of the 'Ingoldsby Legends' a chance to condense the story in comic verse, and to give it at least one keen hit:—

> "De Guise grasped her wrist
> With his great bony fist,
> And pinched it, and gave it so painful a twist,
> That his hard iron gauntlet the flesh went an inch in:
> She did not mind death, but she could not stand pinching!"

'Henri III. et sa Cour' is not a play of the highest order, and it has sufficiently obvious blemishes; but it is a strong and stirring drama, and one of the very best of its class, of which it was also almost the first. It is a very much better play than 'Christine,' written before it, and brought out after it, or than 'Charles VII. chez ses Grands Vassaux,'—a second attempt in rhymed Alexandrines scarcely more successful than the first. It is a better play than either of the two other dramas he produced in 1831. Of these the first was the frantically immoral and preposterously impossible

'Antony,' of which Dumas, strangely enough, was so proud that he was wont to declare it and his son his two best works; and the second was 'Napoléon Bonaparte,' which he had cut with a hasty pair of scissors from the many memoirs of the time, and which is more of a panorama than a play. The author had to confess that it made no pretence to be literature, except in so far as a single character gave it value, — the character of a magnanimous and heroic spy, omniscient, ubiquitous, and ever ready to sacrifice himself for Napoleon.

The Napoleonic piece may be dismissed thus briefly, but 'Antony' is too important and too powerful a play to be glanced at cursorily. It is a play one cannot help pausing over. Even in the thick of the battle between the Classicists and the Romanticists, when the latter opposed to the staid decorum of the former the most glowing pictures of fiery passion, free from all bond or limit, — even at such a time 'Antony' gave a sharp shock to those who saw it, and owed its success to the sudden and startling surprise upon which the curtain fell, and which left the first spectators too astonished to protest. Byronic influence, always powerful among the exuberant young iconoclasts, had peopled the dramas of the day with fellows of the Giaour, haughty, self-contained, and passionate bastards, bearing their bar sinister as though it were the grand cross of a mighty order. The re-action against the cold conventionalities of the Classicist tragedies had given birth to a long line of lovely ladies, sad and suffering, sentimental and sinning. As the contemporary epigram had it, —

> "À croire ces messieurs, on ne voit dans nos rues,
> Que les enfants trouvés et les femmes perdues."

Nowhere are these two figures more puissantly fashioned and more powerfully put upon their feet than by Dumas in this play; and Antony and Adèle d'Hervey are types of the great lengths to which the revolutionary zeal of the revolting Romanticists could carry them.

Antony had loved Adèle before she was married, but did not dare ask her hand, because he was illegitimate. He absents himself for three years, and then returns, to find her a wife and a mother. In the first act he saves her life from a runaway before her door, and is brought into her house seriously injured; and, to remain under the same roof with her, he tears the bandages from his wounds. In the second act his passion is so powerful, that Adèle thinks it best to seek safety for her fragile virtue by secretly joining her husband, who is at Frankfort. The third act passes in an post-inn on the road to Frankfort. Antony has learned Adèle's flight, and discovered her destination, and contrived to pass her on the road. He engages the only two rooms in the house, and hires all the horses, sending them on with his servant; and, when Adèle arrives, she is forced to wait for fresh horses. The landlady asks Antony to cede one of his rooms to a lady travelling alone; and Antony gives up one room, having seen that the balcony affords a means of communication with the other, which he retains. Adèle, forced to pass the night by herself, is lonely and nervous: at last, however, she retires to sleep in the alcove bed-room. Antony appears outside the window, breaks a pane, passes in his arm, shoots back the bolt, and steps into the room. As he locks the door through which the landlady went out, Adèle comes back. The act comes to an end after this abrupt dialogue and action : —

Adèle. — Noise ! . . A man ! . . . Oh !

Antony. — Silence ! (*Taking her in his arms, and putting a handkerchief over her mouth.*) Tis I ! . . . I, Antony ! (CURTAIN.)

In the fourth act we are back in Paris again. The relations between Antony and Adèle are beginning to be talked about. Both are present at a party, and after much talk about the new literary theories, in the course of which Dumas follows the Aristophanic precedent, and, in a sort of parabasis delivered by one of the secondary characters, makes a personal defence, as well as a direct assault on the 'Constitutionel,' the newspaper most opposed to the new views, Antony retorts severely on a scandal-monger, who reflects by innuendo on Adèle. Made wretched by this attack, Adèle withdraws early ; and Antony follows her hurriedly aş soon as his servant arrives post-haste from Frankfort, announcing the hourly return of Adèle's husband. He gets to Adèle's house, in the next and last act, before the husband ; and the guilty pair make ready for flight. All of a sudden Adèle bethinks herself of her child. Antony consents to take the child along. But the mother cries out that her open shame, confessed by her flight, will surely be visited on her daughter in the future, and that death would be better than exposure and humiliation. In the midst of the heated talk of Adèle and Antony, a double knock is heard at the street-door. The husband has got back. Flight is no longer possible. There is no way of escape. Adèle begs for death in preference to shame. She is one of those who hold, with Tartuffe, that, —

"Le scandale du monde est ce qui fait l'offense,
Et ce n'est pas pêcher que pêcher en silence!"

Now, when silence is not possible and scandal is inevitable, she cries aloud for death. As a sharp knock is heard on the door of the room, Antony asks her if she means what she says, if she would welcome a death which might save her reputation and her child's, if she would forgive him for slaying her. Adèle, out of her mind with the excitement of the moment, begs for death. Antony kisses her and stabs her. Then the door is broken in. The husband and servants rush in, and stand in horror as they see Adèle lying in death. "Dead: yes, dead!" says Antony heroically. "She resisted me, and I assassinated her." On this the curtain falls finally.

Of course this story is simply absurd, if you consider it calmly; but this is just what the author will not let you do. He allows no time at all for consideration. He hurries you along with the feverish rush of the action, as resistless as it is restless. As the younger Dumas has told us, 'Antony' is to be "studied by all young writers who wish to write for the stage, as nowhere else is interest, audacity, and skill carried so far." The elder Dumas knew how audacious his story was, and how important to its success was the leaving of as little time as possible to the play-goer for sober second-thought. At the first performance, when the curtain fell on the fourth act there was great enthusiasm. Dumas sprang upon the stage, and shouted to the carpenters, "A hundred francs for you if you get the curtain up before the applause ceases!" By this presence of mind he succeeded in springing his very ticklish fifth act upon the audience while they were still excited over the fourth.

The proud and lonely bastard had been called Didier, and had made love to Victor Hugo's Marion Delorme, before he was Antony, the lover and assassin of Adèle d'Hervey. There was more than a family likeness between Dumas's hero and Hugo's ; and when 'Marion Delorme,' written in 1828, and forbidden by the censors, was at last acted in 1831, not long after 'Antony,' charges of plagiarism were not wanting. Alexandre Dumas came forward at once, and said ingenuously enough, that if there was a plagiarist it was he, as he had heard Victor Hugo read 'Marion Delorme' before 'Antony' was written. In his memoirs Dumas frankly sets down the great effect the hearing of 'Marion Delorme' had had upon him, and confesses that it had greatly enlarged his dramatic horizon. By one of the curious compensations, of which there are a many in the history of literature, it seems as though Dumas was enabled to pay his debt to Hugo in full; for it can scarcely be doubted that for 'Lucrèce Borgia,' Hugo, perhaps and indeed probably unconsciously, was indebted to the ' Tour de Nesle ' of Dumas.

Although we can detect Antony's father in Didier, it would be a hopeless task to attempt to discover or count all the children of Antony himself. A play, like any other entity, is perhaps best judged by its posterity. A very successful play like 'Antony' has a progeny as numerous as a patriarch of old. Antony's offspring are a pernicious brood, from the elder Dumas's own efforts to put him again on the stage, under other names, down to the 'Princess of Bagdad,' the latest play of the younger Dumas, the three chief characters of which all show the hereditary characteristics. In the list of the French plays of the past half-century there is a long line of monsters, violent, headstrong, bloody, and impossible; and all of them own Antony for their father. Of late, as scepticism grows, and passion forcibly repressed is more fashionable than passion forcibly expressed, the play-going public does not take very kindly to Antony or to his children. It is many a long year since 'Antony' itself has been acted in Paris: it is as long, nearly, since any play in which his influence is emphatic and visible has had any success on the French stage. The 'Princess of Bagdad,' the latest play of the younger Dumas, is almost as preposterous an impossibility as 'Antony' itself; and in spite of its modern dress, cut in the latest fashion, and trimmed with the sharp wit of which its author alone has the secret, — in spite of the fame of the dramatist and the aid of some of the chief actors of the Comédie-Française, the 'Princess of Bagdad' has been a distinct and dismal failure. Fifty years ago 'Antony' was as distinct a success. The world moves. Outside of France, neither 'Antony' nor Antony-ism has ever been popular; and, so far as I know, there has never been acted in any English or American theatre any adaptation of 'Antony.'

After 'Antony,' the next of Dumas's dramas which needs consideration here is the 'Tour de Nesle.' This is quite as remarkable a play as 'Henri III.' or 'Antony.' It is a play of the same kind, but more exciting, more terrible, more brutal. The dramatist has given another turn to the screw, and the pressure is more intense. Considered solely by its effect in the theatre, the 'Tour de Nesle' is one of the most powerful plays ever written. The clash of conflicting interests and emotions catches the attention in the first scene, and holds it breath-

less till the last.   There is a resistless rush of action :
improbabilities so glaring that on other occasions you
would cry aloud, are here so dexterously veiled, and so
promptly turned to advantage, that you have neither
time nor wish to protest.   Situation presses after situation, each stronger than the other ; a complicated plot,
intricate in its convolutions, unrolls itself with the
utmost ease and simplicity : the eye is kept awake, and
the ear alert ; and the interest never flags for a moment,
from the rising of the curtain to the going-down thereof.
Then, oh, then ! with a final pause, there is at last and
for the first time a chance for reflection, and you begin
to wonder what manner of monster this is which has
held you motionless, and almost panting, for so many
hours ; and you begin, it may be, to suspect that the
drama is a series of absurdities, — a phantasmagoric
nightmare.   But whatever it is, and however much sober
second-thought may find to cavil at, its power, its sheer
brute force, is indisputable.

Outcry has been made about the immorality of 'Henri
III.' and the 'Tour de Nesle,' surely without reason.
'Antony' is immoral, it is true, shamelessly and grossly
immoral ; but not 'Henri III.,' or the 'Tour de Nesle.'
The latter has been termed a tissue of horrors, because
it contains murder and adultery and incest.   But Dumas
tries to get no sham pathos out of these sins ; and they
are not dallied with, or in any way palliated.   Dark
crimes were frequent enough in the dark days in which
the action of the 'Tour de Nesle' is laid.   Nor are these
crimes so revolting that they are without the pale of art,
as are some of the subjects Calderon treats for example.
The horrible is not necessarily immoral ; rather, if any
thing, the reverse.   The accumulation of sin in the

'Tour de Nesle' is not more horrible than it is in the 'Medea,' nor is it as horrible here as it is in the 'Œdipus.' It must be confessed at once that the effect is more horrible in the modern play than in the ancient, because the Greek tragedians were poets, and their later imitators have tried to catch also something of the poetic spirit. But Dumas's handling of a similar situation has no touch of poetry : it is prosaic, baldly prosaic ; and the horrors stand forth in their nakedness. The modern French play may be more shocking, but essentially it is no more immoral, than the old Greek tragedy. After all, morality is an affair, not of subject, but of treatment ; and Dumas's treatment, while not as austere and ennobling as the Greek, is not insidious or vicious. Except in so far as all over-exciting exhibitions are harmful, I do not believe that any one ever has been injured by the 'Tour de Nesle,' which has been acted in half the theatres of the United States at one time or another during the past half-century.

It was with intention that reference was made to Calderon. There is something in the exuberant prodigality of Dumas's production which recalls the most brilliant days of the Spanish stage. Dumas can stand the comparison with Lope de Vega and Calderon : it is not altogether to his disadvantage. In the qualities in which they were most eminent, — ease and fertility and skill, — he was also most abundant. In the vastness of his production he recalls Lope de Vega ; but it is perhaps rather Calderon than Lope de Vega with whom Dumas may be compared when one considers quality more than quantity. He lacked the simple faith of Calderon, and Calderon was without the self-consciousness which was so strong in Dumas ; and the points of

resemblance are scarcely more than the points of dis-
similarity. Archbishop Trench dwells on the technical
playmaking skill of Calderon, in which Dumas was
assuredly his equal ; while in fecundity of character, if
not of situation, the French dramatist surpasses the
Spanish. Where Dumas is inferior, is in that indescribable quality we call "style." Calderon, like Victor
Hugo, is a playwright doubled with a lyric poet : in the
highest sense neither is a true dramatic poet, as are
Æschylus, Shakspere, Molière, and Schiller. The distinction between the clever playwright who is also a
lyric poet, and the true dramatic poet, is not at all
trivial, even if it seem so. Much as Dumas was like
Calderon in ease and abundance and skill, he was far
inferior in that he was not a poet, and that he is altogether lacking in elevation.

It was in 1836 that Dumas brought out 'Don Juan
de Marana ; or, The Fall of an Angel,' mystery in five
acts. This is the play of his which puts us most in
mind of Calderon. The story is one which the author
of 'Life is a Dream' might well have told, and would
have told with a simple sincerity and an honest faith not
to be found in Dumas's drama. The bold use of sacred
personages as part of the machinery of the play is more
in the style of the pious and priestly Calderon than of
a worldling like Dumas. The chief figure is a repetition
of the traditional type of Don Juan, accompanied throughout by the good and evil angels of his family, striving
with each other for his soul. Most of the scenes are on
the earth : though there is one under the earth, in a
tomb, in which a dead man comes to life for a moment ;
and another above the earth, in the heavens, in which
the good angel begs permission of the Virgin Mary to

be allowed to go down into the world as a woman, to be more closely united with her beloved Don Juan. In the course of this truly extraordinary production we have duels and deaths by the half-dozen, suicides, seductions, elopements, murders, poisonings, ghosts, and spectral visions; "and what is more, is more than man may know." Calderon handles elements not unlike these without shocking our moral sense: however extravagant the events in his tale, it is easy to see they have been touched by the magic wand of the poet. Dumas had to use a showman's pointer instead of the poet's wand; and so, in spite of all effort to moralize, his precious hodge-podge is not exactly edifying.

'Don Juan de Marana' is one of the plays against which Thackeray particularly protested in his essay on French Dramas and Melodramas, reprinted in the 'Paris Sketch-Book.' With all his liberality and fondness for freedom, this play affected him so unpleasantly, that he cried aloud for government interference, and the putting-down of such indecent entertainments by the stern hand of the law. It is not a little curious that Thackeray, who lost no opportunity of heartily praising Dumas's novels, has only words of reprobation for his plays. For one thing, it must be remembered that Dumas had not regularly set up as a novelist, with a sign over his door and daily office-hours, when the 'Paris Sketch-Book' was written: he was known then only as a dramatist. The charm of the story-teller had not yet disposed Thackeray, whose morality was stout and sturdy, to look with lenity on Dumas's slipshod ethics. Then, again, Thackeray himself had not a very quick feeling for strength of situation and stage-effects in general, and perhaps he was therefore not precisely the critic to appreciate at its full value Dumas's best quality. Whatever the cause of Thackeray's lack of liking for Dumas as a dramatist, it is certain that he did not like him, and showed it plainly in the essay already referred to. Not only does he fall foul of 'Don Juan de Marana,' but he makes fun of some of the rhodomontade which fills the preface to 'Caligula:' harmless enough it seems to us now, and not to be taken seriously. Besides 'Caligula,' which failed, Thackeray also dissected with the finest-edged scalpel of his sarcasm, 'Kean,' a drama the action of which Dumas chose to lay in England. In spite of its success, due no doubt for the most part to the acting of Frédéric Lemaître, 'Kean' can scarcely be considered a fair specimen of Dumas at his best. The hero is Edmund Kean, most erratic and most miserable of Mother Carey's chickens; and Dumas, with a truly Parisian disregard for exact facts, makes Kean indeed a tragedy hero. Thackeray has so thoroughly shown the flimsiness and absurdity of the play that nothing remains to be said.

I have called 'Don Juan de Marana' a hodge-podge, not merely because the drama has no very distinct unity of design, but more particularly because it was compounded of scraps stolen from half a score authors. The outline of plot and character had been borrowed from Molière, of course, and more especially from Merimée; and individual incidents had been taken from Goethe, Musset, Scott, Shakspere, and even "Monk" Lewis. It must be confessed at once that this proceeding was not unusual with Dumas, although the plagiarism is rarely as flagrant as here. All through his earlier plays are scattered little bits of Scott and Schiller and

Lope de Vega, turned to excellent account, and firmly joined to the rest of the work.   The prologue of 'Richard Darlington' is from Scott's 'Chronicles of the Canongate.'   Generally it is but a hint, a suggestion, an effect, an incident, a situation, which he took unto himself.   Sometimes, as in the case of 'Henri III.,' he borrowed from two or three authors.   Sometimes, as in 'Don Juan de Marana,' although the whole play was plainly his own, nearly all the separate scenes could be traced to other authors.   Sometimes he even took a play ready made, and condescended to the vulgar adaptation of which his own plays have only too often been the victims in English.   Dean Milman's 'Fazio' was thus turned into French verse as the 'Alchimiste.' Sometimes, again, only the motive of the action came from outside, and the development was all his own: thus Racine's 'Andromaque' furnished the basis of 'Charles VII.,' and Dumas boldly braved the comparison by the epigraph on his title-page, " *Cur non?* "

Ben Jonson, we are told, once dreamed that he saw the Romans and Carthaginians fighting on his big toe. No doubt Dumas had not dissimilar dreams; for his vanity was at least as stalwart and as frank as Ben Jonson's.   To defend himself against all charges of plagiarism, the French dramatist echoed the magniloquent phrase of the English dramatist, and declared that he did not steal, he conquered.   It is but justice to say that there was no mean and petty pilfering about Dumas.   He annexed as openly as a statesman, and made no attempt at disguise.   In his memoirs he is very frank about his sources of inspiration, and tells us at length where he found a certain situation, and what it suggested to him, and how he combined it with another effect which had struck him somewhere else. When one goes to the places thus pointed out, one finds something very different from what it became after it had passed through Dumas's hands, and, more often than not, far inferior to it. It can scarcely be said that Dumas touched nothing he did not adorn; for he once laid sacrilegious hands on Shakspere, and brought out a 'Hamlet' with a very French and epigrammatic last act. But whatever he took from other authors he made over into something very different, something truly his own, something that had *Dumas fecit* in the corner, even though the canvas and the colors were not his own. The present M. Dumas asserts that "there are no original ideas, especially in dramatic literature: there are only new points of view." Granting this, as we may, it remains to be said that no one ever took more new points of view than Dumas. In a word, all his plagiarisms, and they were not a few, are the veriest trifles when compared with his indisputable and extraordinary powers.

Besides plagiarism, Dumas has been accused of "devilling," as the English term it; that is to say, of putting his name to plays written either wholly or in part by others. There is no doubt that the accusation can be sustained, although many of the separate specifications are groundless. The habit of collaboration obtains widely in France; and collaboration runs easily into "devilling." When two men write a play together, and one of them is famous and the other unknown, there is a strong temptation to get the full benefit of celebrity, and to say nothing at all about the author whose name has no market-value. That Dumas yielded to it now and then is not to be wondered at. There was something imperious in his character, as there was something imperial in his power. He had dominion over so many departments of literature, that he had accustomed himself to be monarch of all he surveyed; and if a follower came with the germ of a plot, or a suggestion for a strong situation, Dumas took it as tribute due to his superior ability. In his hands the hint was worked out, and made to render all it had of effect. Even when he had avowed collaborators, as in 'Richard Darlington,' he alone wrote the whole play. His partners got their share of the pecuniary profits, benefiting by his skill and his renown; and most of them did not care whether he who had done the best of the work should get all the glory or not. At times, too, as in the case of 'Perrinet Leclerc' and of the 'Tour de Nesle,' his name did not appear at all: he tells us in his memoirs that the former was in part his handiwork, and it is not even yet included in his collected plays.

The case of the 'Tour de Nesle' is different, and not a little complicated. Dumas has written a long and somewhat disingenuous history of the play. It seems that M. Frédéric Gaillardet (afterward the founder of the *Courier des États-Unis* in New York) wrote the 'Tour de Nesle,' and took it to Harel, the manager of the Porte St. Martin Théâtre. Harel saw in it the raw material of a strong piece, and accepted it, subject to revision by a more practised hand. He sent the play to Jules Janin, who re-wrote it, and then knew enough to see that the result was hopelessly undramatic. Harel then took Janin's manuscripts to Dumas, who, according to his own account, discarded most of the original play, and wrote a new drama around the central situations. Having thus made what was substantially a new play, Dumas arranged with Harel that M. Gaillardet should get the full author's fee which the Porte St. Martin Théâtre was accustomed to pay, and that his own pay should be independent of M. Gaillardet's. In spite of Harel's repeated requests, Dumas refused to allow his name to be put on the bills. Under such circumstances a play is announced as by MM. Gaillardet and * * * but Harel chose to announce the 'Tour de Nesle' as by MM. * * * and Gaillardet. M. Gaillardet rushed into print, and Dumas retorted, setting forth his own share in the composition of the drama. After a while Dumas and M. Gaillardet fought a bloodless duel. Then there was a lawsuit. After many years, peace was declared, and M. Gaillardet was pleased to acknowledge the great service Dumas had rendered to the 'Tour de Nesle.' Looking back now, one can scarcely have a doubt as to whom the success of the drama was due, — whether to M. Gaillardet, who had not done any thing like it before, and who has not done any thing like it since, or to Dumas, who had shown in 'Henri III.' and 'Antony' his ability to write a play of precisely the same quality. The original sequence of situations was no doubt suggested by M. Gaillardet; but the play as it stands is unequivocally the handiwork of Dumas.

That Dumas plagiarized freely in his earliest plays, and had the aid of "devils" in the second stage of his career, is not to be denied, and neither proceeding is praiseworthy ; but, although he is not blameless, it irks one to see him pilloried as a mere vulgar appropriator of the labors of other men. The exact fact is, that he had no strict regard for mine and thine. He took as freely as he gave. In literature, as in life, he was a spendthrift; and a prodigal is not always as scrupulous as he might be in replenishing his purse. Dumas's ethics deteriorated as he advanced. One may safely say, that there is none of the plays bearing his name which does not prove itself his by its workmanship. When, however, he began to write serial stories, and to publish a score of volumes a year, then he trafficked in his reputation, and signed his name to books which he had not even read. An effort has been made to show that even 'Monte Cristo' and the 'Three Musketeers' series were the work of M. Auguste Maquet, and that Dumas contributed to them only his name on the titlepage. It is foreign to my purpose now to consider Dumas as a writer of romance; but, as these novels were at once cut up into plays, a consideration of their authorship is in order here. I must confess that I do not see how any one with any pretence to the critical faculty can doubt that 'Monte Cristo' and the 'Three Musketeers' are Dumas's own work. That M. Maquet made historical researches, accumulated notes, invented scenes even, is probable; but the mighty impress of Dumas's hand is too plainly visible in every important passage for us to believe that either series owes more to M. Maquet than the service a pupil might fairly render to a master. That these services were considerable is sufficiently obvious from the printing of M. Maquet's name by the side of Dumas's on the titlepages of the dramatizations from the stories. That it was Dumas's share of the work which was inconsiderable is as absurd as it is to scoff at his creative faculty because he was wont to borrow. Señor Castelar has said that all Dumas's collaborators together do not weigh half as much in the literary balance as Dumas alone ; and this is true. I have no wish to reflect on the talents of Dinaux, the author of 'Thirty Years, or a Gambler's Life,' and of 'Louise de Lignerrolles,' or on the talents of M. Maquet himself, whose own novels and plays have succeeded, and who is so highly esteemed by his fellow-dramatists as to have been elected and re-elected the president of the Society of Dramatic Authors ; yet I must say that the plays which either Dinaux or M. Maquet has written by himself do not show the possession of the secret which charmed us in the work in which they helped Dumas. It is to be said, too, that the later plays taken from his own novels, in which Dumas was assisted by M. Maquet, are very inferior to his earlier plays, written wholly by himself. They are mere dramatizations of romances, and not in a true sense dramas at all. The earlier plays, however extravagant they might be in individual details, had a distinct and essential unity not to be detected in the dramatizations, which were little more than sequences of scenes snipped with the scissors from the interminable series of tales of adventure. How could the plot of the 'Three Musketeers,' — so far as it has any single plot, — how could it be compressed within the limits of five, or even of six or seven acts ? How could there be any of the singleness of impression which is a necessary element of good dramatic art in a dramatization so bulky that it took two nights to act ? 'Monte Cristo' was brought out as a play in two parts, Dec. 3 and 4, 1848 ; and three years later two more divisions of the same story were put on the stage. Obviously enough, pieces of this sort are like the earlier 'Napoléon Bonaparte,' not plays, but panoramas : slices of the story serve as magic-lantern slides, and dissolve one into another at the will of the exhibiter.   Full as these pieces are of life and bustle and gayety, they are poor substitutes for plays, which depend for success on themselves, and not on the vague desire to see in action figures which the reader has learned to like in endless stories.   These dramatizations were unduly long-drawn, naturally prolix, not to say garrulous.   When his tales were paid for by the word, when he was "writing on space," as they say in a newspaper office, Dumas let the vice of saying all there was to be said grow on him.   On the stage, the half is more than the whole.

Side by side with these dramatizations, Dumas continued to bring out now and then dramas in his earlier manner ; for example, the already mentioned 'Alchimiste' (1839) and 'Hamlet' (1849), and also a 'Catilina' (1849), likewise in verse, besides an occasional play in prose, including, for one, an adaptation of Schiller's 'Kabale und Liebe.'   None of these, however, is as interesting or as important as any one of his earliest four or five successes.   The only works of his more mature years which enlarge his reputation are his comedies.   He brought to the making of comedy the same freshness, facility, fecundity, and force, that he had brought years before to the making of drama. After all, it is not inexact to say that the two chief qualities of Dumas were abundance and ease.   Other writers of his time were abundant : none were so easy. Contrast his running sentences with the tortured style of Balzac, and we can understand how it was that Dumas could write a volume in a few hours, and that Balzac once spent a whole night toiling over a single sentence. Now, ease and abundance are invaluable to a writer of comedy. Although the half a dozen comedies Dumas wrote vary in value, all are equally facile and flowing. 'Mlle. de Belle-Isle' and the 'Demoiselles de St. Cyr' and the 'Jeunesse de Louis XIV' (which his son edited for the Parisian stage a few years ago) are as simple and unaffected plays as you can find; and they are plays of a new kind. The comedies of Dumas are unlike the comedies of any other French dramatist. They are as different from the more philosophical comedy of the seventeenth and eighteenth centuries as they are from the Realistic comedy which his son brought into fashion. They are a little like the best of the comedies which Scribe wrote for the Théâtre Français, although they had a boldness and a freedom Scribe could never attain. Perhaps, more than anything else, they resemble the English comedies of intrigue and adventure imitated from Spanish models, such as Cibber's 'She Would and She Would Not.'

In Dumas's plays, however, both situation and dialogue seem less forced, although it is unfair ever to speak of either as though it were at all forced. Dumas had little humor, as we understand the word, and what he had was on the surface; but he was witty without effort and without end. It is a quality he seems to have discovered after he had written his earlier and more famous plays; for in these there is little to relieve the tensity of emotion. In his comedies, however, his wit had a chance to show its nimbleness. This wit is lightsome and buoyant, rather than penetrating. It is not epigrammatically sparkling with a hard brilliance like Sheridan's and Congreve's; nor is it biting and vitriolic like his son's: it seems less

studied and more natural than either, and more to be
compared to the graceful and clever wit of a ready man
of the world; and, as I have said, it is as unfailing as it
is unforced.   I can recommend a little comedy in one
act called the 'Mari de la Veuve,' and written during the
desolation caused by the cholera, to all who may desire
to see as bright a little play as one could wish.   In his
memoirs Dumas tells us that the primary idea of this
tiny piece was one friend's, and that the development
and construction were another's, and that all he did
was to take their plan, and write the dialogue.   But it
was dialogue such as none but he could write.

This very play contains an admirable instance of his
tact in turning a difficulty.   A husband has written to
his wife bidding her to announce his death, for reasons
not given but imperative.   It is from the false position
thus created for the wife, who is supposed to be a
widow, that the comedy is evolved.   Shortly after the
rise of the curtain, the husband appears, but too much
in a hurry to explain why he has had to conceal his
existence.   At the end of the play even, he had not
yet told; then, when all is attention, the servant an-
nounces the notary to draw up the contract for the
marriage which brings every comedy to a happy end.
Interrupted, the husband says, "I will tell you all about
it to-morrow."   And the curtain falls, leaving the spectator amused and entertained, but still in ignorance
why the husband found it necessary to give out his
own death.   I am inclined to surmise that the pair of
collaborators who planned the play devised a reason for
this, and that Dumas found this reason insufficient.
Not having time to concoct another, he made the difficulty disappear by not giving any reason at all.

From the sombre 'Antony' to the laughing 'Mari
de la Veuve' is a long stride; but Dumas took it without straining; and many another beside. Even more
remarkable than the range of Dumas's work is its general level of merit. He had, at least, one element of
greatness, — an inexhaustible fecundity. More than
this; when we consider the quantity of his dramas, the
quality of the best of them seems singularly high.
There is but one dramatist of his generation who will
stand comparison with him; and even Victor Hugo,
master as he is of many things, is less a master of the
theatre than Dumas. He was the superior of Dumas
in that he was a poet, and had style, as Dumas was
willing to confess. But for success on the stage,
poetry and style are not so potent as other qualities
which Dumas had more abundantly than Hugo. He
had an easy wit which Hugo lacked, and which is of
inestimable service to the playmaker. He had a flexibility of manner to which Hugo could not pretend.
We have seen how many different kinds of dramas
Dumas attempted, while all Hugo's pieces are cast in
the same mould. As Heine said, "Dumas is not so
great a poet as Victor Hugo; but he possesses gifts
which in the drama enable him to achieve far greater
results than the latter. He has perfect command of
that forcible expression of passion which the French
term *verve;* and he is, withal, more of a Frenchman
than Victor Hugo is." Elsewhere Heine credits Hugo
with a Teutonic want of tact, and suggests that his
muse had two left hands. Now Dumas's muse had a
right hand, and it never forgot its cunning. Dumas's
dramas, extravagant as some of them are, strike one as
more natural than Hugo's, perhaps because the latter

reveal too openly the constraint of their construction, which the former never do. Dumas was frank to praise Hugo, and to acknowledge his own indebtedness to him; yet he spoke his mind freely about his competitor. He is reported as saying that "each had our own good points; but mine were better. Hugo was lyrical and theatrical: I was dramatic. Hugo, to be effective, could not do without contrasting drinking-songs with church hymns, and setting tables laden with flowers and flasks by the side of coffins draped in black. All I wanted was four scenes, four boards, two actors, and a passion." It is easy to smile at this as mere vanity and vexation of spirit; but, magniloquence apart, it is sound criticism nevertheless.

Like Hugo, Dumas was the son of a revolutionary general, and both were as militant in literature as their fathers had been in life. From his father, Dumas inherited little but the physical force which sustained him in his reckless waste of energy, and which helped to give him the abundant confidence in himself: these two things indeed, strength and confidence, are at the bottom of his career of marvellous prodigality. It was confidence and strength combined which made possible his unhasting, unresting life of toil in so many departments of literature. This life is in many respects a warning, rather than an example. With his great powers one feels he ought to have done something higher and nobler: that he had great powers, admits of no cavil. The present M. Alexandre Dumas, who is as restrained as his father was exuberant, and who looked on his father as a sort of prodigal son, upholds the honor of the family, and pushes filial reverence to the extreme verge of extravagance; yet, due allowance made, he is not so very far out when he speaks of his father as "he who was and is the master of the modern stage, whatever noise may be made about other names, he whose prodigious imagination touched the four cardinal points of our art, — tragedy, historical drama, the drama of manners, and the comedy of anecdote ; he whose only fault was to lack solemnity, and to have genius without pride, and fecundity without effort, as he had youth and health ; he who, to conclude, Shakspere being taken as the culminating point, by invention, power, and variety approached among us most closely to Shakspere."

CHAPTER IV.

EUGÈNE SCRIBE.

CARLYLE speaks of Diderot as "successful in criticism, successful in philosophism, nay, highest of sublunary glories, successful in the theatre." Accepting this last dictum, we may venture the assertion that no writer ever enjoyed so much of the highest of sublunary glories as Eugène Scribe; for no maker of plays, either before or since, was ever so uniformly successful, and over so wide an area. Æschylus and Aristophanes did not always get the prize they strove for; and even when they did triumph, their fame was limited to their own city, or at most to Greece and its chain of colonies. Scribe's luck rarely failed him; and his best pieces were carried, not only all over France, but around the world. His fertility was as unfailing as his good fortune. The output of his fiction-factory is enormous. In the year 1823 alone, he brought out nearly a score of plays. In the half-century of his incessant production he wrote more than four hundred dramatic pieces, of one kind or another, beside a dozen or more novels. In bulk his work is barely equalled by Lope de Vega's, or by Hardy's, by De Foe's, or by Voltaire's, or, in our own day, by the elder Dumas's. His complete works are now in course of publication. Sixty closely-printed volumes, of some four hundred pages each, have already appeared; and the end is not yet. He began life with a trifling patrimony. By his pen he made sometimes as

much as one hundred and fifty thousand francs a year
For the one long novel he wrote for serial publication
in a newspaper, he received sixty thousand francs; and
when he died he left a fortune of quite two millions
of francs. To these material gains, there was added
the honor of a seat among the illustrious forty of the
French Academy.

Born in 1791, Scribe began to write for the stage
before he was twenty. Like many another dramatist,
he was intended for the law, before his success on the
stage justified his giving up the bar. Like many
another dramatist, moreover, his earlier dramatic attempts proved failures. If we may credit M. Ernest
Legouvé, his fellow-craftsman and sometime literary
partner, Scribe saw fourteen of his plays miss fire
before he made his first hit. Then, turning from the
servile imitation of Picard and Duval, he began to look
at the life around him, and determined to place on the
stage the petty foibles of the day. His first attempt
at what an American dramatist has called "contemporaneous human interest" was 'Une Nuit de la Garde
Nationale,' a vaudeville in one act, brought out in 1816.
It attracted instant attention. The citizen-soldiers it
made fun of chose to take offence. There was much
bluster, and some talk of a challenge to mortal combat. The piece, in the mean time, set everybody laughing; and Scribe saw, that, after prospecting vainly, he
had found at last the lead he could work to advantage.

The vaudeville, when Scribe took it up, was in a
middle stage of its long evolution. Originally it had
been a sort of satirical ballad, or a string of epigrams,
telling pointedly an anecdote of the hour, or girding
sharply at an unpopular official or favorite. This

is the vaudeville whereof Boileau speaks when he
says, —

> " Le Français, né malin, forma le vaudeville."

About the beginning of the last century this versified anecdote came to be cast into dialogue, and sung
in public, appropriate action aiding. For the theatre
in the fair first, and afterward for the Italian comedians, Lesage and Piron wrote vaudevilles of this type,
rudimentary plays, the words of which were all in
rhyme, ready for the vocalists. By the end of the
century the vaudeville had got a little more dramatic
consistence, remaining, however, either the parody of a
play or opera popular at another theatre, or a brief
and brisk setting on the stage of an anecdote. Such
it was when Scribe began to write, and to him was due
its final transformation. First he freshened it, as we
have seen, by attacking the follies and the fashions of
the day ; then, as soon as he felt himself secure, he
broadened its scope. The versified anecdote, dramatic
only by courtesy, gave place to a complete play, which,
slight as it might be, had a beginning, a middle, and an
end. Traces of the old form survived in the frequent
sets of verses written to well-known airs, and almost
meant to be said rather than sung. In these *couplets*,
as the snatches of song were called, were put the
special points of the dialogue and the best jests. But
in Scribe's hands reliance was had on the situation,
rather than on the dialogue. For the first time a
vaudeville was seen with an imbroglio as involved and
as full of comic uncertainty as might have sufficed
hitherto for a play of far greater pretensions.

In 1820, four years after Scribe's first success, M.

Poirson, his collaborator in that play, opened the
Gymnase Théâtre, and at once bound Scribe by contract not to write for any rival house for the space of
ten years. This is the decade of Scribe's most copious
production. Aided by a host of collaborators, he
brought out at the Gymnase a hundred and fifty pieces,
nearly all of them vaudevilles. Sure of his public,
Scribe gave the vaudeville still greater extension.
From one act he enlarged it often to two, and at times
to three acts. From a merely jocular and hasty representation of scenes from every-day life, he raised it
now into comedy, and again into drama. As he trust-
ed more and more to his plot, to the situations which
his wondrous constructive skill enabled him to present
to the best advantage, the couplets, although still retained, became of less and less importance : they could
even be omitted without great loss. In at least one
case this was done. Scribe had written a vaudeville
in one act for the Gymnase, intending the chief part
for Léontine Fay, who, however, fell sick before the
piece was put in rehearsal. The author cut out the
couplets, and cut up the play into three acts, changing
but one line of his original prose in so doing. Then
he took 'Valérie,' a comedy in three acts, to the
Théâtre Français, where it was accepted at once, and
where Mademoiselle Mars acted the blind heroine with
her usual graceful perfection. This anecdote shows
how the vaudeville had grown in Scribe's hands. A
vaudeville which a skilful touch or two will turn into a
comedy fit for the Comédie-Française is very far from
the vaudeville which is only a hastily dramatized anecdote. Of this comédie-vaudeville, then, Scribe was
really the inventor, as well as its most industrious
maker.

The new comédies-vaudevilles varied in range from
pretty and semi-sentimental comedy, like 'Valérie,' to
light farce, like the 'Intérieur d'un Bureau.'   As fast
as they appeared in Paris, they were adapted to the
London market by Planché, Dance, Poole, or Charles
Mathews the younger.   As typical as any is 'Zoé, ou
l'amant prêté,' which Planché turned into the 'Loan
of a Lover.'   Those who recall that well-worn little
comedy can form a not unfair idea of the hundred
other plays of its kind which Scribe wrote for the
Gymnase.   Those who will take the trouble to compare the English play with the French will see that
the adaptation is a better bit of work than the original.
Planché, having a story ready to his hand, could spend
time and give thought to the consistency and coher-
ence of the characters who were to take part in it.
To Scribe the situations were of first importance ; and
no more strength was imparted to the characters than
was needed to get them through the ingenious intrigue.
There is a sharp contrast between the innate and
carefully cultivated tact with which Scribe handled
the succeeding situations of these lively little dramas,
and the careless way he set on their legs the people
whom he was to guide through the labyrinth.

I do not pretend to have read all of Scribe's four
hundred and more dramatic pieces, or even the half
of them ; but I have read or seen acted all those which
the consensus of criticism has indicated as the most
typical and the best ; and in all these plays I can recall only one single character thoroughly thought out
and wrought out, breathing the breath of life, and
moving of its own will.   By an effort of memory I
can call up a crowd of pretty faces with a strong family

likeness, or a lot of young gentlemen who have got themselves into a most unpleasant scrape. But that is all. The people who pass through these plays are merely profiles : they are like the plane of the geometricians, — without thickness and impalpable. Scribe had some knowledge of human nature, but it was only skin deep. He had insight enough; but it went just below the surface, and no further. Now, nothing is more temporary than superficial human nature. Scribe never got behind the man of the time to find man as he is at all times. His characters are silhouettes, into which the scissors have cut also the date. The fifteen years of the Restoration were the years when Scribe wrote the most of his comédies-vaudevilles, and it does not need the titlepage to tell us that they were acted before 1830. Scribe had looked around him, and seen the mighty industrial progress of France, freed at last from the bondage of the old Bourbon rule, from the uneasiness and ferment of the Revolution, and from the military strain of the Empire. Sick of martial glory, all France was trying to make money; and yet in picturesque juxtaposition to the new brood of bankers and merchants and manufacturers, stood the survivors of the Empire and the Revolution. So these comédies-vaudevilles are full of old soldiers, sergeants, and colonels and generals, all singing bits of verse in which *guerriers* rhymes with *lauriers ;* and in contrast with these are the money-makers, and the usual young men and pretty dolls of women, more or less witty and wicked. By dint of off-hand sketching of these as they floated by on the current of middle-class society, Scribe had made for himself a full set of the personages which might be needed in any comédie-vaudeville ; and, having once got a stock of these figures, he used them again and again, much as the deviser of one of the old Italian *commedia dell' arte* used the pedant and Brighetta, the captain and the doctor, and the rest of the instantly recognizable masks.

A comparison, not without interest, might be instituted between the comédie-vaudeville of Scribe and the commedia dell' arte as it became naturalized in France by the harlequin Dominique and his fellows, the friends of Molière. In each case, it was especially the amusement of the people of Paris, of the shop-keeping class above all; and, as I have said already, in each case, characters and dialogue were of less importance than plot and situation. The fecundity of Scribe in providing new subjects far surpassed that of his Italian predecessors. Goethe told Eckermann that Gozzi said that there were only thirty-six tragic situations, and added that Schiller had thought there were more, but could never succeed in finding even so many. Granting that the comic situations outnumber the tragic, there must be an end to them at length; yet Scribe seemed inexhaustible. When one turns out from ten to twenty new plays every year for ten years, there must be some repetition, some use of stale matter, some attempt at a *réchauffée*. But France is not a country with ten religions and only one sauce; and a French play-maker, if he be as skilful as Scribe, can serve you over again any old drama with a new dressing, so deftly disguised that you would scarce know it. Scribe took suggestions everywhere. From Marryat he borrowed 'Japhet in Search of a Father;' from Mrs. Inchbald, 'A Simple Story;' from Hertz, the lovely 'King Réné's Daughter;' and from Cooper's

'Lionel Lincoln' he got the germ of the 'Bohémienne, ou l'Amérique en 1775,' a highly comic drama of our Revolution, which might have been adapted to advantage during the centennial excitement. Scribe was fond also of doing over again in his more modern manner some of the masterpieces of the past; and so we have the 'Nouveaux Jeux de l'Amour et du Hasard' and the 'Nouveau Pourceaugnac:' even Molière did not scare him. Then, too, he did his own plays over again. M. Legouvé tell us that he quite forgot his own work sometimes, and would sit and listen to it, criticising it freely, without recalling it as his own. And I have seen somewhere an anecdote of his saying, as the curtain fell on a piece which was an obvious failure, "No matter: I will do it again next year." He did over not only his own failures, but those of other dramatists, when they bungled a good idea.

Beside all his borrowing from himself and from others, borrowing in which there was no deceit or dishonesty, — a more straightforward and upright man than Scribe never lived, — he had the assistance of the crowd of collaborators who encompassed him about. Scarce a tithe of his earlier plays were written by Scribe alone. First and last he must have had half a hundred collaborators, most of them unknown now out of France, and well-nigh forgotten even there. Not a few were men of mark on the French stage at that time. Three or four may be known to the world at large : Saintine, for instance, the author of 'Picciola;' and Bayard, the author of the 'Gamin de Paris;' and Saint-Georges, the author of the libretto of 'Martha' and of many another opera; and M. Legouvé, the author of 'Medée.' So many were his partners, that he was accused of keeping a play-factory, under the style of Scribe & Co., just as Dumas had been charged with keeping a novel-factory. But Scribe's treatment of his collaborators was in marked contrast with Dumas's. Scribe always did more than his share of the work, and was ready to give them more than their share of the credit. He never tried to grasp all the gold or the glory for himself.

His collaborators remained his friends, every one of them; and it was to them collectively that he dedicated the complete edition of his plays. One brought him a suggestion, another a plot in detail, a third a few couplets: whatever the share in the work, they were always named in the bill of the play, and on the titlepage, and they always drew a proportion in the profits. The most of the labor was always Scribe's; and sometimes the contribution of the partner was so slight that he could not point it out. M. Dupin once brought Scribe an ill-made two-act vaudeville, from which, however, Scribe got a suggestion that he immediately worked over into a one-act play of his own, 'Michel et Christine.' To the first performance he invited Dupin, who never knew he was seeing his own piece until it had succeeded, and the chief actor had announced as its authors MM. Scribe and Dupin. Again: M. Cornu came up from the country with a bag full of melodramas, one of which he begged Scribe to glance at. When he next called, months afterward, Scribe asked him if he had time to listen to a play. M. Cornu was pleased with the compliment, pleased with the vaudeville Scribe read, and astonished as well as pleased when told that he was its author. "I found an idea in your melodrama," said Scribe: "to me an idea is

enough." So on its titlepage the 'Chanoinesse' declares itself to be by MM. Scribe and Cornu. M.
Dupin had not written a line of one play, nor M. Cornu
of the other, nor had they even recognized their ideas
in Scribe's work; yet he acknowledged his obligation
to them, and shared his profits with them. In 1822
M. de Saint-Georges brought him a piece turning on a
game of lansquenet. "You have lost your labor," said
Scribe; "your play is impossible. If you want to
make dramatic use of a game of cards, you must
choose a game familiar to play-goers now, — *écarté*, for
example." And then he went on showing how such a
play might be written, what its plot might be, and
what might be done and said. When he paused,
Saint-Georges suggested that he had just sketched a
play, only needing to be written out. "So I have!"
said Scribe, smiling; and in November, 1822, there
was acted at the Gymnase a vaudeville called 'Écarté,'
by MM. Scribe and Saint-Georges. Now, M. Saint-
Georges had contributed nothing whatever to the
piece; but as his play had been the cause of the talk
out of which 'Écarté' sprang, Scribe chose to consider
him as a collaborator. Surely delicacy can go no farther than this.

Perhaps the making of a vaudeville like 'Michel et
Christine,' or the 'Chanoinesse,' or 'Écarté,' was such
an easy thing to Scribe that he held it lightly, although it must not be forgotten that he shared the
substantial profits of the play as well as the more
immaterial honor. When however he took a higher
flight, and rose from the comédie-vaudeville, never
longer than three acts, to the full-length five-act comedy of manners, meant for the Théâtre Français, he

renounced all outside aid, and relied on himself alone. The only fault his collaborators had ever found with him was his insisting on doing more than his share of the work. When he began to write for the Comédie-Française he cast them aside altogether, and did all the work. Dumas, whose assistants were as many, but not as loyally treated, as Scribe's, once defended himself over Scribe's shoulders, and declared that collaboration is a hindrance, and not a help. When Scribe was received at the French Academy, one of his dissatisfied colleagues is said to have murmured, "It is not a chair we should give him, but a bench to seat all his collaborators." And there were not wanting those who insinuated that his literary partners supplied all the ideas, and deserved all the credit. On these he turned the tables by doing alone and unaided his· most important, and in many respects his best work.

Fifty years ago the Théâtre Français, owing to the strict division of styles among the theatres of Paris, and the reservation to it of the masterpieces of classic tragedy and comedy, was an institution more august and of higher dignity than it is even now. Scribe, broken to every ruse and wile of theatrical effect by the experience gained in a hundred plays, and speaking on the stage as one having authority, turned from the Gymnase (though without wholly giving up the comédie-vaudeville), and brought out at the Théâtre Français a series of comedies of higher pretensions. Valérie was produced by the Comédie-Française in 1822, half by accident, as we have seen. Five years later, in the midst of his incessant production at the Gymnase, he brought out at the Théâtre Français his first five-act comedy, the 'Mariage d'Argent.' It failed. "Here, at last," said Villemain, when receiving Scribe into the French Academy, "is a complete comedy, without couplets, without collaborators, sustaining itself by its dramatic complexity, by the unity of its characters, by the truth of the dialogue, and by the vivacity of its moral." But at first the old play-goers, who were wont to meet in the house of Molière, keen to protect its traditions, would not hear of Scribe's comedy. It was the work of a vaudevillist only too obviously, they said; and they sent him back to his couplets and his collaborators. Though the piece failed in Paris, it succeeded amply in the provinces.

Soon the Théâtre Français was bearing the brunt of the Romanticist onslaught; and soon a more material revolution overthrew the Bourbon throne. Scribe was the only French dramatist of prominence who took no part in the struggle between the Romanticists and the Classicists, who went quietly on in his own way, and who held his public as firmly after the success of 'Antony' and 'Hernani' as before the publication of the preface to 'Cromwell.' But the revolution of July affected him more closely. The Gymnase had been called the "Théâtre de Madame," and on the withdrawal of the princely protection its future seemed less favorable. Besides, the turn of the political wheel had brought into view subjects for which the stage of the Gymnase was too small. So Scribe went to the Théâtre Français again, and 'Bertrand et Raton, ou l'Art de Conspirer,' was acted there in November, 1833, nearly six years after the check of the 'Mariage d'Argent.' In the next fifteen years, seven other five-act comedies, written by Scribe alone, were acted by the Comédie-Française: the 'Ambitieux' (1834); the 'Camaraderie, ou la Courte Echelle' (1837); the 'Calomnie' and the 'Verre d'Eau, ou les Effets et les Causes' (1840); 'Une Chaîne' (1841); the 'Fils de Cromwell, ou une Restauration' (1842); and the 'Puff, ou Mensonge et Vérité' (1848). These comedies, notwithstanding their well-jointed skeletons, are already aging terribly; they show the wrinkles of time: even the young lovers are now gray-haired, and the language is hopelessly rococo. The taste for sub-titles has died out, and some of Scribe's seem very ridiculous now.

His fancy for reflecting fully the changing hues of the hour has given his plays a color now faded and out of fashion forever. What is contemporary is three parts temporary. Language, for one thing, is always shifting. A far-seeing literary artist borrows only as many phrases from the jargon of the day as he may need to give life to his dialogue, and never enough to weight that dialogue down with dead words after they have dropped out of use. Scribe's subordination of every thing to the demands of an immediate stage-success makes most of his dialogue now lifeless and wooden. And unfortunately, though Scribe had a very pretty wit of his own, and was capable of writing dialogue of no little sparkle, he was never above making use of the ready-made jests, the commonplaces of joking. Théophile Gautier, to whom picturesqueness was the whole duty of man, somewhere says, that, after a witticism had been worn threadbare by hard usage, it was still sure of a freshening-up in some one of Scribe's plays. Here again we see Scribe's knowledge of the play-goer: if he made the new jest he was so well capable of making, perhaps the public might not see it ; but if he used the old joke, the public could but laugh. On the same principle, the clown in the circus gives us the most obvious and antique wit ; and the people needs must laugh at it, just as Diggory had been laughing at the story of the grouse in the gun-room these twenty years. Taught by his experience as a playwright, Scribe distrusted his own higher powers, assuredly capable of further development, and chose instead to rely on his well-tried, and indeed truly wondrous, constructive skill.

To consider in detail the comedies acted at the Théâtre Français would take too long. 'Valérie' is, no doubt, much improved by the cutting out of its couplets : it is a simple and touching little story, lacking only in depth and pathos, in the one touch of nature. It is made, not born ; and there is no blood in it. The 'Mariage d'Argent' seems to me the least satisfactory in structure of Scribe's long plays, and I do not wonder it failed. The subject might suffice for a comédie-vaudeville in three acts ; and the strain of stretching it into a five-act comedy is unfortunately only too evident. But in 'Bertrand et Raton' is a great improvement : for the first time Scribe strikes the true note of high comedy. All the characters are cast in worn moulds, and have no sharpness of edge, save Bertrand, the incarnation of the ultimate diplomacy. Here is real observation and the real comic touch. In Bertrand the world chose to see a portrait of Talleyrand, then ambassador to England ; and when the play was acted in London, Mr. Farren wore a wig, which made him the image of Talleyrand. To the horror of the English authorities, the French ambassador came to the play ; but with characteristic shrewdness he refused to see the likeness, and led in applause of the actor. Bertrand is Scribe's one rememberable character. It leavens the whole play, of which the plot however is interesting and possible, and not without irony.

What would the great writer who invented Queen Anne have thought of the 'Verre d'Eau,' in which the Duchess of Marlborough and the lady-love of Lieut. Masham are rivals of the queen for the affection of that inoffensive young man? Scribe takes as many liberties with Queen Anne — who is dead, as we all know, and has no Churchill now to fight her battles — as Hugo took with Queen Mary; but he is never melo-dramatic like Hugo. The emotion is rarely tense; and even the shock of surprise evokes no more startling ejaculation than "O Heaven!"—a lady-like expletive which recurs half a dozen times in the play. The 'Verre d'Eau,' indeed, is a very lady-like comedy, wherein high affairs of state are shown to hang on the trifles of feminine feeling. While Scribe has no enthu-siasm, no poetry, no passion, so also has he no affec-tation, and no false and forced emotion. In 'Une Chaîne,' for instance, which remains the most modern of Scribe's comedies, and which tells a familiar tale, there are no ardent scenes between the lover and the mistress, and no dwelling on the raptures of illicit pas-sion. On the contrary, the play, as the title shows, turns on the lover's struggles to break the toils that bind him to his enchantress. Scribe was a *bourgeois*, a Philistine if you will; and he worshipped respectability with its thousand gigs. Mr. Henry James, Jr., has said that the grand protagonist of Balzac's 'Comédie Humaine' was the five-franc piece: I am inclined to think that money plays an even more important part in Scribe's plays than in Balzac's novels. Money, for one thing, is eminently respectable; and Scribe was nothing if not respectable. In 'Oscar, ou le Mari qui trompe sa Femme,' for example, a three-act comedy done at the Théâtre Français in 1842, there is abundant sacrifice to decorum, though the subject is disgusting. Outwardly all is proper: inwardly it is of indescribable indelicacy. But so skilfully has Scribe told his story, that it is only by taking thought that one sees into it: we are hurried so swiftly over the quaking bog, that we scarcely suspect its existence. In 'Une Chaîne' the subject is commonplace enough now, though it was less so in Scribe's day. What is remarkable about it is not only the matter-of-fact treatment of a passionate situation, — this was possibly Scribe's protest against the Romanticist code, which set passion above duty, — but the curious way in which his instinct as a playwright had anticipated the formulas of a quarter of a century later. 'Une Chaîne,' written in 1841 by Scribe, is in construction very much what it would have been had it been written by M. Victorien Sardou in 1881. It has the external aspects of a comedy; but lurking behind and half out of sight is a possibility of impending tragedy, — a possibility which stiffens the interest of the comedy, and strengthens it.

We try a play by a triple test, — for plot, for character, for dialogue. Scribe, who was a born playwright, well knew, what so many would-be dramatists do not know, that plot alone, if it be striking enough, will suffice to draw the public. But he either ignored or was ignorant of the fact that only character, that only a true fragment of human nature, can confer immortal-

ity. Panurge and Sancho Panza and Bardolph and Tartuffe are as alive to-day as when they came into being.
Plot and situation and intrigue, however clever, become
stale in time : we weary of them, and they are forgotten. Unless a story is kept alive by the immortality
of character, it soon gets old-fashioned, and drops out of
sight till another generation takes it up, and dresses it
anew to suit the changing fancy. If it then fall into
the hands of a true poet, a real *maker*, and he put into
it the human nature it has hitherto lacked, it has a
chance of long life ; though the first arranger is remembered only as having suggested the story, and the great
credit is given to the creator of the character. Thus
Shakspere and Molière have worked over the plots of
the Latin comic dramatists, and so stamped these with
their marks, that no one has since dared to question
their ownership, or to replevin what, after all, belonged
to the public domain. Even when a man is without
this puissant gift of making men in his own image,
he has a chance of immortality if he be but sincere and
simple, and if he but put himself into his work. As
the saying is, every man has one book in him : however
he may halt in the delivery of his message, the world
will listen to him so long as he tries to deliver it in
straightforward fashion. There was nothing halting or
hesitating in Scribe's manner. He had practised till he
could talk on the stage better than any one else ; but
he had absolutely nothing to say, he had no message
whatsoever to deliver. No sooner did there come
to the front men like Émile Augier and the younger
Dumas, who believed in a new gospel, and preached it
heartily and boldly, than all men flocked to hear them,
deserting Scribe. There was even an audience for M.

Sardou, who has hardly more to say than Scribe him-self, but who is young enough to say nothing in a style fifty years younger than Scribe's.

Scribe has left his impress on the stage; but it is as the inventor of the comédie-vaudeville, as the improver of grand opera, as a play-maker of consummate skill, not as the maker of character. He was full of appreci-ation of a comic situation, and wrung from it the last drop of amusement : it never re-acted to the creation of a truly comic character. No one of Scribe's people lives after him. They were in outline only, faint at best, and soon faded : time has had no difficulty in rubbing them out. "Outline" is perhaps scarcely the right word : one may say, rather, that they are pastels, not sketches in black and white. Indeed, there is little black any-where in Scribe. He took a rose-colored view of life ; and, as M. Octave Feuillet pointed out in the eulogy he delivered as Scribe's successor in the French Academy, nowhere in all his plays will you find a villain of the deepest dye. Few of his characters are even vicious : they are ridiculous only. We can laugh at them with-out any feeling that we ought, perhaps, to weep. His is a benevolent muse, and all's for the best in the best of worlds.

The most easily recalled of Scribe's characters is one which shows some of the complexity of real life, — Ber-trand, the cold and subtle diplomatist, who turns the zeal and the generosity of others to his own account, and makes the rest of his fellow-men serve as his cat's-paws and scapegoats. Here is a figure not all of a piece : he has some life of his own ; he could stand on his own legs, even if the directing wire of the manager of the show were withdrawn. After Bertrand, one can

bring up with least effort Michonnet, the old prompter
in 'Adrienne Lecouvreur.' Here, also, is a man with
the blood of life coursing through his veins. And of
all Scribe's countless women no one has such a glow of
human nature, fragile and feminine, as Adrienne herself.

It is hard to have to grudge Scribe the credit of
these last two characters; but it is a fact that in writing 'Adrienne Lecouvreur,' Scribe had again taken
unto himself a partner, this time M. Ernest Legouvé.
Scribe was asked by the Comédie-Française to write a
comedy for Rachel. He doubted, and wisely, whether
the task was not beyond him, and whether Rachel, who
was great in tragedy, would in comedy either be easy
herself, or be accepted by the public. He casually
consulted M. Legouvé, who said the task was lighter
than it seemed. "It will be enough to put into a new
frame and another period Rachel's ordinary qualities.
The public will believe it a transformation, while it will
be only a change of costume." — "Will you look up
a subject for us to treat together?" said Scribe at
once. M. Legouvé sought; and at last he happened on
the anecdote of Adrienne Lecouvreur acting Phèdre,
and throwing into the teeth of the Duchess de Bouillon,
who sat in the stage-box, these scorching lines of her
part : —

> "Je ne suis point de ces femmes hardies
> Qui, goûtant dans le crime une tranquille paix,
> Ont su se faire un front qui ne rougit jamais!"

M. Legouvé hastened to carry his find to Scribe, who
fell on his neck in delight, crying, "A hundred performances at six thousand francs!" M. Legouvé kindly
tells us that this was not a mercenary outbreak : it was
the natural expression of the enthusiasm of a trained

playwright who knew that in the box-office receipts
are figures that never lie, or flatter, or disparage, but
tell the author with brutal frankness what the public
thinks of his work. M. Legouvé has also described to
us how Rachel refused the piece, and how artfully he
persuaded her to play it. Its success tightened the
link between Scribe and M. Legouvé; and they wrote
three other plays together, of which the best known is
'Bataille de Dames,' turned into sturdy English by Mr.
Charles Reade as the 'Ladies' Battle.'

If I had to select one play of Scribe's showing him
at his best, I should choose this 'Bataille de Dames.'
I can recommend it as agreeable reading, and quite
harmless. It takes no great study to see that the
plot of the play is a wonderful work of art. The
neatness with which the successive links of the simple
yet ever-changing action are jointed together is beyond
all praise. The comedy of intrigue can go no farther:
this is its last word. And there is not only ingenuity
of incident, there is some play of character; not much,
to be sure, but a little. Nature in Scribe's plays has
as poor a chance as it had at the hands of the French
gardeners who bent the yew and the box into shapes
of strange animals. But 'Bataille de Dames' is far
better in this respect than the 'Camaraderie' of fifteen
years before. Ingenious with a Chinese-puzzle ingenuity, all the pieces fit into each other, and fill the box
exactly, and so completely that there is scant room for
the least human nature. In the 'Camaraderie' there
is no air at all, and you cannot breathe; but in 'Bataille
de Dames' the people show some little will of their
own, thanks possibly to M. Legouvé. In the plays
Scribe wrote with M. Legouvé there is more life, and

less insufficiency of style, than in his other pieces. Scribe had little of the literary feeling, and cared less for the art of writing than even M. Zola. It is a rare thing for a Frenchman to attain prominence as an author, and yet write as ill as Scribe: and it is only as a dramatist that he could have done it; on the stage purely literary merit is a secondary consideration. Scribe had far more real ability than M. Legouvé, but he lacked the tincture of literature which the latter had: so their conjunction was fertile. Together they made a better play than Legouvé alone, who with no great poetic endowment tried to be a poet, or than Scribe alone, who was satisfied to be theatrically effective. So the 'Bataille de Dames' is the best of Scribe's comic imbroglios; and 'Adrienne Lecouvreur' is the best of his more dramatic attempts.

In his lighter comedies, as in his position in the theatrical world, Scribe recalls Lope de Vega. Each was in his day the chief purveyor of plays; both relied on the ingenuity of plot to sustain the interest; neither left behind him a single memorable character. With due allowance for the differences of time and place, some of Lope de Vega's comedies are very like Scribe's. Take the 'Perro del Hortelano:' is it not in suggestion and handling much what it would have been had Scribe written it? A little more sprawling, may be, not so economical in its effects, but still much the same. The Gardener's Dog is Spanish for the Dog in the Manger. In this case it is a woman lightly and easily sketched: she loves, and she is jealous; and yet she cannot make up her mind to marry the man she loves, because of his lowly birth. Even the nincompoop of a lover is not unlike some of Scribe's uncertain heroes. The art of play-making is constantly improving, and Scribe could have given points to Lope in the game of the stage. The Spanish dramatist, on the other hand, had a Spanish dignity and grandiloquence, and some stirrings of poetry. Scribe's Pegasus had no wings; and so his attempts to rise to the romantic and historical drama did not succeed. He had a telescope rifle, unfailing in shooting folly as it flies; but the handling of a siege-gun was beyond his power.

In 1819 Scribe had written the 'Frères Invisibles,' a sufficiently absurd melodrama of the Pixérécourt school. In 1832, in the midst of the Romantic ferment, he tried his hand at 'Dix Ans de la Vie d'une Femme,' something in the style of Dinaux and Ducange's 'Trente Ans; ou, la Vie d'un Joueur.' But the dagger and the bowl were too heavy for him to lift. If any one wants to see a delightful specimen of the competent criticism one dramatist can visit on another, as candid and as cutting as may be, notwithstanding its good nature, he should glance over Scribe's drama, and then read Dumas's analysis of it in his 'Souvenirs Dramatiques.' Perhaps the rattling raillery of Dumas convinced Scribe of his error. It was twenty years later, and only after 'Adrienne Lecouvreur,' a comedy-drama, had succeeded, that he ventured on the 'Czarine,' an historical drama acted by Rachel in 1855. Scribe could do a dainty pastel or a delicate miniature, but he lacked the robust strength which historical painting calls for. Strange to say, the play is wanting even in the picturesqueness of stage-effect when compared with Scribe's own libretto for the 'Star of the North,' or with the beginning of a play sketched by Balzac,

both of which have for their heroine the mistress and
wife and successor of Peter the Great. A complicated and petty intrigue dwarfs the figure of one who
fills so large a place in history and in the imagination
as Catherine. Scribe's feebleness in character-drawing
is shown in the way his historic figures slip out of
mind in spite of every effort to lay hold on them, and
in spite of their pretence to be portraits of Richard
Cromwell and Marshal Saxe, of Queen Anne and the
Duchess of Marlborough, of Francis the First and
Charles the Fifth.

Scribe's device was a pen crossed over pan-pipes,
with the motto, *Inde Fortuna et Libertas,* — a proud
saying, for all its humility. He owed what he was to
his pen, and he acknowledged the debt. The pan-pipes,
I take it, are meant to symbolize, more modestly than a
lyre, his operatic labors : still they seem somewhat out
of place, as no man was ever less given to the warbling
of native wood-notes wild. Scribe's share in the development of grand opera, and in the maintenance of
opéra-comique, important as it is, must be dismissed
briefly. Nowhere is skilful scaffolding more needed
than in an opera-book, and nowhere did Scribe's un-
equalled genius for the stage show to better advantage
than at the opera. It was he who constructed the
'Jewess' for Halévy, and 'Robert the Devil,' the
'Huguenots,' the 'Prophet,' and the 'Africaine,' for
Meyerbeer. It was he, in great measure, who made
possible Herr Wagner's art-work of the future by
bringing together in unexampled perfection and pro-
fusion the contributions of the scene-painter, the ballet-
master, the property-man, and the stage-manager, and
putting them all at the service of the composer for the

embellishing of his work. As the First Player says, in the 'Rehearsal' of his Grace the Duke of Buckingham, "And then, for scenes, clothes, and dancing, we put 'em quite down, all that ever went before us; and these are the things, you know, that are essential to a play." They are essential to that passing show we call an opera; and no one handled them more effectively than Scribe.

His operas, ballets, and opéras-comiques fill twenty-six volumes in the new edition of his works; and among them are the librettos of the 'Bronze Horse,' 'Crown Diamonds,' the 'Sicilian Vespers,' the 'Star of the North,' 'Fra Diavolo,' the 'Dame Blanche,' the 'Domino Noir,' the 'Favorite,' 'Masaniello,' and the 'Martyres;' which last he had taken from Corneille's 'Polyeucte,' just as he had taken another opera-book from Shakspere's 'Tempest.' Many of his comédies-vaudevilles he made over as operas. The 'Comte Ory,' was set by Rossini, and the 'Sonnambule' was arranged as a ballet. An Italian librettist afterward took this ballet, and used it as the book for Bellini's 'Sonnambula,' just as other foreign librettists have used his plots for the 'Ballo in Maschera,' the 'Elisire d'Amor,' and more recently for 'Fatinitza.'

Consider, for a moment, Scribe's extraordinary dramatic range. He began with the vaudeville, which he improved into the comédie-vaudeville; he rose to the five-act comedy of manners; he invented the comedy drama; he failed in Romantic and historical drama, but he succeeded in handling tragic themes in grand opera; he devised the ballet-opera, and he gave great variety to the opéra-comique. He was ever on the lookout for new dramatic forms. One of the most curious of those he attempted is to be seen in the three-act play of 'Avant, Pendant, et Après.' The first act, 'Before the French Revolution,' is a comedy; the second act, 'During the Revolution,' is a drama; and the third act, 'After the Revolution,' is a vaudeville.

The same impulse to seek new forms led him also to discover a new country, in which he laid the scenes of all his plays. Scribe called this new land England, or France, or Russia, or whatever else he wanted to make it pass for; but the critics called it Scribia. This is a country where the people are all cut and dried, where the jokes are generally old jokes, where every thing always comes out right in the end, where waiting-women twist queens around their fingers, where great effects are always the result of little causes, and where, in short, Scribe could have every thing his own way. This uniformity of local color made his plays more easily understood in foreign countries, and facilitated the task of the adapter. Beaumarchais and Augier lose fifty per cent. in transport to another land and tongue. Scribe's tare and tret is trifling. Manners are local: but a plot might be used as well in England as in France, and in Germany or Italy as in England; and so the universal borrowing from France began. Before Scribe, the nations had borrowed from each other all round: no one race had a monopoly of the dramatic supply. The Restoration comedy of England was derived from France; but Germany and France were both copying from England toward the end of the last century; and England and France were imitating Germany in the early part of this. Since Scribe's plays began their tour of the world, and since his re-organization of the French Dramatic Authors' Society made writing for the stage the most profitable form of literary labor, France has ruled the dramatic market.

It is instructive to note that the French playwright who has had the most foreign popularity, after Scribe, is M. Victorien Sardou, who came to the front in 1861, the year of Scribe's death, and who, like Scribe, places his main reliance on his situations. M. Sardou is the direct disciple of Scribe. We have been told, that, when M. Sardou was learning the trade of play-making, he modelled himself on Scribe, seeking to spy out his secret. He would take a play of Scribe's, read one act, and then write the following acts himself, comparing his work with his model, and so learning the tricks of the trade from its greatest master. Proof of this study can be seen by a glance at the list of M. Sardou's works: the 'Pattes de Mouche' is his 'Bataille de Dames;' 'Rabagas' is his 'Bertrand et Raton;' and in 'Nos Intimes' and 'Fernande' we have the formula of 'Une Chaîne.' To M. Sardou, as to Scribe, a play is a complex structure, whose varied incidents fit into each other as exactly as the parts of a machine-made rifle, lacking any one of which, the gun will miss fire. M. Sardou is not as rigid in his construction as Scribe was, and he has a broader humor, and is more open to the influences of the day, — perhaps too much so; and the disciple is consequently more in accord with the taste of the times than was the master as his career drew to a close. Toward the end of his life Scribe complained that his pieces did not meet the old success, and wondered why it was, sure that he made plays as well as ever. The fact was, that taste had changed, and the public did not ask for well-made plays; or rather, it demanded something more than a

well-made play, something more than mere workmanship. Fortunately for his own peace of mind, Scribe
passed away before the full effect of the change in
public taste was apparent.

To sum up, Scribe's qualities are an inexhaustible
industry, an unfailing invention, an easy wit, a lively
feeling for situation, great cleverness, and supreme
technical skill. He paid little attention to human
nature ; he showed no knowledge that life is more than
mere work and play, that there can be grand self-sacrifice, noble sorrow, or any large and liberal sweep of
emotion. He had neither depth nor breadth. A good
man himself, and a generous, in his plays he took a
petty, not to say an ignoble, view of life. Even in his
comedies there is no great comic force : it is easy to
understand how Philarète Chasles came to call him a
Marivaux-*épicier*. And it is no wonder that Heine,
whose eyes were wide open to the iniquities, the sufferings, and the struggles of mankind, should regard
Scribe as the arch-Philistine, the guardian of the gates
of Gath, and should have risked a dying jest against
Scribe. As breath was fast failing him, Heine was
asked if he could whistle (in French, *siffler*, meaning
also "to hiss"), to which he replied with an effort,
"No, not even a play of M. Scribe's."

CHAPTER V.

M. ÉMILE AUGIER.

In criticism, as in astronomy, we must needs allow for the personal equation; and I am proud to confess a hearty admiration for the sincere and robust dramatic works of M. Emile Augier, to my mind the foremost of the French dramatists of our day, with the possible exception only of Victor Hugo. M. Augier inherits the best traditions of French comedy. He is a true child of Beaumarchais, a true grandchild of Molière. He has the Gallic thrust of the one, and something of the broad utterance of the other and greater. One of the best actors in Paris told me that he held the 'Gendre de M. Poirier' to be the finest comedy since the 'Mariage de Figaro.' It would be hard to gainsay him; and in the 'Fils de Giboyer' there is more than one touch which recalls the hand of the great master who drew 'Tartufe.'

It is not a little curious, that, while the plays of M. Alexandre Dumas and M. Victorien Sardou are familiar to the American theatre-goer, M. Augier's virile works are but little known here. Three or four years ago the case was the same in Germany; and in an appreciative study of M. Augier's career, published in *Nord und Süd*, Herr Paul Lindau asked the reason of this, and gave the answer; which is simply that M. Augier appeals to a higher (and smaller) class than either M. Dumas or M. Sardou. In the preface of 'Cromwell,'

Victor Hugo divides those who go to the theatre into three classes: (1) The crowd, who look for action, plot, situations; (2) Women, who expect passion, emotion; and (3) Thinkers, who hope for characters, studies of human nature. M. Sardou suits the first class, M. Dumas the second, and M. Augier the third. It is much easier to transfer to an alien soil the situations of M. Sardou, or the emotions of M. Dumas, than the social studies of M. Augier, in whose plays plot and passion are subordinate, and subservient to the development of character. Startling incidents can be set forth in any language, and strong emotion loses little by change of tongue; but a fearless handling of burning questions, and a scorching satire of society, can be fully appreciated only among the social surroundings in which they first came forth. The note of M. Augier is a broad and liberal loyalty; while M. Dumas's chief characteristic is a brilliancy often misdirected, and M. Sardou's a cleverness always ready to take advantage of the moment. M. Dumas is too complex a problem to be considered in a sentence or two; but M. Sardou is simpler, and one may venture to define the difference between his work and M. Augier's as not unlike the difference between journalism and literature. M. Sardou's puppets live, move, and have their being in some city forcing-house, where their master keeps them under lock and key. M. Augier's characters are as free as all out-doors; and they breathe the open breeze which blows from seashore and hilltop, and which has the odor of the pines, and not a little of their balsamic sharpness.

That M. Augier's plays, in spite of their lack of sensational scenes, should not have found favor in the eyes of Anglo-Saxon managers, is the more remarkable, because he is the most moral of modern French dramatists. He is not one of "them that call evil good, and good evil; that put darkness for light, and light for darkness; that put bitter for sweet, and sweet for bitter." Unlike M. Dumas, he does not let his emotions run away with him. It is not that the moral is violently thrust through each play, as a butterfly is impaled on a pin, to use Hawthorne's apt figure. No: the morality in M. Augier, as in all really great authors, "is simply a part of the essential richness of inspiration," to quote from that other American writer who has recently rapidly sketched Hawthorne's life. "The more a work of art feels it at its source, the richer it is," continues Mr. James; and in this respect M. Augier's work is of royal richness.

Although the French drama of to-day is not so bad as many believe it to be, still the dramatists, like the novelists of France, have not taken to heart Dr. Johnson's warning: "Sir, never accustom your mind to mingle vice and virtue." Mr. Matthew Arnold quotes with approval Michelet's assertion that the Reformation failed in France because France did not wish a moral reform; and he adds that the French are lacking in the "power of conduct." Admitting the rule, M. Augier is a noble exception: he has an abiding sense of the importance of conduct in life, and he strenuously seeks to strengthen that sense in others by dwelling on the influences which make for it. 'Home,' the name which the English dramatist, Robertson, gave to an English comedy, for which he had borrowed the plot of M. Augier's 'Aventurière,' is characteristic of all M. Augier's work. Home in his eyes is a sacred thing; and throughout his plays we can see a steadfast setting-forth of the holiness of home and the sanctity of the family. This feeling will not let him be a passive spectator of assaults on what he cherishes. His is a militant morality, ever up in arms to fight for the fireside. The insidious success of the 'Dame aux Camélias' — in which a courtesan's chance love purified her so far as it might — drew from him the indignant 'Mariage d'Olympe,' and gave him the opportunity of showing what might be expected when the courtesan wormed her way into an honorable household. The Third Person is as important to many French dramas of this century as was the Third Estate to the nation in the last century: but he is in no way aided and abetted by M. Augier; there is one French dramatist who can always be counted on for the husband and the home.

This love for the fireside is not merely literary capital: it is part of his actual life. In the preface to one of his plays he explains how it happens that he has written more than once in collaboration: it is owing to his fondness for chat by the hearth with a friend; and if, in course of talk, they start a subject for a piece, and run it down, to which of the two does it belong? M. Augier's whole life has been given to literature: his career is that of a true man of letters, passing his time quietly by his fireside, or in his garden in the study of men and things. Herr Lindau quotes his answer to a would-be biographer, perhaps the German critic himself, who asked for adventure or anecdote: "My life has been without incident." And Mr. W. E. Henle has pointed out that M. Augier's love for the family may be seen even in the externals of his works, — in the dedication of his collected plays to his mother's memory, and of individual pieces to his sisters and to other intimate friends. There is in all this nothing namby-pamby : on the contrary, his manly tenderness is joined to a hearty scorn of sentimentality. Indeed, the first tribute he paid to his family was an act of courage. He inscribed his earliest play to the memory of his maternal grandfather, Pigault-Lebrun, who traced his descent from Eustache de St. Pierre, the burgher of Calais. Pigault-Lebrun himself was a curious product of the revolutionary effervescence : put in prison twice by his father for youthful freaks, he went through a series of Gil-Blas adventures : — he was shipwrecked ; he fought at the frontier ; he wrote for the stage ; and finally he brought forth certain free-and-easy tales, which were so successful that his father forgave him. The dominant quality of Pigault-Lebrun was what the French call " verve," and the English " go." M. Augier seems to have inherited his independence and his frank gayety : perhaps he has a portion of the imperative will of the imprisoning father ; and, it may be, also some share of the stout heart of Eustache de St. Pierre.

M. Augier began modestly. A two-act comedy of antique life, called the ' Ciguë,' — from the draught of hemlock which the hero has determined to take, — tendered first to the Théâtre Français, was finally brought out at the Odéon in May, 1844. It met with instant success, ran three months, and has since been taken into the repertory of the Comédie-Française. In classic purity of form this first of his plays remains the best : it is a picture of self-seeking greed, treated with a firmness of touch and a masculine irony unusual in a young writer. M. Augier, born in 1820, was not twenty-four when the 'Ciguë' first saw the light of the lamps. He had studied for the bar; but the entice-ments of poetry were irresistible, and, after the success of the 'Ciguë,' he devoted himself wholly to the drama.

He came upon the stage just in the nick of time: both play-goers and professional critics accepted him as the most promising of a new school of dramatists. Just at this moment there was a lull in the fierce strife between the Romanticists and the Classicists. A year before the 'Ciguë,' the Odéon had acted 'Lucrèce,' a tragedy by François Ponsard, a classic tale told in verses of romantic variety and color. The unwitting poet was hailed at once as the chief of a new school, — the School of Common Sense — which was, to seek safety in the middle path, and to join the good qualities of both the opposing styles, without the failings of either. The 'Ciguë,' on its appearance, was claimed as the second effort in the new manner. Neither Ponsard nor M. Augier — warm personal friends, and both men of modesty — ever set up as leaders of a new departure; just as it has been said that John Wilkes was never a Wilkite. M. Augier gave in no adhesion to the School of Common Sense, yet was tacitly accepted as its lieutenant: when its day had passed, he stepped out of its narrow limits, and walked on toward his own goal with a sturdy tread. But for convenience, and not in-accurately, we may consider his earlier work as belong-ing to this school. Beautiful as much of it is, taken by itself, we see at once, when we survey his writings as a whole, that the earlier pieces were only tentative, and that he had not yet discovered where his real strength lay. In the first ten years after the 'Ciguë' was acted, he brought out six other plays in verse; in

1845 the 'Homme de Bien;' in 1848 the 'Aventurière,' the finest and firmest of all his metrical comedies; in 1849 'Gabrielle,' a noteworthy success; in
1850 the 'Joueur de Flute,' a weaker return to the
classic, and akin in subject to the 'Ciguë;' in 1852
'Diane,' a romantic drama written for Rachel, and acted
by her without any great effect, owing, perhaps, to its
use of the historical material which had already served
Victor Hugo in 'Marion Delorme;' and in 1853 'Phili-
berte,' a charming comedy of life in the last century.
All these comedies belonged to the new school, in that
they had common sense without commonplace. In the
best of them were to be seen simplicity, without the
weakness of the Classicists, and vigor, without the brutality of the Romanticists.

'Gabrielle,' as we consider it now after thirty years,
does not seem the best, even of these earlier attempts :
it lacks the easy sweep of the 'Ciguë,' and the manly
strength of the 'Adventurière;' it is almost wholly
wanting in the wholesome humor which plays so freely
around the characters in M. Augier's other comedies ;
and, although the play is well constructed from a technical point of view, its climax is reached by means
which seem inadequate to the end attained. Yet so
noble was its intention, and so clean its execution, that,
in spite of its vulnerable points, it created a profound
sensation, enjoyed success beyond its fellows, and received from the Academy the Monthyon prize of virtue.
It shows how M. Augier fought for the fireside and the
home before he gave up a didactic for a purely dramatic
method. In 'Gabrielle' we have, briefly, a young husband devoted to his wife and child, and toiling unceas-
ingly for their future : therefore is he unable to divine,

much less to satisfy, the somewhat sentimental aspirations of his wife. Unfortunately a friend of his falls
in love with her, and tenders the ideal passion her heart
craves. Fortunately the husband is warned in time;
and he fights bravely for his home, — not with his
hands, but with his brain. Giving no sign of suspicion,
he appeals to the lover to help him loyally to win back
his wife's heart; then, getting them both together, he
seizes an occasion to set before them with heartfelt
eloquence the consequences of a false step. So per-
suasive and so powerful is he, that, when they are left
alone for a moment, the wife dismisses the lover, who
accepts his sentence without a murmur. By herself,
she compares the two men: how small looks the lover
by the side of her husband! On his return she confesses, whereupon he declares the fault to be his own,
in that he has neglected her, and asks if he may hope
to win back her love. Conquered by his strength and
his tenderness, the wife seizes his hand, and, as the
curtain falls, exclaims, —

"O père de famille! ô poëte! je t'aime!"

To understand the startling effect of such a comedy,
we must consider the state of the stage in France at
the time. It was a cutting rebuke to the followers
of Scribe and to the disciples of Dumas. "There is
something about murder," Mr. Howells tells us, "some
inherent grace or refinement perhaps, that makes its
actual representation upon the stage more tolerable
than the most diffident suggestion of adultery." M.
Scribe and the crowd of collaborators who encompassed
him about were of another opinion. The fracture of
the Seventh Commandment, actual or imminent, was to

be seen at the centre of all pieces of the Scribe type. "There was a need of hearing something which had common sense, and which should lift up, encourage, or console mankind, not so egotistic or foolish as M. Scribe declares it," wrote the younger Dumas ; adding, that a writer "robust, loyal, and keen, presented himself ; and 'Gabrielle,' with its simple and touching story, with its fine and noble language, was the first revolt against the conventional comedy."

M. Dumas saw distinctly the blow M. Augier gave to Scribe ; but he did not acknowledge, that at the same time were shaken the foundations of the school in which his father was a leader. As M. Émile Montégut has said, only once did M. Augier take up arms against the Romanticists. "The re-action of the School of Common Sense had, as a whole, but little success, because it especially attacked the literary doctrines of Romanticism, which were sufficiently solid to resist. But Romanticism presented more vulnerable points than its doctrines ; for example, the false ideals of sentimentality it made fashionable, and the brilliant immorality of its works, which had again and again exalted the superiority of passion over duty." With this feeling M. Augier had no sympathy : he is always for duty against passion ; and 'Gabrielle' was a curt rebuke to 'Antony.' Yet one can but regret, with M. Montégut, that the object was attained by this mild piece, in the author's earlier and gentler manner, rather than by a true comedy in the hardy and satiric style of his later work. Sham sentimentality and misplaced yearnings call for the hot iron of satire ; and the weapon which M. Augier soon forged for use against the hypocrites and schemers of the 'Effrontés' and the 'Fils de Giboyer' would have served effectively against personified Romanticism. But, like many another young warrior, M. Augier was a long time finding his right weapon. After writing without aid the seven plays in verse which have been grouped together, he changed about, and took to prose and to collaboration. In the 'Pierre de Touche' (1853), in which M. Jules Sandeau was a partner, and in 'Ceinture Dorée' (1855), in which M. Foussier was a half-partner, a distinct advance can be noted toward what was soon seen to be M. Augier's true road; and in the 'Gendre de M. Poirier' (1855) he struck the path, and walked straight to the goal.

To my mind the 'Gendre de M. Poirier' is the model modern comedy of manners : its one competitor for the foremost place, the 'Demi-Monde' of M. Dumas, is fatally weighted by its subject.   M. Augier gives us a picture of the real world, and not of the half world. M. Montégut truly calls it "not only the best comedy of our time, but the only one which satisfies the idea formerly held as to what a comedy should be." Most modern French comedies are melodramatic ; and more than one successful play by Dumas or Sardou is but a Bowery drama in a dress-coat.   But the 'Gendre de M. Poirier' is pure comedy, and would be recognized as such by Congreve and Sheridan, Lessing and Beaumarchais.   It is simple and straightforward in story, and it has no petty artifices or cheap machinery.   The interest arises from the clash of character against character, and not from external incidents or ready-made situations.   The subject is the old, old strife between blood and wealth, between high birth and a full purse. M. Poirier is a shop-keeper, who, having made a fortune, has political aspirations, which he seeks to advance by an alliance with the aristocracy. The Marquis de Presles is a young nobleman without money, but with blood and to spare. The daughter of M. Poirier becomes the wife of M. de Presles, and is the innocent victim of both father and husband; and the situations of the play are called forth by the unexpected development of her character under the pressure of suffering, — a character which M. de Presles, although they have been married three months, has hitherto held to be colorless. From idle carelessness the husband gets into trouble, and the young and plebeian wife has twice a chance of saving his patrician honor. There is no palliation of his vice, still less any pandering to it. Nakedly it stands before us, and we see the pain which the empty pursuit of pleasure may bring even on the innocent. A chance of reconciliation is offered to the marquis at a heavy cost of honor; and this brings about the beautiful scene — one of the most pathetic known to the modern stage, and ending in a truly dramatic surprise — where the wife nobly rejects the sacrifice, and sends her husband forth to battle for his name. Besides these three characters there are but two others; and to carry through a full four-act comedy with but five parts is an instance of that calm simplicity which only a very high art can attain.

The 'Gendre de M. Poirier' is truly dramatic in every sense, above all in the rare merit of impartiality. The authors do not take sides, and the scales are held with an even hand. Altogether the tone of the play is so honest, healthy, and hardy, and its literary quality is so high, that I am never tired of reading it and praising it. I see in it an almost Molièrian inspiration: indeed, it seems to me not only the best French comedy

since Beaumarchais, but better than any between Beaumarchais and Molière. Beside the noble simplicity of
its subject, it has more than one characteristic of the
great sad humorist's style : for one thing, it unites, in
true Molièrian manner, humor and good humor. The
humor is searching and liberal, and the good humor is
abundant enough to light the whole play with healthy
laughter. In the evolution of the characters again we
catch a glimpse of Molière : every one of the five persons of the play is at once a type and an individual,
true to eternal human nature. In all five can be seen
a masculine sturdiness of conception allied to an almost
feminine delicacy of delineation.

This remark reminds me, that, although I have hitherto spoken of the 'Gendre de M. Poirier' as M. Augier's,
it is signed also by M. Jules Sandeau. However, no substantial injustice is done ; for, while there is nothing
else of M. Sandeau's which will bear comparison with
the 'Gendre de M. Poirier,' it is but the best expression of M. Augier's genius. Both M. Augier and M.
Sandeau are men of too marked an individuality to
gain by collaboration, although in this play the manly
vigor of the former and the caressing gentleness of
the other blend harmoniously. Not always has the
union been so easy. In the 'Pierre de Touche,' for
instance, as it has been neatly said, the characters are
by the author of the 'Effrontés,' and the situations and
scenery are by the author of 'Mlle. de la Seiglière.'
And in their latest joint-production, 'Jean de Thommeray,' M. Augier had obviously only borrowed the
idea of M. Sandeau's charming tale, and had himself
written the whole play, stamped throughout by his
muscular hand. "Dans tout *concubitus*," wrote M.

Augier in regard to M. Labiche's collaborations, "il y a un mâle et une femelle."[1] Now it is not to be doubted that M. Augier is the male. To him that hath shall be given : *on ne prête qu'aux riches.* So much the worse for M. Sandeau.

The effect of collaboration is to raise the general level of dramatic workmanship. Partnership makes it easier to learn the difficult trade of playmaking. The beginner full of ideas serves his apprenticeship with the veteran full of experience ; and the association is for mutual profit. But, if we get more good plays, we gain no more great ones. Two minds can rarely have the singleness and simplicity needed to conceive and carry out a truly great idea. Indeed, since Beaumont and Fletcher, the 'Gendre de M. Poirier' is the first masterpiece ; and its strength and beauty are in great measure owing to the fact that M. Augier and M. Sandeau, like Beaumont and Fletcher, are kindred intellects, thinking alike in important matters, and happily correcting each other in minor details. Generally the two natures either clash irreconcilably, or else emphasize each other's virtues and vices with a consequent loss of proportion. This is to be seen even in M. Augier's case, although he has only collaborated with first-rate men, — Alfred de Musset, M. Jules Sandeau, M. Eugène Labiche, and M. Edouard Foussier ; the first three, like himself, members of the Academy. In 1849 he wrote a little one-act trifle, the 'Habit Vert,' with Musset ; and in 1877 he joined M. Eugène Labiche in writing the 'Prix Martin,' a three-act farce ; and neither of these is equal to the average of either of its author's other plays.

" In every consorting, there must be a male and a female."

To the partnership with M. Foussier we owe one, at least, of M. Augier's most important plays,—the 'Lionnes Pauvres' (1858). I can but think that the play would have been better, had M. Augier written it alone. M. Sandeau's gentleness may have corrected M. Augier's occasional acerbity; and the 'Gendre de M. Poirier' is artistically a finer piece of work than any thing M. Augier did by himself: but M. Fouisser simply says "ditto" to M. Augier, and so their joint work shows an over-accentuation and almost a harshness of tone not to be found in the other plays of the author of the 'Fils de Giboyer.' A comparison of the 'Mariage d'Olympe' (1855), written alone, with the 'Lionnes Pauvres' (1858), written with M. Foussier, will show what I mean. In the latter there is an over-emphasis not to be detected in the former; and the conception and dramatic construction is feebler in the joint work than when M. Augier relied on himself alone. These two plays are linked together here, because, although a comedy in verse intervened, in them M. Augier came before the public in an entirely new manner. The 'Dame aux Camélias,' first acted in 1852, changed the whole aspect of contemporary dramatic literature. The merely amusing comedy was pushed from the front rank, to which the skill of Scribe had advanced it; and, as Scribe fell from his high estate, M. Dumas came to the front as the demonstrator of social science set forth upon the stage. A quarter of a century ago M. Dumas had not developed into the moral philosopher who now so calmly surveys mankind from the summit of a preface; and the morality of his earlier plays was easy, to say the least. The success of these pieces of M. Dumas's was the one

thing needful to the full fruition of M. Augier's genius.
Orderly, fond of home, full of love for the family, and
a bitter foe to any insidious attack on these ideals, he
saw in the 'Dame aux Camélias,' its successors and its
rivals, formidable adversaries with whom to do battle.
The school of easy morality offered a shining mark
for his satire ; and, in the new dramatic form which
Dumas had introduced, Augier found a sure weapon
ready to his hand.   In the 'Mariage d'Olympe' and in
the 'Lionnes Pauvres' he first showed his willingness
to sound a note of warning against social dangers, and
displayed a power of grappling with social problems.
In both plays the subject is repulsive, and of a kind
not now tolerated on the English-speaking stage.   An
adaptation of the 'Lionnes Pauvres,' called 'A False
Step,' and made with due decorousness of expression,
was refused a license in London in 1878.   Plays written in English, like novels written in English, must be
made *virginibus puerisque;* and so only half of life
gets itself into our literature.   In France, fortunately
or unfortunately, the dramatic moralist labors under
no such limitations.   Yet it is to be recorded that the
French censors tried to prevent the production of the
'Lionnes Pauvres' unless it were made more moral;
one of their suggestions, as M. Augier tells us in his
preface, being that the vicious woman should, between
the fourth and fifth acts, have an attack of small-pox as
a "natural consequence of her perversity."

The late G. H. Lewes, one of the best of dramatic
critics, wrote of a revival of this play in 1867: "The
comedy — or shall I not rather call it tragedy ? — was
terribly affecting : the authors have shown us what
comedy may be, should be.   They have boldly laid bare

one of the hideous sores of social life, and painted the
consequences of the present rage for dress and luxury
which is rapidly demoralizing the middle classes of
Europe." The hideous sore was the possible change
from passionate adultery to salaried prostitution for the
continuance of luxury and extravagance. The scene
is laid in two households; and we see in one the wife
awakening to desertion, and in the other a husband
discovering his dishonor. The subject was indeed a
bold one; and, if the play had succeeded, it would go
far to contradict the assertion, made now and again in
Théophile Gautier's dramatic criticisms, that the stage
never becomes possessed of any idea until it has been
worn threadbare in print. Unfortunately the play,
although more than once revived, and always well received, never makes a long stay on the stage. It owes
this lack of stability, perhaps, to the very boldness of
its subject: this, at least, is the suggestion of M.
Sarcey, formulated when the play was last revived, —
in the fall of 1879. The subject was so novel in 1858,
and so hazardous, that the authors did not dare to
paint the wicked woman in the vivid colors which the
situation demanded: they attenuated the drawing, and
filled it in with half-tints, to the obvious weakening of
the effect. In spite of this blemish, the 'Lionnes
Pauvres' remains a work of extraordinary vigor and
value, — one which the future historian of Parisian society under the Second Empire cannot afford to neglect.

Yet as a work of art it is inferior to the 'Mariage
d'Olympe,' which M. Augier wrote alone, and which
had no success at all. Olympe is a courtesan who
tricks an inexperienced young man into a marriage,
and by a skilful comedy gets herself recognized by

his family. Once sure of her position in an honorable household, she is seized by the *nostalgie de la boue*,
the longing for the mud, the homesickness for the
gutter from which she has been lifted, and in which
she had her natural growth. A lover appears, and she
sells herself to him from mere wantonness. Brought
to bay by her husband's grandfather, the head of his
noble house, she threatens to publish a scandal about
an innocent young girl, the youngest member of the
family. Unable to buy her off, the old marquis shoots
her down like a dog. While this was a fit solution of
the situation, so violent a method of meting out poetic
justice revolted the play-going public ; and the final
pistol-shot killed the play as well as the heroine. It
came before its time : the public was not ripe for it.
Since then the stage has taken a bold stride forward,
and a sudden shot has cut the Gordian knot in two of
M. Dumas' plays, — the 'Princesse Georges,' and the
'Femme de Claude.' On two occasions the 'Mariage
d'Olympe' has been revived to see if a more favorable
fortune might not be found for it ; but although re-
spectfully received, and although its many good qualities are admitted, it has never been able to captivate
the general public and to compel admiration from the
common throng.

The heroine of the 'Mariage d'Olympe' is not so
vicious as the heroine of the 'Lionnes Pauvres,' for
whom there is no excuse to be made ; and the sudden
taking-off of the former is more merciful than the awful
perspective opened before us as the certain course of
the latter. In each play we have a sickening picture
of depravity ; and the stronger the artist's hand, and
the finer his art, the more we wish that he had chosen

another subject. The orgy in the second act of the
'Mariage d'Olympe' is as typical in its way as Couture's
picture of the Romans of the decadence ; but it is set
forth with a decorous pen by an author who respects
himself. There is nothing in it of the unspeakable
filth of M. Zola's 'Nana ;' besides, Olympe is true, and
in the highest degree artistic, and Nana is conventional
in spite of her minute Naturalism. One feels that
the mere mention of M. Augier in the same breath with
M. Zola is a mistake in taste; yet in the portrait of
Olympe there is an impression of main strength which
one feels M. Zola must appreciate. I should be
tempted to characterize it as violent and brutal, if these
were not altogether too harsh words to apply to a
writer so well-bred and so keen as M. Augier. It is
perhaps safe to say, that, had it been treated by another
hand, "violent and brutal" would surely be the exact
words to employ. It is not that the note is forced, or
that there is any thing false in the treatment : on the
contrary, no work of M. Augier is more sober or direct.
The painful impression is no doubt due to the repulsion
inherent in the subject, and it is this painful impression which has kept the play from attaining general
popularity.

Between the 'Mariage d'Olympe' (1855) and the
'Lionnes Pauvres' (1858), M. Augier had reverted to
verse in 'La Jeunesse,' acted in 1857. Eleven years
later, in 1868, came 'Paul Forestier,' another poetical
play. These two are his latest attempts in verse, and
may therefore be considered together. 'La Jeunesse'
is closely akin to Ponsard's 'L'Honneur et l'Argent'
in subject and style. Its verse is not so academic in
its elegance as Ponsard's; but it is fresher, and it has

more freedom : the flowers of M. Augier's poesy always have their roots in the soil. In spite of the dates, it seems as though ' La Jeunesse ' must have been written just after ' Gabrielle : ' they are informed by the same spirit, and in each is a warning to be seen.

In as marked contrast as may be to both of these is ' Paul Forestier,' M. Augier's last drama in verse. Indeed, it is so unlike the rest of his plays, that it might almost be taken for the work of another. It is a play of pure passion surchanged with hurrying emotion, and culminating in what one cannot but think, in spite of all the skill with which it is done, is a conventional conclusion, only caused by a wrenching of the logic of the characters, wherein vice is punished, and virtue rewarded, in spite of themselves. M. Augier's comedies are generally moral in another and nobler manner than this. Here one feels that, given the characters and situation, the outcome would have been different. In general, M. Augier's logic is so inexorable, and the moral so entirely a part of the essence of his story, that to come upon this play, in which the moral seems merely tacked on, is something of a shock. The only excuse at hand is that the poet had run away with the moralist, and that the latter got the upper hand only in time to pull up as best he might.

In America the divorce between poetry and the stage seems to be as final, and as unhealthy for both parties, as the divorce between politics and society. In France one has a chance now and then of hearing an actor speak the language of the gods. The habit of writing in verse is dying out slowly ; yet, as M. Augier has shown us, the poetic attitude is possible even to those who use the language of men. It may well be doubted whether the gradual disappearance of French dramatic verse is greatly to be deplored. The rhymed Alexandrine is not a fit dramatic instrument : it is, of all metrical forms, the one least suited to the stage. The theatre requires action, and the Alexandrine is lazy and slow. The theatre requires simplicity, and, above all, directness ; and the Alexandrine lends itself only too easily to the employment of drum-like words, loud-sounding, empty, and monotonous. M. Augier succeeds in overcoming this temptation : so close at times is his verse, that it would be no light task to turn his Alexandrines into English verse, line for line. Style is generally on a level with the thought it clothes. In M. Augier's poetry we find none of the haziness of expression which results from weakness of conception. He sees clearly, and speaks frankly : his verse is flexible, full, and direct. In his antique and mediæval plays, especially in the 'Aventurière,' it abounds in grace and color ; and the metre helps to keep up the artificial remoteness of the illusion.

It is, perhaps, my duty to give a specimen of M. Augier's verse, although I dare not attempt a translation. Here, then, is the indignant rebuke of Fabrice, when Clorinde, the adventuress, claims the right to be treated with the courtesy due to a woman : —

> "Vous une femme ? Un lache est-il un homme ? Non . . .
> Eh bien ! je vous le dis : on doit le même outrage
> Aux femmes sans pudeur qu'aux hommes sans courage,
> Car le droit au respect, la première grandeur,
> Pour nous c'est le courage et pour vous la pudeur.
> La sainte dignité que vous avez salie
> Au lieu de l'invoquer, souhaitez qu'on l'oublie.
> Vous seule, songez-y, mais pour pleurer sur vous.
> O femme sans amour, sans enfants, sans époux ;

Étrangère au milieu des tendresses humaines,
La glace de la mort est déjà dans vos veines,
Et quand vous descendrez au néant du cercueil,
Il ne s'éteindra rien en vous qu'un peu d'orgueil!
C'est votre châtiment! Aussi, je vous l'atteste,
Vous me feriez pitié, si vous n'étiez funeste . .
Mais lorsque je vois, vos parcelles et vous,
Repandre vos poisons dans les cœurs les plus doux,
Quand surtout vous voulez, par d'odieuses trames,
Prendre dans nos maisons le rang d'honnêtes femmes,
A côté de nos sœurs lever vos fronts abjects,
Et comme notre amour nous volez nos respects! . . .
Tiens, va-t'-en!"

(Act iv. sc. 5.)

Well as M. Augier could handle the Alexandrine, his admirable artistic instinct told him that it could only be used to great disadvantage in attacking the weak points of a more modern and complex civilization. In a play of passion like 'Paul Forestier,' or in a more or less didactic and idealized comedy like 'La Jeunesse,' it might serve; but in a direct assault on a crying evil, as in the 'Mariage d'Olympe' or the 'Lionnes Pauvres,' metre would hamper rather than help; and so verse was discarded for a prose as pointed and as nervous as any dramatist could wish. M. Augier's practice as a poet was of great aid in giving to his prose its form and color: it is a true poet's prose, — a prose lifted at times on the wings of poetry, but never to soar out of sight. M. Augier's prose is seemingly hurried at times: it shows, besides the effect of its author's poetic experience, a study of Beaumarchais: one catches at times a faint echo of the "rusé, rasé, blasé" manner of Figaro. It is as picturesque, in its nineteenth-century way, as was Beaumarchais's; and it is far more correct and more natural. Indeed, it is the model of dramatic dialogue of our day, — terse, tense, racy, and idiomatic.

Nowhere is M. Augier's style seen to better advantage than in the series of startling comedies of contemporary life which he brought forth between 1861 and 1869. The avenging pistol-shot was abandoned for the whip-lash of satire. At bottom, both the 'Mariage d'Olympe' and the 'Lionnes Pauvres' were dramas. There can be no doubt that the 'Effrontés' and the 'Fils de Giboyer' are comedies : they are models of what the modern comedy of manners should be ; they show no trace of melodrama, and the interest arises naturally from the clash of character against character. Therefore it is not a little difficult to convey an idea of their high merit ; for no rehearsal of the plot fairly represents the play, because the plot is a secondary consideration ; and any description of character is pale and weak copying of what in the comedies moves before us with all the myriad hues of life.

"There has never been a literary age," so Joubert tells us, "in which the dominant taste was not sickly. The success of an excellent author consists in making healthy works agreeable to sickly tastes." M. Augier boldly surmounted this difficulty by making the sickly tastes of his age — a literary one beyond all question — the theme of his satire. He attacked contemporary demoralization in four comedies, — the 'Effrontés' (1861), the 'Fils de Giboyer' (1862), the 'Contagion' (1866), and 'Lions et Renards' (1869). No one of them was so calmly artistic or symmetrical as the 'Gendre de M. Poirier,' but all four of them, taken together and considered as one, are more exactly typical of his

genius, and give us an even higher opinion of it. The
'Gendre de M. Poirier' remains M. Augier's best play;
but in his series of satiric comedies there are characters
who linger in the memory even longer than M. Poirier
himself, — Giboyer, for instance, who ties together the
first two plays; and d'Estrigaud, who links the other
pair.

In the 'Effrontés' an assault was made on discredit-
able speculation, and undue respect for mere money
whencesoever derived. In the 'Fils de Giboyer' — in
which Giboyer, a Bohemian of the press, and the
Marquis d'Auberive, a representative of the old nobili-
ty, re-appeared from the preceding play — a plain picture was presented of clerical intriguing in politics.
All at once M. Augier found himself in a wasp's nest.
Clericalism was in arms; and M. Augier received hot
shot and heavy from newspaper and pamphlet, accus-
ing him of odious personalities, calling him Aristophanes, and recalling the legend that the death of Socrates
was due to the attacks of the great Greek humorist.
The likeness to Aristophanes was not altogether inapt;
for, without the license of the Greek, the Frenchman
had the same directness of thrust. He indignantly
repelled the accusation of personality, while frankly
admitting that one character — and but one — was
drawn from the living model. This was Déodat, in
which everybody had recognized Veuillot, the ultra-
montane gladiator and papal-bull fighter. The denial
availed little. A disreputable pamphleteer who called
himself Eugène de Mirecourt, author of a series of
prejudiced and inaccurate contemporary biographies,
professed to recognize himself in Giboyer (without warrant, surely; for, in spite of his vice and venality, Gi-

boyer was sound at the core) ; and this fellow published, in answer to the 'Fils de Giboyer,' a stout volume called the 'Petit-fils de Pigault-Lebrun,' in which he tried to hit M. Augier over the shoulder of his grandfather, gathering together stores of apocryphal anecdotes and doubtful jests.

Nothing daunted by this rain of invective, but holding it rather as proof that he had hit the mark, M. Augier returned to the assault. One may guess that he delights in the combat, and is never so happy as when giving battle for the right. In this case he showed that he had what we Yankees call "grit." He brought out a new pair of plays. In the 'Contagion,' as in the 'Effrontés,' he attacked a general evil, — the cheap scepticism of the hour, the want of faith in the future, the ribald scoffing at things hitherto held sacred. Then in 'Lions et Renards,' as in the 'Fils de Giboyer,' he used one of the characters, fully developed in the earlier play, as a mainspring of the polemic action of the later. In the 'Contagion' we see the Baron d'Estrigaud, most keen and quick-witted of rascals, carrying off his rascality with an easy grace, and taking things with a high hand. In 'Lions et Renards' clericalism re-appears again in the person of a M. de St. Agathe, mentioned already in the 'Fils de Giboyer,' and here brought boldly upon the stage: he is one who has sacficed every thing, even his identity, to the order of which he is an unknown instrument, from sheer lust of power wielded in secret. The struggle between these two, D'Estrigaud and St. Agathe, for a fortune which neither of them captures, is exciting. In the end, by a sudden irony, the beaten D'Estrigaud abandons the world, forgives his enemies, and, under the eyes of St.

Agathe, takes to religion, — the last resort of rascals, to paraphrase Dr. Johnson.

While no one of these four comedies, as I have said, is artistically equal to the 'Gendre de M. Poirier,' yet taken together they give us a still higher opinion of M. Augier's genius. No other dramatic author of this century can point to four such pieces : no other dramatist of our day has put before us so many distinct individualities, and shown them before us in action, each after its kind. There are no longer preachments ; there are a bit of action and a single line instead, — and the evil is summed up better than by a score of sermons. The dialogue is sharp and short : it has a satiric wit, which cuts like a lash when it does not bite like an acid. The wit is really wit, a diamond of the first water, transparent and clear. There is none of the rough-and-ready repartee only too common in many modern English plays, the rudeness of which recalls Goldsmith's assertion, that there was no arguing with Dr. Johnson ; for, if his pistol missed fire, he knocked you down with the butt. M. Augier's pistol does not miss fire.

The series of comedies of manners which I have here grouped together was interrupted in 1865 by 'Maître Guérin,' as well as by the poetic drama 'Paul Forestier' (1868). 'Maître Guérin' is analyzed at length in Mr. Lewes's valuable volume on 'Actors and the Art of Acting.' Although showing many of M. Augier's everadmirable qualities, it is lacking in the symmetry of the 'Gendre de M. Poirier' and in the sharp savor of the later satires : it pales by the side of either. In the same year (1869) that he brought out 'Lions et Renards' he gave us also the 'Postscriptum,' one of the brightest and most brilliant little one-act comedies in any language, and to be warmly recommended to American readers. The next year came the war with Prussia and the two sieges of Paris.

The first play which M. Victorien Sardou brought out after France had gone through these terribles trials was the trivial 'Roi Carotte,' a fairy spectacle; and the second was the illiberal and re-actionary 'Rabagas.' M. Augier's first play was the stirring and patriotic 'Jean de Thommeray' (1873) : love for home and love for the fatherland are rarely separated. 'Jean de Thommeray' was a series of energetic pictures of the demoralization which had led to defeat : its fault was that it was only a series of pictures, and not a homogeneous drama. M. Augier had borrowed his hero from M. Sandeau's tale ; and Jean de Thommeray himself was almost the only link connecting the succeeding acts. The play thus lacked backbone ; its parts were not knit together by the bond of a common life : it was rather a polyp, any one of whose members, when detached, is as capable of separate life as the original whole.

M. Augier's later plays call for little comment. In 1877 was acted the 'Prix Martin,' signed by M. Augier and by M. Eugène Labiche. It is not noteworthy ; and M. Augier has himself told us that his share of the work was confined to a partnership in the plan and to a slight revision of M. Labiche's dialogue. The year before, M. Augier brought out 'Mme. Caverlet,' and the year after, the 'Fourchambault.' The latter was very successful, but neither is in M. Augier's best manner. The first is a plea for divorce, and the second a plea for the solidarity of the family ; and both are what on the English stage are called "domestic dramas."

In all, M. Augier has written twenty-seven plays,

great and small. Of these, nine are in verse. Eight times he had a literary partner. At least ten out of the twenty-seven are plays of the first order, not to be equalled in the repertory of any contemporary drama-tist ; and of these ten, three — the 'Aventurière,' the 'Gendre de M. Poirier,' and the 'Fils de Giboyer' — are surely classics in the strictest sense of the term. According to Lowell, "a classic is properly a book which maintains itself by virtue of that happy coales-cence of matter and style, that innate and exquisite sympathy between the thought that gives life and the form which consents to every mood of grace and dig-nity, which can be simple without being vulgar, elevated without being distant, and which is something neither ancient nor modern, always new, and incapable of grow-ing old." Judged by this test, the 'Aventurière,' the 'Gendre de M. Poirier,' and the 'Fils de Giboyer,' are classics beyond all peradventure.

The first thing which strikes one who surveys M. Augier's literary career is the combination of original-ity and individuality with great susceptibility to external influence. He is a self-reliant man, but quick to take a hint. He was at first accepted as a disciple of Pon-sard ; and perhaps the 'Ciguë' did owe something to 'Lucrèce,' and 'La Jeunesse' to 'L'Honneur et l'Ar-gent.' But to my mind, even in Augier's comedies of antiquity, there was a greater obligation to Alfred de Musset. They wrote together a little piece of no consequence ; and Musset's influence may be traced in all M. Augier's earlier plays of fantasy, in which the scene, wherever the poet may declare it to be, in reality is laid in the enchanted forest of Arden, or in that

Bohemia which is a desert country by the sea. In the technical construction of 'Diane' there was something of the manner of Victor Hugo : that M. Augier's verse was indebted to Hugo for its freedom from the eigh-teenth-century shackles goes without saying. Neither Scribe nor the elder Dumas tempted him ; but, with the first work of the younger M. Dumas, M. Augier saw at a glance the prospect it opened. Combined with this suggestion of new worlds to conquer, given by M. Dumas, was a study of Balzac's methods. With-out the 'Recherche de l'Absolu' we should not have had 'Maître Guérin,' just as, if there had been no 'Dame aux Camélias,' there had also been no 'Mariage d'Olympe.'

I have ill expressed myself, if, from the paragraph above, any one infers that M. Augier has been guilty of any servile copying. Nothing could be less true. He is a man of marked individuality, and in his works strongly self-assertive. Nothing like imitation is to be discovered in his dramas. Another man's work is to him only an exciting cause, to use a medical phrase. The analogies to Ponsard, Musset, and Hugo, are sub-tile and probably unconscious ; and the indebtedness to M. Dumas is comprised in the assertion that the author of the 'Dame aux Camélias' turned over a new leaf of the history of French dramatic literature, — a leaf upon which M. Augier wrote his name with his own pen. The obligation to Balzac is no more than that M. Augier studied human nature with Balzac as his master. It is by his knowledge of human nature, and by his skill in turning this knowledge to account, that poster-ity judges an author. M. Augier is fit to survive : he is a great creator of unforgettable figures, a true poet in the Greek sense, — a "maker." Giboyer is one of the most puissant characters of the nineteenth century; he seems to sum it up; he walks right out of literature into life. He is no mere profile silhouette, such as M. Sardou cuts so cleverly: he is rounded and ruddy flesh and blood, — one of the glorious company of Sancho Panza, Falstaff, Tartuffe, and Captain Costigan. Scarcely less extraordinary in their absolute truth to life are D'Estrigaud and D'Auberive, who, like Giboyer himself, are made to appear in more than one work, — a device Balzac may have borrowed from Molière. Who is there, having any knowledge of French character, does not see the marvellous reality of Poirier and of his noble son-in-law, the Marquis de Presles? And is not the high-art cook whose resignation M. Poirier receives, — is he not a worthy descendant of the coachman-cook who was in the service of Harpagon?

M. Zola — who looks forward to an impossible regeneration of the stage, from which convention is to be banished, and every thing is to be as dull as every day, in the interest of naturalistic exactness — recognizes in M. Augier a creator of actual characters, and calls him the master of the French stage. "Séraphine," says M. Zola of the heroine of the 'Lionnes Pauvres,' "is a daring figure, put squarely on her feet, of an absolute truth." And M. Zola praises Guérin, who "has a final impenitence of the newest and truest effect." He objects that some of M. Augier's characters are too good to live, and that others change front in an instant before the curtain falls. In M. Zola's eyes any noble character is unnatural: Colonel Newcome, for instance, is too good to live. But his other criticism has some slight foundation: there are characters of M. Augier's

who reform with undue haste, — in 'Gabrielle' for
example, and in 'Paul Forestier.'

M. Augier's women are all admirable. In his devotion to the family he has drawn woman fit to be the
goddess of the fireside. He excels alike in the young
girl, clear-headed and warm-hearted, perfectly *jeune fille*
according to French ideas, but with a little spark of
independence, with a head of her own, and a willingness
to use it if need be; and in the clever woman of the
world, skilled in all the turns and tricks of society,
quick-witted and keen-tongued, and able to hold her
own. His women, good or bad, are thoroughly feminine and human : they are neither men in women's
clothes, nor dolls ; they have hearts and *sex*. He has
drawn brilliant portraits of wicked women, — Seraphine
and Olympe, and, above all, Navarette, — and he delights in showing their true womanhood, and, as in the
'Aventurière,' redeeming them almost at the last with
a few words of simple dignity and pathos. In none of
these qualities can any trace of foreign influence be
detected : they are purely personal.

Purely personal also are his hatred of hypocrisy, his
trust in the future, his belief in progress, his respect
for toil. To these last two qualities is due his liking
for modern invention and discovery. In the 'Beau
Mariage' the hero is a chemical experimenter ; in the
'Lions et Renards' he is an African explorer ; while in
the 'Fourchambault' he is a specimen of the highest
type of mercantile sagacity. National, rather than personal, is the occasional note of bad taste. In general,
the French pay an exaggerated respect to the Fifth
Commandment, to balance, perhaps, the frequent fracture of the Seventh : so the scene in the 'Contagion,'

where the hero chances on his mother's love-letter in the midst of a disreputable supper, comes with an unexpected shock. There is another scene in the 'Fourchambault,' this time directly between the mother and the son, which no Anglo-Saxon pen could have written. But these taints are rare. For the most part, M. Augier's characters live, move, and have their being, in a clear, pure atmosphere, as different as may be from the moral miasma which hangs over Balzac's landscapes.

Mentally and morally M. Augier is a well-balanced writer, and his works are symmetrical. We see in him an intellect in equilibrium, well poised on itself, and sure of its stability. A great critic has told us that the grand style is not the so-called classic, with its finish and polish and point, but something larger, freer, ampler; something not incompatible with a homely realism in matters of detail, — if, indeed, a truly grand style does not demand a rigorous calling of the thing by its right name, be it never so humble. As Molière in his day and Beaumarchais in his were in the grand style, so is M. Augier, — each in his degree. The progressive civilization of the nineteenth century is perhaps as hampering as the pseudo-classic formality of the seventeenth. It is high praise to say that the words which describe one of M. Augier's characters, and which Herr Lindau aptly applies to their author, are as fitting to him as they are to his great master, Molière : "Un cœur simple et tendre, un esprit droit et sûr, une loyauté royale." A simple and tender heart, an upright and sure spirit, a royal loyalty, these are noble gifts which no one can deny the author of the 'Gendre de M. Poirier,' of the 'Aventurière,' of the 'Fils de Giboyer,' and of the 'Mariage d'Olympe.'

CHAPTER VI.

M. ALEXANDRE DUMAS *fils.*

WITH the appearance on the stage of the younger Alexandre Dumas, a fresh force came into the French drama. To say this is easy; but to qualify this force adequately, and to define its limits, is no light task. The two other dramatists, each in his way remarkable, who stand to-day with M. Dumas at the head of French dramatic literature, are comparatively simple problems. In M. Sardou we see the utmost cleverness and technical skill, heightened by a girding wit: he continues the tradition of Scribe, adding all the modern improvements. In M. Augier we behold a high and genuine literary value, a broad and humorous humanity he inherits by right of primogeniture from Molière, and observes mankind with the large frankness of his master. But M. Dumas continues no tradition. He is that rare thing in literature, — a self-made man. He derives from no one. He expresses himself, and with emphasis: he is a personal force. Not condescending to the ingenious trickery of M. Sardou, and never rising to the lofty liberality of M. Augier, his place in the dramatic hierarchy is not so readily fixed as theirs, his character is not so simple: in fact, it may fairly be called complex and even contradictory. Here, for instance, is a bundle of inconsistencies: with a real power for creating character, there is no dramatist who has more often and more boldly than he brought forward the same faces and figures. While declaring in one volume that he knows no immoral plays, but only ill-made ones, in another volume he asserts that the stage of itself is immoral. Setting forth in one piece the right of assassinating the wife taken in adultery, he sets forth in the next the duty of forgiving her. In comedies inherently vicious he pauses to preach virtue, but with a bluntness of language at times shocking even to vice. He has written the 'Ami des Femmes' and the 'Visite de Noces,' two plays which imply that their author does not suspect what "good taste" means; and yet he has been elected a member of the French Academy, constituted to be a tribunal of taste. The historian of the ' Dame aux Camélias,' and the discoverer of the 'Demi-Monde,' — a word with which he has enriched the vocabulary of the world, — he has stood forward in the name of the Academy to bestow prizes of virtue. The son of a prodigal father always poor, he himself is wealthy and frugal. And finally, brought up in all the looseness of the lightest Parisian society, he has the Bible at his fingers' ends, and quotes the Scripture as freely as an orthodox New-Englander. With such a character and such a career, M. Dumas is one of the most interesting and curiously complex figures of our century.

The literary baggage of M. Dumas is not over bulky. Exclusive of about a dozen juvenile novels of little or no value, it is contained in eleven volumes. The collected edition of his plays — in which each piece was accompanied by a preface, wherein the author frees his mind — began to appear in 1868: the sixth, and, for the present, final volume was issued late in 1879. Under the apt title of ' Entr'actes ' a collection of his miscel laneous essays came out in three volumes in 1878–79. The dramaturgical chapters are of great value; the general literary papers are interesting; and so competent a critic as M. Auguste Laugel has at length, in letters to the *Nation*, praised the political portions. A later novel, the 'Affaire Clémenceau,' put forth in 1867, and two pamphlets on divorce and the woman-question, published within two years, complete the list of M. Dumas's acknowledged works. More or less anonymously he has had a hand in half a dozen plays not wholly his own: chief among these are the 'Supplice d'une Femme' of M. Girardin, and the 'Danicheff.' Another play, the 'Filleul de Pompignac,' acted anonymously, and not yet included among his collected plays, seems, however, to have been acknowledged by him. It is as a dramatist only that M. Dumas is now to be considered. Such portions of the books mentioned above may be passed over as do not either relate directly to the stage, or reveal peculiarities of the author's character. As far as may be, attention will be confined to the twelve important plays which M. Dumas produced in the twenty-five years, 1852–76.

M. Alexandre Dumas *fils* was born in Paris in July, 1824, a few days after his father was twenty-one years old, and a few years before his father had begun that career of literary notoriety and inexhaustible production which was to end only with his death. Like his grandfather, he was an illegitimate son, — a fact which seems to have given a congenital bias to his future writings. In one of his many autobiographic fragments the elder Dumas referred grandiloquently to the birth of his son: "The 29th of July, 1824, whilst the Duke of Montpensier was coming into the world, there

was born to me a Duke of Chartres." M. Dumas himself, in a letter to M. Cuvillier-Fleury, which serves as
a preface to the 'Femme de Claude,' speaks of the circumstances of his birth with real eloquence: he protests against the law which marked him, an innocent
babe, with the stigma of illegitimacy. "Happily my
mother was a noble woman, who worked to bring me
up, my father being a petty employee at twelve hundred
francs a year. And by a happy chance it turned out
that my father was impulsive, but good. . . . When,
after his first successes as a dramatist, he thought he
could count on the future, he formally acknowledged
me as his son, and gave me his name. This was much.
The law did not compel him; and I was so grateful to
him for it, that I have borne the name as nobly as I
could."

The boy was then put to school under Prosper
Goubaux, one of the authors of 'Thirty Years, or A
Gambler's Life,' and of 'Louise de Lignerolles.' His
school-fellows bullied him unmercifully because he was
a natural son. "My torture, which I have depicted in
the 'Affaire Clémenceau,' and of which I did not speak
to my mother, so as not to worry her, lasted five or six
years." These years of suffering gave him the habits
of observation and reflection. Removed finally to another school, he regained his strength and his growth.
At twenty he was a healthy lad, who, having known
misery, was only too eager for pleasure enough to
balance the account. His father, making and spending
hand over fist, was glad to have his son share in his
prodigalities; and M. Dumas soon plunged headlong
into the vortex of Parisian dissipation. But, to quote
again from his letter, "I did not take great delight

in these facile pleasures. I observed and studied more than I enjoyed in this turbulent life." Yet he was swept along by the current for several years, writing juvenile novels, more or less imitations of his father's inimitable fictions, gathering a load of debts, and laying up a stock of adventures and experiences for future literary consumption. In all his earlier plays he drew from the living model. The 'Dame aux Camélias,' and 'Diane de Lys,' and even the 'Demi-Monde,' were, as he tells us, "the echo, or rather, the re-action, of a personal emotion to which art gave a development and a logical conclusion happily lacking in life." One may, perhaps, hazard the suggestion, that since M. Dumas has exhausted his personal experiences, and has had to rely altogether on his invention, as in the 'Étrangère' and the 'Princess of Bagdad,' his plays are not nearly so good : whence we may fairly infer that the early adventures of the man were necessary for the full development of the author.

"It was the play of the 'Dame aux Camélias' which began to free me from the slavery of debt and of the society to which I owed both the debt and the success. I promised myself not to fall back, either into debt or into this society ; and I kept my promise at the risk of being called ungrateful." Written when the author was but little older than twenty-one, the novel of the 'Dame aux Camélias' had been published with striking success just before the Revolution of 1848. It decked out afresh a figure of which the French seem fonder than any other race. Manon Lescaut gave birth to Marion Delorme, and Marion Delorme was the mother of the Dame aux Camélias, who, in turn, may vainly deny her latest offspring, Nana. Truly it is an unsavory brood. The popularity of the novel suggested its dramatization. The elder Dumas thought ill of the project; and it was not until a melodramatist showed the author the *scenario* of a black melodrama which he had taken from the novel, that, in sheer revolt at such treatment, M. Dumas himself set to work at it.

In eight days the play was finished, so the author tells us; and the statement does not seem extravagant. As in the case of the 'Supplice d'une Femme,' which he wrote later with extraordinary rapidity, he had his material all under his hand; and the play was not comedy, which calls for slow incubation, but a drama of simple passion, which could be struck off at white-heat. In spite of the speed of its production, the 'Dame aux Camélias,' of all plays which an author has made out of his novel, shows least traces of a previous existence. One would suppose that every stage-door in Paris would open wide to receive a dramatization of his successful novel by the son of one of the foremost novelists and dramatists of France. But it was more than three years before the play was tried by the fire of the footlights. Rejected by nearly every theatre in Paris, it was at last accepted at the Vaudeville, only to be vetoed by the censors. Patronized by the Duke of Morny, the government interdict suppressed it until after the bloody 2d of December, 1851, when the duke himself entered the ministry. He believed in providing sensations for the people of Paris, and, if possible, in diverting attention from politics to the playhouse. The 'Dame aux Camélias' was brought out at the Vaudeville Theatre, Paris, Feb. 2, 1852. It was an instant success, holding the stage for a hundred nights or more. It has since been revived in Paris half a dozen times, and always with the same success. A mutilated and innocuous alteration of it, prepared by Miss Jean Davenport (afterward the wife of Gen. Lander), was acted by her in America: it was called 'Camille, or the Fate of a Coquette,' an absurd title, which shows how the story suffered in the interest of Procrustean morality. Later the piece was taken up by Miss Matilda Heron. An Italian version of the play served Signor Verdi as the book of his 'Traviata,' an opera of which the lord-chamberlain permitted the performance in London while prohibiting the acting of the original French play.

The 'Dame aux Camélias' was at once simple, pathetic, and audacious. It emancipated French comedy, and gave it the right of free speech. To judge it fairly, one must consider the comedies which held the French stage before its coming. There were Scribe and his collaborators, with their conventional and machine-made works; and there were Ponsard and M. Augier, with their plays, poetic in intent and finely polished, but as yet reflecting nothing vital and actual. The great merit of the 'Dame aux Camélias' is, that it changed the face of modern French comedy by pointing out the path back to nature, and the existing conditions of society, and by showing that life should be studied as it was, and not as it had been, or as it might be. There is no need to dwell on the character of the play. As M. Montégut pointed out over twenty years ago in the *Revue des Deux Mondes*, the story of a courtesan's love may be a poetic subject if treated with elevation, or it may be a degrading subject if treated realistically; adding that M. Dumas had chosen a middle course, and that the result was little more than a vulgar melodrama.

Before M. Montégut wrote, the subject had been treated poetically in Hugo's 'Marion Delorme;' since, it has been set forth with unspeakable realism, or Naturalism rather, in M. Zola's 'Nana.' In M. Dumas's play we avoid the offensiveness of the latter, but we miss wholly the poetry of the former. On one of its revivals a competent French critic declared that it bore itself, even in its old age, like a masterpiece; and an equally competent American critic recorded that he had had a hearty laugh over its "colossal flimsiness." It is, in fact, not to be taken too seriously. It carries one along by the rush of youthful strength; yet one has time to note phrases horribly out of tune, and to detect a sort of sentimentality run mad. Its morality is cheap, not to say tawdry: in short, the play seems to me youthful in the objectionable sense of the word, and I am half inclined to think that the Dame aux Camélias herself is doing exactly what she is best fitted for when she serves as the heroine of an Italian opera.

This may seem a harsh judgment. It is perhaps only fair to add, that, although the 'Dame aux Camélias' is not at all a work of genius, it is a work which could have been written only by a genius. It is a work of the Werther type, in that it is the result of youthful effervescence and the period of ferment which needs must precede the riper, richer, purer work of the author's maturity. Flimsy it is, if you will, and of a shabby morality; but it is not insincere. The author said what he thought when he wrote it, or, rather, what he felt; for he had scarcely begun to think then. When he did begin to think, his views of the courtesan changed entirely, and so did his treatment of her. It is in the treatment of Marguerite Gautier, and not in the mere bringing forward of such a character on the stage, that the 'Dame aux Camélias' is immoral. A courtesan is the chief figure of M. Augier's 'Mariage d'Olympe,' and no play is more moral. Where the ethics of the ' Dame aux Camélias' are at fault is, not in the taking of a courtesan for the heroine : it is in the failure to show that so self-sacrificing a courtesan as Marguerite Gautier was an exception. In any later play, M. Dumas, had he chosen to treat the subject anew, would have proved conclusively, and by a few simple and direct touches, that a Marguerite Gautier was as rare as a white blackbird, and as little likely to be chanced upon by the wayfarer. Here occasion offers to say, once for all, that the 'Dame aux Camélias' is not now to be judged by the light of Dumas's later plays. It has no thesis ; it was meant to point no moral ; it was written off-hand and carelessly, with no thought but to tell a touching story as touchingly as possible.

The second play of M. Dumas, 'Diane de Lys,' calls for no detailed criticism. Like its predecessor, it was taken from an earlier novel ; and, as M. Dumas himself suggests, the second play is inferior to the first. It cost but a few days' work, and was written to pay off lingering debts ; and it shows that the impulse which called it into being was wholly external. It is a manufactured product, a re-working of old material, lacking wholly the youthful freshness which gave the 'Dame aux Camélias' so individual a savor. Paul, the hero, like his forerunner Armand, is obviously a projection of the author's own profile. Neither Armand nor Paul comes up to our standard of a gentleman. In his first scene with Diane, Paul heedlessly and needlessly betrays the confidence of the friend who has just presented him

to her. Diane herself is none too ladylike : she seems
a sort of study for that much finer portrait, the Duchess
in the 'Étrangère.' But with time M. Dumas's touch
had become firmer and more delicate. The Duchess
would be above the brutal frankness of Diane, who,
when her husband's sister begs her to guard the family
honor, and to remember that she bears the family name,
retorts point blank, " There's no danger that I forget it :
your name costs me enough. I paid four millions for
it."

'Diane de Lys,' however, did one thing : it freed the
author from debt, and enabled him to devote eleven full
months to the execution of his next and best play, —
the 'Demi-Monde.' Intended for the Gymnase Theatre,
the author was constrained to offer it to the Comédie-
Française, dexterously choosing his time, however, so
that it might be rejected. Acted at the Gymnase in
1855, a score of years later it was triumphantly adopted
by Comédie-Française, where it is now a chief comedy
in the current repertory. A word as to the title, before
we consider the comedy itself. By the phrase *demi-
monde* M. Dumas meant, not the class of courtesans,
but the class of exiles from society. The half-world
is peopled by those who have fallen from grace, and
not by such as have always been outcasts and sinners.
It is, in the main, an association of repudiated wives.
As de Jalin, the witty Parisian of the play, tells de
Nanjac, the soldier just fresh from Algeria, " The first
wife who was thrust from the door went to hide her
shame, and weep over her sin, in the most sombre retreat
she could find ; but — the second ? The second set out
to find the first ; and, when they were two, they called
their fault a misfortune, and their crime an error ; and

they began to console and excuse each other. When
they were three, they invited each other out to dinner.
When they were four, they had a quadrille." And then
de Jalin goes on to account for the later recruits, —
imitation widows, and brevet wives : "in short, all the
women who wish to have it believed that they have been
what they are not, and who do not wish to appear what
they are." There is a distinct boundary-line between
this society and that of the venal courtesans who have
since arrogated to themselves the title of the *demi-
monde*. There is an equally distinct boundary-line between this society and the real *monde*, — the world of
fashion and society at large : " it is to be known best
of all," says de Jalin, " by the absence of the husband."
In what is the most celebrated speech in the comedy,
de Jalin likens the *demi-monde* to a basket of peaches
in the window of a Parisian fruiterer. You ask the price
of a basket in which each peach is carefully wrapped in
paper, and protected by leaves : these peaches are thirty
cents apiece. Alongside of this basket is a second, in
which the fruit is seemingly as good, save that it is
somewhat huddled together ; but the price of these is
but fifteen cents. If you ask why there is this difference, the dealer lifts one of the latter carefully, and
shows you a little spot on its lower side. The fifteen-
cent peaches are all speckled, and the *demi-monde* is a
basket of fifteen-cent peaches.

The play sets forth the struggles of a clever woman,
Suzanne d'Ange, calling herself a baroness, to get out
of the troubled waters of this doubtful world into the
haven of matrimonial respectability. M. de Nanjac, a
hot-headed and warm-hearted young soldier, has fallen
in love with her just after his arrival from Africa ; and,

unsuspecting her past, he is about to marry her. But his friend M. de Jalin has the best of reasons for knowing her to be unworthy; and in the end, by despicable trick, he opens de Nanjac's eyes, and prevents Suzanne's marriage. The 'Demi-Monde' is a masterly play. It stands the threefold test: it is good in plot, in dialogue, and in character. The story is one which we follow with interest to the finish, with a growing desire to be in at the death. In dialogue it is as brilliant and as metallic as any M. Dumas ever wrote. The characters are splendidly projected against the dim background of a dubious society, and contrasted one against the other with the utmost skill: M. de Nanjac's heat, for instance, sets off the coolness of M. de Jalin. In M. de Thonnerins we see a second edition of the old duke, invisible in the 'Dame aux Camélias;' and in Valentine we see the first sketch of the future Iza of the 'Affaire Clémenceau' and of the wife of Claude. The chief person of the comedy, Suzanne, is a boldly drawn character, almost worthy of a place by the side of the nobler and more poetic figure of M. Émile Augier's 'Aventurière:' four years later she re-appears with a hardened outline in the Albertine of the 'Père Prodigue.'

M. Dumas is fond of these reduplications of a favorite character. He confesses that he took a certain Count de R. as the model for Gaston in the 'Dame aux Camélias,' for Maximilien in 'Diane de Lys,' and Olivier de Jalin. The same character also appears as Réné in the 'Question d'Argent,' as M. de Ryons in the 'Ami des Femmes,' and as Roger de Taldé in the 'Danicheff.' If the author had not told us distinctly that he had copied M. de Jalin from the Count de R., one would

have called him a rib from M. Dumas's own breast, the
more especially as M. Dumas has twice used the name
of "de Jalin" to sign plays to which he did not wish
to put his own name.   And yet, in spite of the author's
liking for him, one cannot help thinking him a contemptible fellow.   He is lacking in the instincts of a
gentleman.   He has neither delicacy nor frankness.
He ought to keep a secret sacred, but he leaks by in-
sinuation all the time.   Granting that it is his duty to
prevent the marriage of an adventuress to an honest
man, it should be done somehow honorably and openly,
not underhand and stealthily, by ignoble trickery.
Surely so clever a man as M. de Jalin could find some
other means than the unworthy device by which he
traps Suzanne into a confession of love for him.   And
surely nothing ·is to be said for the brutality of his
outburst of laughter when his stratagem has succeeded,
and he holds her in his arms in the sight of the man
she had hoped to marry.   On top of this the author
goes out of his way to give M. de Jalin a certificate
of honor.   As the curtain falls, M. de Nanjac declares
him "the most honest man I know."   And even M.
Edmond About, reviewing the 'Demi-Monde' in the
Revue des Deux Mondes, called M. de Jalin a type
sympathetic to the audience.

The 'Demi-Monde ' is the model of nineteenth-century comedy, just as the 'School for Scandal' is the
model of eighteenth-century comedy.   The contrast of
the two plays would be pregnant, did space permit.
The seemingly careless ease with which Sheridan has
sketched his characters, and the airy humor which in-
forms the whole comedy, make us accept a story and
special scenes far more dangerous than any thing in

M. Dumas's piece. And yet the impression left by the 'School for Scandal' is pleasant; while the 'Demi-Monde' is almost a painful spectacle. We cannot help liking some of Sheridan's characters, — Lady Teazle for instance, and Sir Peter, in spite of his uxuriousness, and Charles too; while even the scandalous college, after making due allowance for the tone of a bygone century, is not wholly repulsive. But no woman in the 'Demi-Monde' should we wish a wife to visit, and no man in it should we care to shake by the hand.

It was, perhaps, M. About's reproach, — that in the 'Demi-Monde' M. Dumas had painted only a certain society, and not society at large, — that led him in his fourth play, the 'Question d'Argent,' brought out in 1857, to attack a more general subject. It is a play of no great value, much inferior in interest to its predecessors, but differing from them in that it is really a comedy. Both of M. Dumas's earlier plays were dramas; and even in the 'Demi-Monde' the situations at times are on the verge of melodrama. But the 'Question d'Argent' is pure comedy: its incidents are entirely the result of the clash of character on character; and its central figure, though marred by a touch too much of caricature, is one of which any comedy might be proud. We are shown boldly and with novel effect Jean Giraud, a self-made man, with unbounded skill in scheming, and no sense of right or wrong. He is a restless, uneasy speculator, young, and already very wealthy, but never quite sure of his footing. In 'Ceinture Dorée,' and again in the 'Effrontés,' M. Émile Augier has pointed out how vainly ill-gotten riches can live down the bad repute of their origin. In 'L'Honneur et l'Argent' Ponsard was emphatically

moral in his denunciation of peculating financiers.   But
Ponsard was serious and poetic ; while M. Dumas chose
to see the comic side of the speculator's career, and to
hold up to ridicule the suddenly enriched snob.   Ponsard preached : M. Dumas at least enlivened his sermon
with wit and humor.   The comedy is less tainted with
M. Dumas's views and theories than any other of his
plays written before or since : it is more wholesome ;
and it might be read or seen by any one without damage or danger.   Unfortunately the fable is weak ; and
the figure of the financier,— who believes that money is
absolute monarch,— though boldly outlined, is not always
artistically filled in.

"Here is a comedy for which I confess my predilection : this comes, perhaps, from its having cost me a
great deal of work," writes M. Dumas at the head of
the preface of the 'Fils Naturel,' acted in 1858 at the
Gymnase, and, like the 'Demi-Monde,' revived at the
Théâtre Français a score of years later.   In the last
century the founder of modern drama, Diderot, wrote
a 'Natural Son,' which was the illegitimate father of a
play of the same name by Kotzebue, adapted to the
English stage by Mrs. Inchbald, to the American by
William Dunlap, our first playwright, and often acted
by the American Infant Roscius, John Howard Payne,
who had cleverly amalgamated the Inchbald-Dunlap
versions for his own use.   There is a fine theatrical
situation in Kotzebue's play, when the natural son, seeing his mother sick unto death from want, takes to the
highway, and puts a knife to the breast of the first
passer-by, — his own father, as it chances.   But even in
technical excellence M. Dumas's play does not yield to
Kotzebue's.   It is an admirable specimen of stage-craft ;

and it is no wonder that two such experts in dramatic art as M. Sarcey and M. Perrin, the director of the Théâtre Français, should incline to considering it M. Dumas's masterpiece. No wonder is it, either, that such praise should revolt M. Zola, who has a fresh theory of throwing nature on the stage raw and crude as in a photograph. M. Zola holds that M. Dumas "never hesitates between reality and a scenic exigency : he wrings the neck of reality." And he says that M. Dumas "uses truth only as a spring-board to jump into space." In the 'Fils Naturel,' for the first time, M. Dumas sought to set a social problem on the stage; and yet nowhere else has he shown so full a share of the constructive faculty which is the birthmark of the true dramatist, but which M. Zola chooses to contemn.

Kotzebue had treated the demand of the illegitimate child for bread for physical support : M. Dumas chose rather to consider his claim to a place in his father's family, and his right to his father's name. M. Dumas has a prologue specially to show how it was that his young hero had a large fortune left to him by a stranger. Then in the play we have the story over again of d'Alembert and Mme. Tencin : the natural son first seeks his parent's name, and then refuses it. The play is a model of equilibrium. In the first half we see the hero gradually discovering his illegitimacy. At the end of the first act he is told his father's name.

"Where are you going?" asks his informant.

"To my father's."

"What for?"

"Why, to see him, since I have never seen him."
And on this exit-speech the curtain falls. In the next act is the scene between the father and the son, in

which the former refuses to give the latter any satisfaction whatever. Then in the last half of the play we see how the son becomes more important to the father, and well-known in the world at large. Finally, to further his own interests, the father offers the son the name he refused at first ; and the son, in turn, refuses, preferring to keep the name he has made for himself, — his mother's.

The choice of the subject and title of the 'Fils Naturel' by M. Dumas was scarcely in the best of taste : still worse was the name of his next play, the 'Père Prodigue,' acted in 1859 without any great success. What the elder Dumas was we all know. He was truly a prodigal father. His son is reported to have said of him, "My father is a child I had when I was young." But the bad taste is confined to the title : in the comedy itself there was no trace of unfilial personality ; the son of Dumas was not a son of Noah to uncover his father's nakedness. As the 'Fils Naturel' tries to show the result of depriving a son of his father, so the 'Père Prodigue' was intended to set forth the bad effects of giving a son a false education ; and thus one play completes the other. The 'Père Prodigue,' however, is not remarkably good : it is overladen with incident ; and, as a French critic remarked when it was first acted, it might almost begin with the second act, or the third, or even the fourth. The picture of prodigality in the first act is full of typical touches, all compactly accumulated, until an irresistible effect is produced.

The same highly-wrought brilliance is to be seen throughout the play, which contains one of M. Dumas's most successful characters. The prodigal father is in the true high-comedy vein. By the side of M. Dumas's

bull-headed and sentimental heroes, and of his preter-
naturally witty heroes, — projections of his own impulses
and cleverness, and reduplicated to fatigue, — is a series
of comic characters of great force and originality. No
dramatist of the nineteenth century has enriched literature with more amusing comic portraits. The prodigal
father in this play, the self-made speculator in the
'Question d'Argent,' the broken-down and philosophic
artist Taupin in 'Diane de Lys,' the clear-headed and
good-hearted notary Aristide in the 'Fils Naturel,' the
outspoken Madame Guichard in 'M. Alphonse,' and the
profligate duke in the 'Étrangère,' — these are figures
firm on their feet, and worth, any one of them, more than
all the interchangeable MM. de Jalins and de Ryons.

Better by far than these mere figments of cleverness
are the fresh faces of sprightly and self-reliant young
girls seen now and again in M. Dumas's comedies, and
bearing a family likeness one to another. They are
somewhat too knowing to please the French critics, and
they have a little too much decision of character. The
Mathilde of the 'Question d'Argent' is only a little less
decisive than the Hermine of the 'Fils Naturel ;' and,
had either of them grown up in the *demi-monde*, she
would not have been unlike Marcelle. In Jane de
Simerose, in the 'Ami des Femmes,' we see the same
type. The 'Ami des Femmes' was not acted until
1864, five years after the 'Père Prodigue ;' and, although
it called forth greater controversy, it had no greater
success. It is, in fact, by far the poorest of M. Dumas's
plays. There is really little or nothing to admire in it :
there is less wit than usual, and no action to speak of.
It may be passed over with the remark that its subject
was bad, and the taste with which it was treated worse.

Its subject, indeed, is one wholly unfit for stage treatment, unless, as M. Dumas sometimes hints, the theatre ought to be an amphitheatre for gynecologic clinics.

Here I must break off the criticism of successive plays to consider a change which had gradually come over M. Dumas himself. In all the comedies written before this transformation, even in the ' Fils Naturel,' Dumas was first of all a dramatist; and the writing of the best play he could was his aim. Afterward he became a moralist, a teacher, a leader of the people; and to set an example and to prove something was M. Dumas's object in writing plays. This change in the author's views had been brought about by a curious change in the man himself, — a change which may be described as an evolution to virtue from an environment of vice. It seems as though M. Dumas had found out by experience what most other men are fortunate enough to get by inheritance and training. Having grown to manhood without strict or severe education, having seen laxity from his youth up, and having lived years of his life in the *demi-monde*, where morality is but a word, M. Dumas has been surprised to discover that it was also a thing. As he says in ' M. Alphonse,' a young man left to himself, badly brought up and badly surrounded, may most likely fall into errors ; "but little by little, if he have intelligence, he will learn for himself what others have not taught him." So M. Dumas taught himself. He knows by experience, as one may say, that honesty is the best policy, and that vice does not pay. He is at the end of a course of practical ethics; and his experiments have been made *in corpore vilo*, — on his own body. He has been taught by his own sufferings. As far as morals go, one might call him "a self-made man." Of course there are many things he has not yet found out. The world is older than he, and has suffered more, and likewise learned more. But what to many well-meaning persons are but commonplaces, M. Dumas holds to firmly as precious discoveries of his own ; and he is so pleased with these discoveries, that he seeks to cry them aloud from the housetop. Like all converts, he has undue zeal. He is seized with a burning impatience to spread abroad the glad tidings ; and to this is coupled an emphatic intention that they shall not be misunderstood. In all his later plays there is the viciousness of vice and the virtuousness of virtue in every third line : unfortunately his taste has not always improved with his morals, and the other two lines often offend more than the one line benefits. M. Dumas has always shown the tendency toward mysticism not infrequent in men of his temperament. Even in the 'Dame aux Camélias' the curtain finally fell on a quotation from the New Testament. Now he frankly takes to preaching, and puts his audacity, his patience, and his ingenuity at the service of the strange system of sociology which he has evolved from his inner consciousness. His skill as a dramatist is bent to the making of purely didactic dramas. He comes forth in the purple and fine linen of the stage to set forth a doctrine of sackcloth and ashes. In the expounding of his new views his style is harder and more brilliant than ever ; and he explains his latest moral kinks with no sign of sweetness or light, but with great rigor and vigor.

In the 'Idées de Madame Aubray,' acted in 1867, and the first-fruits of this new philosophy, the preacher fortunately has not yet overmastered the playwright.

The piece is a marvel of polemic literature, a model in the art of teaching by example. Mr. John Morley instances it as one of the very few modern plays which Diderot would recognize as belonging to the *genre sérieux,* which began with his own 'Père de Famille.' It treats an important subject honestly and with intellectual seriousness : there is none of the petty begging of the question which disfigures two other works on the same subject, — the 'Fernande' of M. Victorien Sardou, and the 'New Magdalen' of Mr. Wilkie Collins ; both clever men, lacking, however, in the courage and the candor needed to face the problem fairly. There is a fourth work of fiction, published not long after M. Dumas's, which approaches the subject with the same appreciation of its demands and its difficulties. This is a novel, 'Hedged In,' by Miss Elizabeth Stuart Phelps, as representatively New England as the 'Idées de Madame Aubray' is French.

It is of course a mere paradox to say that M. Dumas, since his regeneration, appears to me as a typical New-Englander ; but he has something of the New-England spirit, and he stands at times in the New-England attitude. He recalls, in a way, both Nathaniel Hawthorne and Oliver Wendell Holmes. His theology is in essence Unitarian. I have before made mention of his very New-England knack of biblical quotation ; and, as his recent volume on divorce shows, he is as prone to search the Scriptures for a text wherewith to smite his adversary, as any of those chips of Plymouth Rock who "take to the ministry mostly." Without pushing the analogy too far, we can see it stand out plainly when we set the 'Idées de Madame Aubray' by the side of 'Hedged In,' and see that both the American and the

French writers, though differing greatly in mental equipment, approach the subject from the same point of view,
and give it the same austerity of treatment. M. Dumas
lights up his logic with flashes of his Parisian wit;
while Miss Phelps relieves the stress of undue sentimentality by a sort of imported English humor. But
these are externals.

In considering the problem of the redemption of the
woman who has fallen but once, each author gives us a
picture of a sincere Christian woman who believes in
the gospel of doing good. Madame Aubray and Mar-
garet Purcell are close enough akin to be twin-sisters.
Each of them has a child of her own, — Mme. Aubray, a
son; Mrs. Purcell, a daughter. To each of them, abundant in good works, comes the opportunity of befriend-
ing a young and unmarried mother. In each case the
father of the nameless child re-appears on the stage.
Mme. Aubray and Mrs. Purcell have each to choose
between her sense of duty and her ardent affection for
her own child. Both Miss Phelps and M. Dumas fight
fair; there is no begging of the question; the problem
is looked in the face; the objections to the thesis
are plainly shown. M. Dumas even turns his honesty
to advantage: the philosophic observer who acts as
Greek chorus sums up bluntly the feelings of the
average spectator, *"c'est raide"* —- "it's pretty steep!"
— and the audience, hearing the author thus give vent
to their own verdict, go away without shock or resent-
ment. For in the French play the actions take a
more personal turn than in the American novel: Mme.
Aubray has to consent to her only son's marriage
with the redeemed sinner, while Miss Phelps kills off
her penitent. It cannot be said that either play or

novel has a satisfactory ending, or that the conclusion of either is in any sense a true *dénoûment,* — an untying; and this because no work of fiction, however clever, can at best do more than show one way of cutting the knot.

Just what moral M. Dumas meant to advance in his next piece, a comedy in one act, called the 'Visite de Noces,' and acted in 1871, I cannot imagine. It is an inquest on the internal corruption of man. Perhaps the verdict is just, in view of the evidence produced; but the impulse of a healthy man would be to let such matter drop into the gutter, where it belongs. To lift it thence is to stir up muddy depths of degradation to no purpose.

In a novel, the 'Affaire Clémenceau,' published just before the 'Visite de Noces,' and in the two plays he brought out after it, the 'Princess Georges' (1871) and the 'Femme de Claude' (1873), M. Dumas returned to an early theme. Indeed, we may consider 'Diane de Lys' as the first of these dramas of adultery and death. In 'Diane de Lys' and in the 'Princess Georges' the husband kills the lover. In the 'Affaire Clémenceau' and in the 'Femme de Claude,' in which M. Dumas has treated a situation essentially identical, the husband kills the wife. And in a later play, the 'Etrangère,' it is the husband who is killed.

Neither the 'Princess Georges' nor the 'Femme de Claude' can be called a good play, or even a well-made play. Knowing that Mlle. Desclée acted the heroine of each, one is inclined to see in them scarcely more than two strong parts. The thesis in each case has proved too heavy for the plot. In the 'Princess Georges' the thesis seems to be the duty of feminine forgivenness, in the 'Femme de Claude' the duty of summary justice. I say *seems;* for the exact target of M. Dumas's bullet is not unmistakable, despite much talk about it. Unfortunately the theorist got the better of the playwright, especially in the 'Princess Georges,' in which two ladies of the highest society explain the bad character of the Comtesse de Terremonde at immoderate length, and in M. Dumas's own style, with recondite historical and scientific allusions; and, shortly after they have done, another of the actors, this time a notary, takes up the parable, and preaches another page of the same sort of stuff. After reading these diatribes, with all their pseudo-scientific parade, one can scarcely help wondering whether M. Dumas is not laughing in his sleeve at us. But no: I think his sincerity beyond dispute; only — well, only I wish he would not believe in himself quite so emphatically. If, indeed, he were not so sincere, there would be only one word to describe his attitude with exactness; and that word, unfortunately, is yet waiting its passport into good society: if I may venture to use it, however, I shall say that M. Dumas has sublime *cheek*.

In this very 'Princess Georges,' the general verdict was that the catastrophe was a mistake. The Princess Georges, knowing that her husband is about to go off with an adventuress, and knowing her own helplessness, declares her intention of taking the law in her own hands. She warns the jealous husband of her rival that his wife has a lover; then, when the husband of the Princess Georges is going into the trap which the jealous man has set for the unknown lover of his wife, the princess does what she can to prevent his going, but without avail, when suddenly, as she is clinging to him ineffectually, a shot is heard, and we are told that the jealous husband has brought down a young man whom we have seen making juvenile love to the adventuress. Now, this ending is all wrong, and wholly unworthy of M. Dumas, who, however, defends it by saying that the princess would be guilty of cold-blooded murder if she let her husband go to certain death. This is all very true. I do not ask that the prince should be shot; but I do ask that M. Dumas should not take me in by a petty trick ; that, having led me to think that the prince was to be killed, he should balk this legitimate expectation by a wrench of probability. M. Dumas can afford to leave such clever devices to M. Sardou : they do not become a teacher and a preacher. Unfortunately, M. Dumas at bottom is governed by his emotions : he sees things passionately, and drives on to a vehement conclusion. But he has even more than average French logic. He always seeks to prove — to himself first of all — that the end his feeling has arrived at is the only orderly one in the nature of things, and, indeed, the best of all possible endings.

One is less disposed to dispute the fatal conclusion of the 'Femme de Claude.' Emerson tells us that "the Koran makes a distinct class of those who are by nature good, and whose goodness has an influence on others, and pronounces this class to be the aim of creation." M. Dumas reverses this : he shows us in the 'Femme de Claude,' and elsewhere, a woman by nature irredeemably bad, and of evil influence on all; and on this class he pronounces destruction. Mr. John Morley, speaking of the startling figure which dominates that tale of unholy passion, Diderot's 'Religieuse,' says that "it is a

possibility of character of which the healthy, the pure,
the unthinking, have never dreamed. Such a portrait
is not art, that is true; but it is science, and that delivers
the critic from the necessity of searching the vocabulary
for the cheap superlatives of moral censure." M. Dumas's
science is not as deep as Diderot's, but the attempt is
the same in kind. In the Valentine de Santis of the
'Demi-Monde' we see the first sketch of this woman;
in the Countess de Terremonde of the 'Princess
Georges' we have a half-length; and the figure re-
appears at full-length in the Iza of the 'Affaire Clémenceau' and in the Cesarine of the 'Femme de
Claude.' Both of these last are creatures governed
wholly by animal wants and instincts; in other words,
they are irresponsible brutes : and in each case the
husband exercises the right of individual justice, and
puts her out of the world. And in the sociological
pamphlet called 'L'Homme-Femme,' and published in
1872, between the 'Princess Georges' and the 'Femme
de Claude,' M. Dumas dissected the same female phenomenon, and came to the same conclusion formulated
in the phrase " Tue-la ! " — " Kill her."

In 'M. Alphonse' (1873) one may note a return to
M. Dumas's earlier manner, or at least a temporary
cessation of his sociological studies. In spite of its
unpleasant subject and the weak-as-water heroine, the
play is one of M. Dumas's best. Its characters are few,
and nervously drawn. In the M. Alphonse, whom even
the coarse Madame Guichard cannot stand, we see a
sort of transition type from the passive Tellier of the
'Idées de Madame Aubrey' to the active duke of the
'Étrangère,' just as we see Claude repeated in Montaiglin, and Jeannine in Montaiglin's wife. There is no-

where any feebleness in outline. All M. Dumas's characters, like their creator, believe in themselves. The
story, which is simple and pathetic, tells itself plainly;
the action is not overladen with philosophical diatribes.
M. Dumas, for once, reaped the benefit of his own improvement in the formula of dramatic construction.
We owe to him the cutting-short of long-winded ex-
positions and the rapid rush of hurrying action. Unfortunately the inventor of this improved comedy has
taken advantage of the time thus saved for illicit indul-
gence in metaphysical stump-speeches, and for the
promulgation of the gospel according to St. Alexandre.
In 'M. Alphonse' there is little of this skirmishing
along the flanks : he sticks close to the issue in hand.
The teaching of the play is only the plainer for this
restraint. "A good work of art," Goethe tells us,
"may and will have moral results; but to require of the
artist a moral aim is to spoil his work." Now, in general, M. Dumas requires of himself a moral aim: so long
ago as 1869 he announced his intention of using the
stage as a moral engine. He seemed to think that
every play should be a dramatized *Tendenz-Roman*, and
that every statue should bear a lamp on its head, or
in its hand; or else what excuse has it for its being?
An epigram of Mr. Austin Dobson's is apt just here : —

> "Parnassus' peaks still catch the sun;
>   But why, O lyric brother!
> Why build a pulpit on the one,
>   A platform on the other?"

In the 'Demi-Monde' can be seen what M. Dumas
could do before he had bound himself by this new law,
and in 'M. Alphonse' what he could do when he chose
to loosen its coils. When he rigidly required a moral

aim of himself, he spoiled his work, as Goethe told
us, and as we can see in his next play, the 'Étrangère.'

M. Dumas himself has propounded the theory that
all great dramatists have built their plays just as well
in the beginning of their career as at the end, — just
as well, if not better. The faculty of dramatic construction being a native gift, in age they are inclined
to push too far, and so lack spontaneity. So is it
with the author of the 'Étrangère,' a sorry comedy,
and utterly wanting in spontaneity or spirit. I think I
can fairly call it the poorest of M. Dumas's plays, and
surely, despite its moral intent, the foulest. There is
but one decent man in the play ; and he, like the most
of M. Dumas's virtuous heroes, is virtuous with a vengeance : he is a good man in the worst sense of the word.
For the rest, the duke, and the duchess, and the rest of
the gang, — the word sounds coarse, but is exactly expressive, — we have no feeling but disgust. All are corrupt :
there is a general odor of corruption. A miasma hangs
over the stage when the curtain is up, and we breathe
more freely when once we get outside. Of the plot
there is not much more to be said. I can understand
the Englishman who told M. Sarcey, when the Comédie-
Française acted the play in London, that it had no common sense. Coming right after so perfect a piece of
workmanship as 'M. Alphonse,' one scarcely knows
what to make of it. As far as one may disentangle it,
there are three acts of talk and theorizing, and two acts
of action. This is the true Sardou formula : ard the
story cast into it was not M. Dumas's either ; it was a
blackening of the 'Gendre de M. Poirier,' the masterpiece of MM. Augier and Sandeau. M. Dumas and

M. Augier stand at the head of contemporary French
dramatic literature, and it is interesting to remark how
often one has trodden in the other's tracks. M. Augier,
having more and higher qualities than M. Dumas, a
wider reach and keener insight, has not had the same
uniformity of success : in the final and fatal shot of
the 'Mariage d'Olympe' he anticipated the "tue-la!"
of M. Dumas and the 'Femme de Claude,' just as he,
in turn, used the mould of the 'Fils Naturel' for his
'Fourchambault.' This may be a digression ; but, in
considering the 'Étrangère,' I cannot help wishing for
the hygienic breeze that blows through most of M.
Augier's manly plays. There is never a breath of poetry
in M. Dumas's dramas, no trace of imagination. One
is never lifted out of matter-of-fact, every-day life : in a
measure the life in his pieces differs from the life around
us only in that the people in the plays are rather wittier
in speech, and worse in character, than those in reality.
All is hard and dry and brilliant. More than that, every
thing is narrow : it is a very tiny corner of even the
little world of Paris which serves as the stage of M.
Dumas's dramas ; and, if one can form a fair idea of
Paris from these plays, then one may well wonder and
regret that fire and sword, and blood and iron, left one
stone on another.

The scene of his latest play — the 'Princess of Bagdad,' acted by the Comédie-Française in February last
— is not even in this little corner of Paris : it is in some
fantastic capital of M. Dumas's own discovery, where
ordinary human motives have ceased to govern, and
every thing goes, as in a dream, by contraries. Indeed,
the play is a sort of evil dream, a nightmare. It was
of the 'Supplice d'une Femme' that M. Dumas wrote,

" The spectator must submit to this play as to an attack of fever, feeling its truth in the beatings of his heart, and only recognizing its danger afterward ; that is to say, too late : " but these words fit the ' Princess of Bagdad ' even better than they do the ' Supplice d'une Femme.' It is needless to analyze the doings of a lot of people, all of whom are lacking in common sense. Heroine, husband, and would-be lover are all clean daft, and ought to be sent back to Bloomingdale or Colney Hatch, where they would find seclusion and a strait- jacket. One of the characters is called a millionnaire Antony, referring to the ' Antony ' of the elder Du- mas. As a fact, all three of the chief characters seem to have walked right out of the pages of ' Antony ' half a century behind time. In the preface to the ' Étran- gère,' M. Dumas discussed the question of naturalism on the stage, and took occasion to praise Molière for the extraordinary delicacy with which he had treated so indelicate a tale as ' Amphitryon.' In the ' Princess of Bagdad,' there was need of a little of the same deli cacy, instead of which we have needlessly plain speech and brutal violence.

In the foregoing pages all the acknowledged plays of M. Dumas have been dealt with : besides these, there are nearly a dozen others in the making of which he has had a hand. He has retouched his father's ' Jeu- nesse de Louis XIV. ' and done over his father's ' Bal- samo.' He lent his skill to George Sand for the dramatizing of the ' Marquis de Villemer.' He was a silent partner in the ' Danicheff ' with M. " Pierre New- sky," and in the ' Supplice d'une Femme.' To him is ascribed the whole of the ' Filleul de Pompignac,' and a half of the ' Comtesse Romani,' and a quarter of

'Héloïse Paranquet.' In many of these his speech bewrayeth him, but on none do we find his signature. He has nobly respected his name, and it has never been lent to joint-stock literary operations. His skill and his time he has been free with, but his reputation is jealously guarded.

The respect which he pays to his name he also has for his art. He is proud of his business. In his book about divorce, published last year, he constantly opposes his calling as a dramatist to the vocation of the priest he is addressing. He contrasts church and stage; evidently and honestly believing that in the contest between them the stage has the right of it, and gets the best of it. His discussion of this burning question is in the form of a letter to the Abbé Vidier, vicar of St. Roch. He has great dialectic superiority over the abbé; and, although he tries to be courteous, he does not spare satire and sarcasm, until the poor priest is in a bad way. He produces the impression that his clerical adversary is hopelessly his inferior, and that the combat is unequal. Just as one may see in the preface to the 'Ami des Femmes' a supplemental chapter to 'L' Homme-Femme,' so one may trace in the preface to the 'Dame aux Camélias' the germ of this plea for divorce. But since 1868, when he wrote these prefaces, M. Dumas's style has sharpened, and his authority is greater. He has wit and eloquence: he appears in these pages as a Bourdaloue-Beaumarchais. Surpassing his eloquence is his wit, though he is too conscious of it, and too reliant on it: as George Eliot says, —

> " Life is not rounded in an epigram,
> And, saying aught, we leave a world unsaid."

M. Dumas half hints, at times, that he can unlock the gravest of problems with the pass-key of a clever phrase. What is most characteristic in this divorce pamphlet is the serried logic of four hundred and sixteen pages, and the sudden lack of logic in the nine lines of the four hundredth and seventeenth and last page, on which M. Dumas — all his arguments having hitherto tended to show the need of a modification of the French law until divorce may be had under some such strict limitations as obtain in New York — concludes by formally asking for the passage of M. Naquet's bill, which he has cited at length in the earlier part of the book, and which allows a freedom of separation shocking even to an Illinois or Connecticut legislator.

M. Dumas's latest utterance in sociology is a bulky pamphlet of some two hundred pages on ' Les Femmes qui tuent et les Femmes qui votent.' This discussion of women who kill and women who vote contains little that is new to any one familiar with M. Dumas's other polemical writings : it is as characteristic as any, but perhaps a little more extravagant and illogical. There have been several variations of the Laura Fair case in France, and there has been a reproduction of the refusal of the Smith sisters to pay taxes. From the first set of examples M. Dumas argues that, until the French code is reformed by the institution of an action for bastardy and the re-establishment of divorce, woman will be justified in taking the law in her own hands, and acting at once as jury and judge and executioner. From the second example M. Dumas argues that woman suffrage ought to be, and that it is only a question of time how soon it will come. His answer to the objection that woman has not the physical force to defend her choice and cannot fight, is to cite (p. 102) Jeanne de France, and Jeanne de Blois, and Jeanne de Flandres, and Jeanne de Hachette, and Jeanne d'Arc, and to add, that " no one of these women, having done in our day what they did in their own time, would be admitted to elect representatives in the country they had saved. This is very comic." To the objections that a descent into the political arena would rob woman of her charms, M. Dumas responds that she would vote as gracefully as she does every thing, having first made herself "hats *à la* polling-booth, waists *à la* universal suffrage, and skirts *à la* ballot-box." I fear that our own reformers would find M. Dumas very flippant.

Among the consequences which would follow the decreeing of divorce in France, M. Dumas told us in his preceding volume on that question, would be a total change in the French drama, as adultery, now the chief stage-stock in trade, would lose its importance in life, and so would see less service in the theatre. If M. Dumas be right, we can only wish that divorce had been established before he began to write, and perhaps then illicit love would not have been found in some form in every one of his plays. There is adultery, or the attempt at it, or the suspicion of it, in eleven out of twelve of M. Dumas's dramas. Once and again Paganini chose to play on one string as an artistic freak, but he owed his greatness to his skill on a violin complete in all its parts. M. Dumas, though his violin had four strings like the rest, has given us little else save solos on a single one. He is, in short, a specialist; and in literature, as in medicine, a specialist is often danger-ous. An illegitimate child himself, the result of illicit affection, he cannot abandon the discussion of one subject : do what he will, his thoughts still turn to it. All his powers as a playwright are at the service of this peculiar predilection : his gift of seeing things theatrically ; his ability in handling a plot, generally simple, and turning frequently on a single strong situation carefully prepared and provided for, and only postponed to come at last with double force ; his gift of characterization ; his skill in skating over thin ice ; his speech, when needed, vigorous to the point of violence ; his knack of breaking the force of all objections to his conclusion by himself advancing them ; and his wit, which cannot be denied, though he is far too conscious of it, as any one may see who notes how he scatters it broadcast through his plays, and then, for fear some of it may have fallen on stony ground, takes care that his characters compliment each other on their cleverness (and one may easily see also that the wit is M. Dumas's own, and not that of the individual character, in spite of some attempt at disguise), —all these remarkable qualifications are held at the beck and call of his desire for the contemplation of illicit love. He even goes out of his way to make wholly unimportant figures, shown to use only in profile, adulterers, —in the ' Fils Naturel,' for instance, and the 'Princess Georges.'

No wonder he warns us not to take our daughters to the theatre. Goethe, it is true, gave much the same advice. M. Dumas says he respects the maiden too much to bid her to his plays, and he respects his art too much to write for maidens. There is some reason in this : it is, at least, an open question whether we do not fetter the artist too tightly when we insist on bringing all literature down to the level of the school-girl. While we may admit, however, that girls have no business in a dissecting-room, one may also protest against always taking the stage for a physiological laboratory. Besides, while true science is clean and wholesome, M. Dumas's is neither. As M. Francisque Sarcey once wrote, "He gives the best advice in the world in a language which recalls at once the manuals of physiology and the *Vie Parisienne* of Marcelin." And a sceptic is tempted to wonder whether by chance M. Dumas has not gleaned the most of his science in the *Vie Parisienne*. A competent critic like M. Charles Bigot doubts M. Dumas's science, and thinks it rather a hap-hazard gathering of physiological and psychological orts and ends picked up here and there in stray newspaper articles. The scientific spirit itself is utterly absent. One may doubt that M. Dumas knows whether there be any scientific spirit or not. In default of it he is fertile in hypothesis and theory. Sometimes he gets so entangled in the jungle of his own philosophy, that it is difficult to discover his whereabouts. Yet, as a French critic has pointed out, he seems to have had in turn, if not at the same time, these three theories : first, love rehabilitates a fallen woman ; second, when she is not capable of rehabilitation, one must kill her ; and thirdly, woman, anyhow, is a being greatly inferior to man, who, indeed, may be said to stand intermediate and mediating between woman and God. It is to prove one or another of these three hypotheses, that M. Dumas has written his later plays, which, fortunately for us, are most of them of more value than the doubtful theories which called them into being.

There are two writers with whom the elder Dumas **is** to be compared : one is Victor Hugo, because they

together led the Romanticists; the other is the younger
Dumas, because both bear the same name. I have
already, in the chapter on the elder Dumas, given his
opinion of the relative qualities of Victor Hugo and
himself: it is fortunately possible also to give his opinion of the relative qualities of himself and his son, of
whom he was truly proud. "Alexandre, being my son,
was born with a few of my good points, and completed
them with those which were his own. I was born in
a poetical and picturesque age. I was an idealist. He
was born in a materialist and socialist age: he was a
positivist. In one play only can our different manners
be traced: it is the first he wrote, — the 'Dame aux
Camélias.' . . . I take my subject in a dream: he
takes his in reality. I work with my eyes closed: he
works with his eyes open. I shrink from the world at
my elbows: he identifies himself with it. I draw:
he photographs. People look in vain for the models
of my characters: they might almost point out his by
name. The work suggests itself to me through an
idea: it suggests itself to him through a fact." A
little later the father summed up the son in these three
sentences, with which we may leave the subject:
"With all this, Alexandre has a fault which will ruin
him if he does not correct himself in time. Alexandre
is over fond of preaching. His favorite book among
the works of Balzac is the 'Médecin de Campagne,' —
a magnificent novel, it is true, but one in which theory
takes the place of plot, and philosophy of action."

CHAPTER VII.

M. VICTORIEN SARDOU.

PERHAPS the most prominent of the French drama
tists of to-day is M. Victorien Sardou. He is probably
better known, both in and out of France, than any of
his rivals. He has written some twoscore plays, good
and bad, in half as many years : at least ten of those
plays have met with emphatic public applause; and
twenty of them, more or less, have, at one time or
another, been acted in the United States. He is just
fifty; he is rich; he is the youngest member of the
French Academy; and it is to his plays that he owes
his riches and his seat with the forty immortals.

M. Sardou was born in Paris, Sept. 7, 1831. His
father was a teacher and the author of elementary text-
books. The son was early entered as a medical student,
but he soon gave up medicine for history. Both of
these early inclinations have left their mark on the
work of the dramatic author. The larger and ampler
literary style of his two historical dramas, 'Patrie' and
the 'Haine,' is no doubt the result of his youthful
reading; and the scientific marvel which is the backbone of the 'Perle Noire' possibly came within his
experience while he was preparing to be a physician.
His change of front just as he began the battle of life
did not lighten the struggle. The ten years between
1850 and 1860 were years of misery and want. M.
Sardou taught, served as an usher in a school, did hack

writing for dictionary-makers and in cheap newspapers, and wrote various plays, which were refused right and left. But in 1854 the Odéon accepted a three-act comedy in verse; and on April 1 — ominous date — the 'Taverne des Étudiants' was hissed. Like many another successful dramatist, M. Sardou saw his first play damned out of hand. After the failure of this 'comedy he fell back into obscurity. He planned a series of semi-scientific tales, after the manner of Poe's, and in some sort anticipating M. Jules Verne's fantastic inventions; but only one or two of them ever saw the light. The 'Perle Noire' is one of these: it is a neat little story, and a translation of it was published not long ago in an American magazine.

In 1858 M. Sardou married Mlle. de Brécourt, an intimate friend of Déjazet. At the house of the cele-brated actress he met Vanderbuch, who had written several plays for Déjazet; and one day, struck by M. Sardou's intelligence, he proposed a collaboration. The two dramatists wrote together the 'Premières Armes de Figaro;' and the play was at once accepted by Déjazet, for whom the leading part had been con-trived. But the actress was out of an engagement, and vainly offered her services and her new play to manager after manager. At last, toward the end of 1859, she took a theatre herself, called it the Théâtre-Déjazet, and on its stage acted the part of the young Figaro. The play was a great success; and M. Sardou soon followed it by others, — 'M. Garat,' a study of the French revolutionary epoch, a period he is especially interested in; and the 'Près St. Gervais,' which in 1874 was re-arranged to serve as a libretto for the light and tuneful music of M. Lecocq. These three neat little pieces, like all plays written for Déjazet, are not so characteristic of the author as of the actress. They are cast in the Déjazet mould, and one seeks vainly for the Sardou trade-mark. Strong or original dramatic work was out of the question, and the most the author could do was to show his ingenuity in variations on the accepted air. The dramas written for Déjazet by M. Sardou were the only new plays in which the sexagenarian actress was successful; and their success drew their author from his former obscurity, and proved his possession of the dramatic faculty, — the rare gift of shaping one's work exactly for the exigencies of the modern theatre; a gift which the greatest genius may be without, and without which the greatest genius cannot hope for success on the stage.

The doors of the Parisian theatre having thus been opened by Déjazet to M. Sardou, he rushed in at once with long-repressed energy, and produced within five years (1860–64) nearly twenty plays of one kind or another, — comedy, farce, drama, or opera. This haste was its own punishment. The 'Papillonne,' brought out in 1862 at the Théâtre Français, failed, and so did most of the others. Two of the score, however, achieved instant and lasting success. The 'Pattes de Mouche' and 'Nos Intimes' were both first acted in 1861; and the triumph they won compensated in a measure for the less favorable reception of their fellows. These are, perhaps, the two plays of their author best known in England and America. Each has been adapted to our stage more than once. 'Nos Intimes' was turned into 'Friends or Foes?' by Mr. Wigan, whose version has been given in New York as 'Bosom Friends.' Another adaptation, called 'Peril,' has been

of the Republican party in France. Warming to his work, he wrote a second attack on republican institutions, setting his scene this time in this country. Already in an early comedy, the 'Femmes Fortes,' he had compared the manners and customs of America with those of France, greatly to our disadvantage. In his 'Oncle Sam' he laid on the blacks and whites with so heavy a hand that the censors forbade the production of the play, as insulting to a friendly nation. But one of the enterprising managers of the friendly nation procured the piece; and it was brought out here in the land it insulted while still under the ban in France. When acted here, it was at once seen to be the result of the most amusing ignorance, giving us good occasion to laugh at the author, instead of laughing with him, and showing but little of his customary smartness. The words which Matthew Arnold uses to criticise the manner of an English historian toward the French generals in the Crimean war can fairly be used here to characterize this incursion of a French dramatist into America: "The failure in good sense and good taste reaches far beyond what the French mean by *fatuité*. They would call it by another word, — a word expressing blank defect of intelligence; a word for which we have no exact equivalent in English, — *bête*."

'Andréa,' which served as a stop-gap, pending the raising of the interdict on the satire on American society, was a hastily-revised edition of a play written to order for a charming American actress, Miss Agnes Ethel, and originally brought out in New York as 'Agnes:' — one would think that M. Sardou had cause to be thankful to America. The censors soon allowed the performance of 'Oncle Sam;' but the comedy was

received with no great favor; and indeed, for the next
five years, M. Sardou saw little of success. A farce
failed at the Palais Royal in 1873, another at the Variétés in 1874; and in the same year his strong but repulsive historical drama, the 'Haine,' was brought out for
but few nights at the Gaîté. In 1875 'Ferréol' had
a little better luck; and in 1877 'Dora' met with an
enthusiastic reception as a return to his characteristic
manner, and as a worthy successor of the 'Famille
Benoiton' and 'Nos Bons Villageois.' Turned into
English none too skilfully, and disfigured by the needless thrusting-in of jingoism, 'Dora,' as 'Diplomacy,'
has been acted with popular applause throughout England and America. In 1878 M. Sardou sought to repeat
his success of 1867, and to set before the visitors to the
Exhibition a dramatic dish resembling closely the fare
which had proved acceptable to their predecessors of
eleven years before. The 'Bourgeois de Pont d'Arcy'
was made on the same lines as 'Nos Bons Villageois,'
and satirized in the same style the petty politics of
country life. The later play was not so well made as
the earlier one: its fundamental situation was most
unpleasant; and Parisian and provincial play-goers felt,
with Joubert, that comedy ought never to show what is
odious. The piece failed in Paris, and was acted in
New York for a while with much the same result.

In 'Daniel Rochat,' acted by the Comédie-Française
in 1880, M. Sardou, true to his habit of trying to tickle
the taste of the hour, and to set on the stage the question of the day, considered the so-called conflict of
religion and science. When the author of 'Oncle Sam'
and the 'Famille Benoiton' tries to handle so important
a topic, it is a little difficult to take him seriously; but

he is so clever, that he compels attention at least, if not admiration. It is curious that the adjective, which, when one writes about M. Sardou, comes of its own accord to the end of one's pen, is "clever;" and the word really sums him up. Conviction, sincerity, truth, — all these may be wanting in 'Daniel Rochat;' but there is no falling-off in cleverness. Now, a really great writer is not clever, he is something more and better; and to dwell on a writer's cleverness is like insisting on a man's good nature: if he had nobler qualities, this would be taken for granted. To say this is to say, that, whenever M. Sardou tackles a living issue, he may be amusing, but he is not likely to be instructive. In 'Daniel Rochat' his treatment is at once insufficient and superficial. Having attacked the church in 'Séraphine,' the original title of which was the 'Dévote,' he now defends religion in 'Daniel Rochat.'

The story of the play is simple to baldness: Rochat, who is an atheist and an eloquent politician, meets in Switzerland two Anglo-American girls, and falls in love with the elder. We say "Anglo-American," because M. Sardou seems never to be able to make up his mind as to their nationality: at one moment they are English, at another American; and of a truth they are all the time French, M. Sardou apparently thinking that to let them go about without a *chaperone* was sufficient to Americanize them. In the first act Rochat proposes; in the second they are married civilly; in the third she insists on a religious marriage also, which he refuses; in the fourth he tries to seduce her from her allegiance to her faith; and in the fifth they agree to separate, and the curtain falls on the signing of the application for a divorce. Rochat begins as a conceited snob, to turn, in the fourth act, into a contemptible cur; and Léa is always a rather priggish young person. The final three acts are filled with the bandying of argument between the two; and, as M. Sarcey said when the play was produced in Paris, "the fifth act repeats the fourth, which repeats the third, which was tiresome." There is no decrease in the technical skill, but the subject is fatal. We are not interested in hero or heroine; and we know that in real life, if they really loved each other, they would not have parted: either he would have so endowed the civil marriage with solemnity that she would accept it, or else he would have put his pride in his pocket, and been married when and how she pleased, — by minister, or priest, or bishop, or pope, or rabbi, or dervish, or what you will. They would have got married somehow, and then would have come the real dramatic struggle. The true drama looms up after the fifth act of M. Sardou's play, had it ended happily: it is in the rending force in a household of religious antagonism, the wife going one way, and the husband another. If the subject is to be set on the stage at all, it is here in married life that incidents and interest must be sought, and not in the petty hesitancies of two people who cannot make up their minds. It is here that it would have been sought by writers honest of purpose, like M. Augier or M. Dumas. The hollowness of M. Sardou's protestations of a desire to regenerate his countrymen by a dramatic discussion of a vital issue is shown most amusingly by the fact that the first play he brought out after 'Daniel Rochat' was an amusing and highly indecent farce called 'Divorçons,' written for the Palais Royal theatre.

In this brief survey of M. Sardou's career as a dramatist during the past twenty years, only those plays have been dwelt on which demand especial attention. The first thing which suggests itself, when one looks down the list of his twoscore of pieces, is the great variety of the styles the author has striven to succeed in. M. Émile Augier and M. Alexandre Dumas *fils* have confined themselves to comedy, — a comedy, it is true, which sometimes crosses the line of drama; but the apparent intention has always been comedy. M. Sardou has written comedies, historical dramas, farces, and operas. In farce and in historical drama his success has been slight. Opera, which he has attempted half a dozen times, has been but little more advantageous to him. Only 'Piccolino,' a recent setting by M. Guiraud as an *opéra-comique* of an early play, seems likely to last. The 'Roi Carotte,' with the music of Offenbach, and the 'Près St. Gervais,' with the music of M. Lecocq, are already forgotten. 'Patrie!' has been used by an Italian composer as the libretto of an opera called the 'Comtessa di Mans.'

On recalling M. Sardou's work in comedy and in the other departments of the drama, with the idea of detecting what his dominant quality may be, one cannot avoid the deduction that it is cleverness. Mr. Henry James, Jr., has called him a "supremely skilful contriver and arranger." And no one who has at all studied M. Sardou's plays will quarrel with Mr. James's other assertion, that he is "a man who, as one may phrase it, has more of the light, and less of the heat, of cleverness, than any one else." That is to say, M. Sardou is very clever: he has cleverness raised to the nth, if I may so express it, and he has little or nothing except cleverness; but it is the cleverness of a man who has the dramatic faculty, the theatrical touch, the dramatizing eye. And just what this precious faculty is, M. Sardou himself has told us in his speech when received as a member of the French Academy. "The gambler is not more haunted by dreams of play," said he, "nor the miser by visions of lucre, than the dramatic author by the constant slavery of his one idea. All things are connected with it, and bring him back to it. He sees nothing, hears nothing, which does not drape itself at once in theatric attire. The landscape he admires — what a pretty scene! The charming conversation he listens to — what good dialogue! The delicious young girl who passes by — the adorable *ingénue!* And the misfortune, the crime, the disaster, he is told of — what a situation! what a drama!"

This dramatic faculty has another side : the author who has it, besides unconsciously dramatizing all he hears and sees, has also an innate power of so setting upon the stage what he has written, that the spectators are affected by it as he was. The days when a dramatist needed merely to write are now gone, — gone with the placards which may have served to indicate where the action of any scene in Shakspere's plays passed. The dramatic author of our day has to fill the eyes as well as the ears of his audience. The stage-setting, the scenery, the furniture, the costumes, the movements of the actors, the management of the many minor characters, often mingled with the action, in short, the *show* part of the play, — all this is now of importance second only to the play itself, and often thrust into the front place, to the almost certain failure of the production. Play-goers are both audience and spectators ; they like to see as well as to hear : but they do not care to see a show at the expense of the drama they have come to hear. Now, expert as M. Sardou is in all details of stage management and of *mise-en-scène*, — to use a French phrase impossible to render in English with exactness, — he sometimes has pushed the merely spectacular into undue prominence. The 'Haine,' a historical drama, and the 'Merveilleuses,' a historical farce, both failed because the play was smothered into insignificance beneath the splendor of the show. M. Sardou seems to have thought with the First Player in the 'Rehearsal,' that the essentials of a play were scenes and clothes, and to have forgotten to put in enough human interest to counterbalance this excess of external adornment. The plays were over-laden with gold, and they sank when they sought to swim.

In general M. Sardou's extreme cleverness does not thus overreach itself : in general his skill in setting his subject on the stage serves him to great advantage. Consider this scene in 'Patrie!' we are outside the gates of Brussels, with snowy rampart and tower, and frozen moat glistening in the moonlight ; a Spanish patrol crosses, — the patriots, who are in consultation, hide as best they may, — another patrol is heard approaching : the patriots will be taken between two fires ; prompt action is needed ; as the second patrol passes across the stage, every man in it is silently seized, and killed, and his body is thrown through a hole in the ice of the moat, — a hole at once filled with masses of snow, so that when the first patrol returns, it walks unsuspect-ingly over the icy graves of its fellow-soldiers.

Not only in the heavier historical dramas, like 'Pa-trie!' is this skill in stage-setting useful ; for it is almost as imperatively demanded in the comedy of every-day life. Here there are no adventitious aids, no moonlight, no snow, no frozen moat : the variety which charms the eye of the spectator must be sought in the constant and appropriate movement of the actors. A long scene between two characters is broken by numberless changes of position, by crossing and recrossing the stage, by rising and sitting down, now right and now left, by taking advantage of the conformations of the scenery, and the placing of the furniture. All this must not be overdone : every movement must seem to be unpremeditated, and to spring naturally from the dialogue. To assist in the delusion, the scenery and the accessories are all carefully considered by the author; they are to be found set down on his manuscript; and they, and the movements of the actors which they assist, are as truly part of his play as the words he puts into the mouths of his characters. M. Charles Blanc, the eminent art-critic to whom was allotted the duty of replying to M. Sardou's reception-speech at the Academy, took occasion to declare that M. Sardou possessed this talent of *mise-en-scène* in the highest degree. It is a talent, "perhaps," he said, "too highly praised nowadays. . . . But I admire the skilful ordering of the room in which passes the action of your characters, the care you take in putting each in his place, in choosing the furniture which surrounds them, and which is always not only of the style required, — that goes without saying, — but significant, expressive, fitted to aid in the turns of the drama."

In this as in many another way, M. Sardou suggests Scribe, who was also a supremely skilful contriver and arranger. Scribe was passing slowly out of sight as

M. Sardou came into prominence; but without Scribe M. Sardou was scarcely possible. In the rapidity with which they gained wealth, in their many successes, in their willingness to suit the public taste rather than to serve any rigid rules of true art, in their conservatism, in their *bourgeois* respectability with its thousand gigs, in their mastery over stage technicalities, in their frequent borrowing of material from a neighbor, in the dexterity with which they can play with an audience, — in all these respects, the two dramatists are alike. If the habit obtained nowadays of naming one writer after another, some few of whose obvious qualities he might have, — as Irving was at one time the American Goldsmith, and Klopstock was hailed as the German Milton (a *very* German Milton, as Coleridge suggested), — if this habit obtained now, M. Sardou would be the later Scribe. The points of unlikeness are almost as many and as marked as the points of likeness. It is in technical skill and in the resulting success that the essential similarity lies. But M. Sardou, who has studied Scribe to the end, early saw that the simple style of the dramatist of the citizen-king was not best suited to please the new Paris of the lower Empire: so he doubled the French playwright with the Athenian dramatic poet, and sought to be Aristophanes and Scribe at the same time. It can scarcely be said, however, that he wholly succeeds: he is at best but little more than a sort of Pasquin-Scribe. Yet he wields a lively wit; and I think Heine, who hated Scribe, might now and then have shaken hands with M. Sardou.

The essential similarity between the two playwrights is, as has been said, the extreme cleverness of each, and the success which rewards that cleverness. In another important point is the likeness between them almost as striking, — in a willingness to make over old material. Here M. Sardou treads in Scribe's footsteps. But while the old dramatist was open and honest, and never claimed what was not his own, the younger one has been more than once sued because he was bearing away in his literary baggage another man's property. It has been shortly and sharply said that M. Sardou "has shown real power in the creation of types, while unhesitatingly using in his plots the commonest effects : he carries through a play with a *verve* and a rapidity of movement, for the sake of which he has been pardoned the frequency of his rememberings and borrowings."

These rememberings and borrowings are not a few. The germ of the 'Pattes de Mouche' (1861) is to be found in Poe's story of the 'Purloined Letter;' the fourth act of 'Nos Intimes' (1861) is said to be singularly like a vaudeville called the 'Discours de Rentrée;' the 'Pommes du Voisin' (1864) is taken from a tale of Charles de Bernard's; 'Séraphine' (1868) seems to be indebted to Diderot's 'Réligeuse' and to Bayard's 'Mari à la Campagne;' 'Patrie!' (1869) owes something to a play of Méry's; the story of 'Fernande' (1870) is to be found in Diderot's 'Jacques le Fataliste;' the 'Roi Carotte' (1872) was greatly indebted to Hoffman; the American 'Oncle Sam' (1873) would not have existed had it not been for two stories of M. Alfred Assolant, who, however, lost the suit he brought against M. Sardou for a share in the profits of the play; in 'Andréa' (1873) is a situation from M. Dumas's 'Princess Georges;' many a hint for 'Ferréol' (1875) was derived from M. Jules Sandeau and from M. Gaboriau; the 'Hôtel Godelot' (1876), a comedy by M. Crissafulli, of which

M. Sardou was anonymously joint author, was founded upon Goldsmith's 'She Stoops to Conquer;' and the final act of 'Dora' (1877) has more than one point of resemblance to the end of the 'Aventurière' of M. Émile Augier.

Besides borrowing freely from his neighbor, M. Sardou has more than once repeated himself, and is evidently fond of falling back on his early works, and presenting them anew. The two-act 'Près St. Gervais,' a comedy in 1862, becomes a three-act *opéra-bouffe* in 1874. The comedy of 'Piccolino,' played in 1861, re-appears in 1876 as an *opéra-comique*. These are of course avowed reproductions, but there is no lack of unconfessed but almost equally obvious repetition. There is in the 'Vieux Garçons' (1865) a strong situation, — a father, whose child is ignorant of his relationship, is so placed that he dare not declare himself; the same situation re-appears in 'Séraphine' (1868): in the former case the child is a boy, and in the latter a girl. The first acts of the 'Famille Benoiton' (1865) and of 'Oncle Sam' (1873) are almost exactly alike. The fast French-women in the first play and the impossible American girls in the second are exhibited one after another: a clever French-woman (a part taken in both pieces by Mlle. Fargueil) acts as showman, while a witty French-man asks the right questions at the right time. And the characters of the two comedies resemble each other singularly. The witty Frenchman and the clever French-woman take part in both. Uncle Sam himself is a first cousin to M. Benoiton: his son is only the calculating young Formichel, and the trick young Formichel plays on his father finds its counterpart in the trick Uncle Sam s son plays on him. In fact, on a careful comparison of the two comedies, it seems as though M. Sardou, in his absolute ignorance of this country, thought that all he need do to satirize America was to push his satire of fast French society a little farther. 'Oncle Sam' is the 'Famille Benoiton,' only the dose is stronger, more pungent, more acrid. In M. Sardou's first assault on the bad habits of the United States, the 'Femmes Fortes' (1860), we see Americans who are just like those in the 'Oncle Sam' of fourteen years later, and who, like them, seem to have walked straight out of the pages of 'American Notes.'

There is to be seen in the 'Femmes Fortes' the same clever woman of great common sense, who re-appears in both the 'Famille Benoiton' and 'Oncle Sam.' In each of these pieces she plays the part of Greek chorus. In 'Rabagas' she is the *dea ex machina.* In the 'Pattes de Mouche,' perhaps the cleverest of all of M. Sardou's clever comedies, she is the protagonist. In each of these five plays the same woman appears under different names ; and in each M. Sardou lauds her cleverness, and skilfully lays her traps for her, and obligingly insists on the victims walking into them blindfold. In the 'Famille Benoiton' and 'Oncle Sam' and the 'Pattes de Mouche,' the clever woman is accompanied and assisted by a clever man ; and in 'Patrie !' and 'Fernande' and 'Nos Intimes' and 'Dora,' the clever man is all by himself, and has to get things settled and straightened out without any aid from a clever woman. In 'Fernande' he is a lawyer ; in 'Patrie !' he is a soldier and a Huguenot ; and so he gets a backbone and a solidity lacking to his equally clever brothers and sisters. I am not sure, indeed, that the Marquis de la Trémouille, the Frenchman in 'Patrie !' is not the most charming of all M. Sardou's characters. He is strong and manly, and true to life. His courtly grace and vivacity lighten and brighten the sombre gloom of 'Patrie!' and it has been suggested, that, if he or some other of his countrymen equally debonair had appeared also in the 'Haine,' the fate of that powerful and painful play might have been more happy.

These repetitions, these frequent rememberings of himself, and borrowings from others, are pardoned, because in the rushing rapidity which M. Sardou imparts to his play, there is scarce time to think of them. The sin at worst is but venial : we are always willing to forgive an author's theft, if he but steal at the same time the Promethean spark to give life to his creatures. This M. Sardou seems certainly to do. His characters are full of motion, and as life-like as may be, although they are rarely really alive and human. His clever men and women are always seen with pleasure, because M. Sardou is clever himself, and he understands cleverness, and these characters are but projections of himself. All his minor humorous characters are skilfully sketched. He has a keen eye for the ludicrous, and a genuine gift of caricature. This latter quality, the keen, quick thrust of the caricaturist, was used in moderation and with great effect in the village apothecary and the rustic louts of 'Nos Bons Villageois,' and in the professional revolutionist and other self-seeking political agitators of 'Rabagas.' But the dramatist's political animosities blunted his artistic perception when he cast the central figure of the latter play in the same mould which had served for its minor characters. In structure the piece is weaker than any other of its author's important plays ; and the character of Rabagas

himself is an overcharged, self-contradictory caricature.
It is very clever, of course, and one can readily understand its startling success at first; but, when one thinks
over the conduct of Rabagas, its weakness is manifest.
He is represented as a type of the uneasy political
lawyer, using the tools of state-craft to carve his way
to fame and fortune, —

> " Ready alike to worship and revile,
>   To build the altar or to light the pile.
>
> .   .   .   .   .
>
>   Now mad for patriots, hot for revolution;
>   Now all for hanging and the Constitution."

This is a fine subject for a comic dramatist. Patriotic hypocrisy gives as good an occasion for grave and
thoughtful humorous treatment as religious hypocrisy.
Rabagas might have been worthy to hang in the same
gallery with Tartuffe. But Molière's creation is firm,
and broadly handled, and consistent to the end : M.
Sardou's is cheap, and sacrifices again and again his
consistency for the sake of making a point. It is a
Punch-and-Judy show : the figure is the figure of Rabagas ; but we know the hand of M. Sardou is inside it,
and makes it move ; and we recognize the voice of M.
Sardou whenever it speaks. Its movements are amusing, and what it says is entertaining, and we must needs
confess that the showman is very clever. But Molière
was something more than clever when he drew Tartuffe. And if this comparison be thought too crushing,
M. Émile Augier was more than clever when he
created Giboyer ; and M. Alexandre Dumas *fils* was
more than clever when he set before us the 'Demi-
Monde.' Molière and M. Augier and M. Dumas worked

with heart as well as head : they put something of themselves into their plays. M. Sardou relied solely on his cleverness, and, if the assertion may be ventured, on his spite.

In the preface to the 'Haine' M. Sardou declares his respect for woman, and his worship of her. Here is perhaps as good an opportunity as any to say that M. Sardou's plays are, for the most part, as moral as one could wish, not only in the conventional reward of virtue, and punishment of vice, but in the tone and color of the whole. He has his eccentricities of taste and of morals, such as we Anglo-Saxons detect in any Frenchman; but he never panders to vice, never pets it, pats it, and plays with it seductively, as M. Octave Feuillet is wont to do. With the present method in France of bringing up young girls, and of marrying and giving in marriage, the dramatist is forced frequently to seek for his love-interest in the breaking, actual or imminent, of the Seventh Commandment. But more often than any other French dramatist of standing has M. Sardou sought to confine himself to the honest love of a young man and a young woman. In 'Dora,' in the 'Ganaches,' and in more than one other of his comedies, there is, if one strikes out a few grains of sharp Gallic salt, nothing to offend the most fastidious Anglo-American old maid. M. Sardou's young girls are charming. One does not wonder at the fondness of the Frenchman for the lily-like innocence of the *ingénue*, if all *ingénues* are really as innocent and as delicious as those in M. Sardou's comedies. To the healthy American the *ingénue* seems almost an impossibility; but M. Sardou endows her with a frankness and grace which relieves the somewhat namby-pamby, goody-goody innocuousness of a bread-and-butter miss whose only preparation for the duties of life is a complete ignorance of the world, the flesh, and the devil. In M. Sardou's hands the *ingénue* is neither sickly nor unwholesome: she is confiding and engaging, and timid if you will, but charming and delightful. M. Sardou, in announcing his great respect for woman, says he has always given her the best part in his plays, — "that of common sense, of tenderness, of self-sacrifice. I say nothing of my young girls. They form a collection of which I am proud. Aside from one or two Americans and the Benoitons, you could marry them all; and this is no slight praise."

He is right to be proud of them. It would be hard to find a more charming scene in recent comedy than the one in the last act of 'Nos Bons Villageois,' in which Geneviève (the *ingénue*) with girlish frankness confesses to her brother-in-law, the baron, that she is in love, and that her lover is coming in a few hours to ask for her hand; this same lover being the man with whom the brother-in-law is about to fight a duel because the lover has been apparently intriguing with Geneviève's sister, the baron's wife. The daughter of Séraphine is almost equally charming: her presence in the play does much toward atoning for the odiousness of her mother, — that despicable creature, a female hypocrite, a Lady Tartuffe, but not as delicately drawn as Mme. de Girardin's. And the tender and clinging grace of the fragile daughter of the Duke of Alba in 'Patrie!' must be accepted as some compensation for the wretchedly vicious heroine. He acknowledges that these two, Séraphine and Dolorès, are dark spots in his white list of women, "and especially Dolorès. Imposed on me by the action of the play, she long haunted my sleep to reproach me for having made her so guilty."

These words — "imposed on me by the action of the play" (*imposée par la donnée même*) — let in a flood of light on M. Sardou's methods of work. His characters are the creatures of his situations. He contrives his plot first, and afterwards looks around for people to carry it out. Here, again, is the difference between M. Sardou and M. Augier. The author of the 'Fils de Giboyer' and the 'Mariage d'Olympe' invents and contrasts characters, and then lets them work out a play. The author of 'Nos Bon Villageois' happens on a striking situation, and then puts together characters to set it off to best advantage. M. Augier is interested in human nature, and trusts for success on man's interest in man: M. Sardou relies, for the most part, on the mechanical ingenuity of his situations. As the proper subject of comedy is to be found in the ever varying phases of human nature, rather than in the external and temporary accidents of life, M. Augier's method is truer than M. Sardou's.

In the preface to the 'Haine,' from which quotation has already been made, M. Sardou tells us how the first idea of a play is revealed to his mind. "The process is invariable. It never appears otherwise than as a sort of philosophic equation from which the unknown quantity is to be discovered. As soon as it is fairly set before me, this problem possesses me, and lets me have no peace till I have found the formula. In 'Patrie!' this was the problem, What is the greatest sacrifice a man can make for love of his country? And, the formula once found, the piece followed of its own accord. In the 'Haine' the problem was, In what circumstances will the inborn charity of woman show itself in the most striking manner?"

This confession, which is probably as exact as Poe's account of the way he wrote the 'Raven,' confirms the assertion that he always starts with a situation. In 'Patrie!' he sought to find the situation which would show in action the greatest possible sacrifice a man could make for love of his country. In the 'Haine' he looked for the situation in which the inborn charity of woman would be most strikingly revealed. In neither case did he set out with a strong character, and ask what that man or that woman would do in a given situation. In both plays he started with a situation, meaning to fashion afterward a man or a woman to fit it. We must confess that the reliance M. Sardou places in his situations is not misplaced. In general they are very strong, and they admit of effective theatrical handling. Although one is indisposed to admit that in 'Patrie!' we have the greatest sacrifice a man may make to his country, still the situation is beyond doubt powerful and pathetic. The patriot leader of a revolt, loving his wife only second to his country, discovers, on the eve of the rising against the oppressor, that she is untrue to him, and that her lover is his second in command, — a man whose services are indispensable to the triumph of the insurgents. He does not hesitate, but sacrifices at once his private vengeance to his patriotism, and fights side by side with the man who has wronged him. In 'Nos Bons Villageois' a young man found in a lady's dressing-room at night, under suspicious circumstances, seizes her jewels, and allows himself to be denounced as a thief, sacrificing himself to save her reputation. In 'Dora' a young girl on her wedding morning is accused, and the proof is overwhelming, of having stolen an important official document from her husband to send it to an emissary of the enemy. In the 'Bourgeois de Pont d'Arcy' the situation is equally dramatic ; but it is fundamentally disgusting, and suggests the reflection that M. Sardou has morally no taste, to use the apt phrase of Henry James, Jr., about George Sand. And this lack of moral taste affects us unpleasantly in other of his plays, — in the 'Haine' for instance, in the 'Diables Noirs,' and in 'Maison Neuve!' — in all of which the strength of the situations is beyond dispute.

Few playwrights have ever had more skill in handling a situation than M. Sardou. He has, as M. Jules Clare-tie neatly puts it, "better than any one the *fingering* of the playwright" (*la doigté du dramaturge*). He prepares his situation slowly, and presents it with full effect ; leaves you in doubt for a while, and then cuts the knot with a single unexpected stroke. After he has got his characters into a terrible tangle, and there is seemingly no way of loosing the bands which bind them, M. Sardou either shows us that the tangle was only apparent, and the slipping of a single loop will set everybody free, or else he whips out his penknife, and, as has just been said, slyly cuts the cords, getting his knife safely back into his pocket while we are all aston-ished at the sudden falling of the ropes. In this super-subtle ingenuity M. Sardou again resembles Scribe, but the disciple has improved on the master. Both drama-tists take delight in producing great effects from little causes, but the methods are different. Scribe had the ingenuity of the travelling conjurer at a country fair :

he showed you a pellet under this cup; in a second it
is passed under that; and, before you know it, he raises
the third, and there it is again.   The trick is done, and
the three acts are over, leaving the pellet-people very
nearly where they were when he began.   But the art
of magic has made great progress of late.   The village
conjurer has given way before the court prestidigitator.
M. Sardou disdains a simple cup-and-ball effect: he has
at his command an electric battery and a pneumatic
machine, and he can do the second-sight mystery.   He
is a wizard of the North, not like Scott, but like Ander-
son.   He handcuffs his hero, seals him in a sack, locks
the sack in a box, has the box heavily chained, then
lowers the lights, and fires a pistol — and hi! presto!
the prisoner is free, and ready to play his part again.

M. Charles Blanc, in his witty and graceful reply to
M. Sardou's reception oration at the Academy, — a
reply in which, as is often the case in the academic
ceremonies, cutting criticism and biting rebuke were
courteously sheathed in suavity, politeness, and compliment, with no dulling of the edge of their keenness, —
M. Charles Blanc satirically praised M. Sardou's skill
in "using small means to arrive at great effects.
Among these small means there is one, the letter, that
you use from preference, and always happily.   The letter! — it plays a part in most of your plots; and all of it
is important, the wrapper as well as its contents.   The
envelope, the seal, the wax, the postage-stamp and the
postmark, and the tint of the paper and the perfume
which rises from it, not to speak of the handwriting,
close or free, large or small, — how many things in a
letter, as handled by you, may be irrefutable evidence
to betray the lovers, to denounce the villains, and to

warn the jealous!" M. Blanc continues by pointing out, that, in the 'Pattes de Mouche,' a letter is the basis of the plot : it is a long time hidden under a porcelain bust ; then, turn by turn, it serves, half-burnt, to light a lamp, then to prop a shaky table, then as a wad in a gun, then as a box for a rare beetle, and then, at last, for a proposal, which settles all things to everybody's satisfaction. In 'Dora' the traitress is exposed because of a peculiar perfume which she alone uses, and which clings to the letter she has touched. In 'Fernande,' in which M. Sardou, as M. Blanc says, "has so well depicted the exquisite elevation of a young soul which has preserved itself pure in the midst of all the impurities of a wretched gambling-hell, the heroine, on the eve of marrying a gentleman, the Marquis des Arcis, writes him a letter avowing the ignominies she has passed through without moral stain ; but this letter, intercepted by an old mistress of the marquis, does not arrive at its destination in time, and the marquis learns, when it is too late, that his marriage was dishonoring. However, as Fernande had loyally confessed *before* what he had only learned *after*, he consents to forgive all ; he wishes to forget all ; he easily persuades himself that he ought to love her whom he does love ; and thus a letter, because it was a day too late, makes happy a girl whom an involuntary stigma does not prevent from being charming." In the 'Bourgeois de Pont d'Arcy' it is a letter again which a son will not allow his mother to see, because it convicts his father of sin ; and this refusal forces the son finally to avow himself guilty of his father's fault. In the 'Famille Benoiton' and in 'Séraphine' letters are again to be found in the very centre of the plot.

In spite of this frequent use of apparently inadequate and trifling means to untie the knots of his story, no playwright has ever shown more skill in getting the utmost possible effect out of a situation : the situation, however, is nearly all there is. The characters are made to fit it, and the dialogue is sufficient to display it. The skeleton may be supple and well-jointed : it is not clothed with living flesh and blood. In spite of all the cleverness, there is no real feeling. There are few words which come straight from the heart, such as abound in M. Augier's work. The language of any of the characters in the moments of intense emotion is always to the point, and vigorous, and all that is needed by the situation ; but it is the clever language of M. Sardou, not the simple words of a heart torn by anguish, or racked by suspense. The characters do not rule events : they are ruled by them. For the most part, they are little more than puppets, to be moved mechanically so as to bring on the situation, or else they are vehicles for the author's wit and his satire.

For M. Sardou is really a journalist playwright. He tries to put the newspaper on the stage. He is rarely content to rely on his dramatic framework, good as it may be ; but he seeks to set it off by an appeal to the temper of the time, and an attempt at reflecting it. To enable him to combine this dramatizing of editorial articles and the latest news, with the proper presentation of a strong situation, M. Sardou has devised a new formula of dramatic construction. What this formula is can be seen on even slight consideration of almost any two or three of his five-act comedies, — 'Dora,' or 'Oncle Sam,' or 'Nos Bons Villageois.' He does not always employ this formula : 'Patrie !' is an exception, and so

in a measure, is 'Fernande.' Indeed, as the Paris corre-
spondent of the *Nation* once said, "Sardou is not ob-
stinate : he changes his manner, not in the course of a
few years, like the great painters ; he can change it three
times a year. He rather likes to change it, to jump
from one thing to another, to alter his system : he is a
sort of dramatic clown."

In spite of these frequent changes of system, there
are nearly a dozen of M. Sardou's plays, and the best
known of them, constructed according to a definite formula. This formula is evidently the result of a sort of
compromise arrived at between the two different men
contained in M. Sardou, — the satirical wit and the
situation-loving playwright, Pasquin and Scribe. The
wit writes the first half of the comedy, and it rattles
along as briskly and as brightly as a revolving firework ;
and then the playwright seizes the pen, and the story
suddenly takes a serious turn, and the interest grows
intense. It is characteristic of his cleverness, that he
is able to join two acts and a half of satirical comedy
to two acts and a half of melodramatic strength so
deftly that at first glance the joint is not visible. The
first act of any one of his plays rarely does more than
introduce the characters, and develop the satirical motive
of the play. Often there is absolutely no action whatever. This is the case in both the 'Famille Benoiton'
and 'Oncle Sam,' the first acts of which, as has been
said, are almost exactly alike. In the second act, the
satire and the wit and the comedy continue to be developed ; and possibly there is an indication of a coming
cloud, but it is not larger than a man's hand. In neither
'Dora' nor 'Nos Bons Villageois' do we get much
nearer the action of the story in the second act than

we were in the first. During these earlier acts M. Sardou is quietly laying his wires ; and in the third act the change comes, the masked batteries are revealed, and strong situation and sensation follow each other in rapid succession. Even in the caustic 'Rabagas,' M. Sardou seemingly had no confidence in his pure comedy, and so lugs in by the ears an extraneous intrigue of the prince's daughter with a captain of the guards.

For this inartistic mingling of two distinct styles of play, M. Sardou has good reasons. In the first place, it pays better to write five-act plays than plays of any other length. A dramatic author in Paris takes fifteen per cent of the gross receipts every night, more or less. If his play is short, he only gets his proportion of this, sharing it with the authors of the other pieces acted the same evening : if his play is long, and important enough to constitute the sole entertainment, he naturally takes the whole fifteen per cent himself. Having thus a motive for writing five-act plays, M. Sardou knows the temper of Parisian play-goers too well to believe that either five acts of satirical comedy or five acts of pathetic interest will please as well as five acts in which both tears and smiles are blended. Five acts of humor would probably begin to pall long before the fifth act was reached, and five acts of pathos would probably prove too lugubrious : so he combines the two. Now, the Parisian play-goer has a very bad habit : he dines late ; and, if he goes to the theatre after a dinner, he arrives certainly after the first act, possibly after the second. Therefore, clever in this as in all things, M. Sardou delays the real movement of his play until the third act, when he is certain to have all his spectators assembled ; and in the first two acts he gives free rein to his satirical instincts.

To amuse the many spectators who may have come in time, he has much bustle, much coming and going, little or no dramatic progress, but much effective theatrical movement, all accompanied by a running fire of witticisms, and hits at the times. His plays are written so distinctly to suit the taste of the moment, that when they are revived in after-years, they seem faded, and have a slightly stale odor, as of second-hand goods. Indeed, it would not be difficult for any one familiar with politics and society in France for the last score of years to declare the date of almost any of M. Sardou's five-act comedies from a cursory inspection of its allusions. 'Fernande,' we note from a remark in the first act, was written about the time a bottle of ink was broken against the Terpsichorean group of statuary which adorns the new opera-house; and the 'Famille Benoiton' marks the fashionable corruption of the lower Empire just before the Exhibition of 1867. As M. Jules Claretie has neatly said, "Sardou is a barometer dramatist, rising and falling with the weather, as it changes or is about to change. . . . Turn by turn, liberal or re-actionary, as liberty or re-action may happen to be at a premium, and pay a profit to him who traffics in it, he will praise, for example, the reconstruction of Paris in the 'Ganaches' when M. Haussmann is up at the top of the hill, and he will scourge it in 'Maison Neuve!' when M. Haussmann draws near his fall." The criticism is not unjust. The incipient re-action against the republic found its reflection in 1872 in 'Rabagas;' the uneasy restlessness in regard to foreign spies furnished the groundwork for 'Dora' in 1877; the provincial election-eering, log-rolling, and wire-pulling of the MacMahonite struggles were used in 1878 to give color to the 'Bour

geois de Pont d'Arcy ;' and advantage is taken of the
agitation in favor of a divorce-law in 1881 to give point
to 'Divorçons.'

In spite, therefore, of M. Sardou's extraordinary
cleverness, of his great theatrical skill, of his undenia-
ble wit, in spite of his many gifts in various directions,
he is not a dramatist of the first rank. He cannot
safely be taken as a model. As Joubert points out, "It
suffices not for an author to catch the attention and to
hold it : he must also satisfy it." M. Sardou often
catches the attention, and for a time he holds it; but
he never satisfies it. In the preceding pages he has
been likened to a conjurer, a clown, and a barometer.
If these comparisons are just, they suggest that there
is an ever-present taint of insincerity in his work ; that
he does not put himself into it; and that we shall seldom
find in it that "one drop of ruddy human blood " which
Lowell tells us "puts more life into the veins of a poem
than all the delusive *aurum potabile* that can be distilled
out of the choicest library," or compounded by the
utmost cleverness.

CHAPTER VIII.

M. OCTAVE FEUILLET.

AMONG the foremost of the French dealers in for-ʋidden fruit, canned for export and domestic use, is M. Octave Feuillet, whose wares are well known to the American public. His novels are the fine flower of the Byzantine literature of the Second Empire. They have been freely translated and widely read in this country. The 'Romance of a Poor Young Man' has the choice distinction of being one of the few French novels harmless enough for perusal in young ladies' boarding-schools. The drama which M. Feuillet made from this novel, and of which a broadened and vulgarized version has been acted in America by Mr. Lester Wallack, is equally familiar. Two other of his plays — the 'Tentation' (skilfully transmuted by Mr. Boucicault into 'Led Astray') and the 'Sphinx' — have been frequently shown to American play-goers. But the novels which have been translated into English, and the plays which have been acted in America, are only a part of M. Feuillet's work; and they are not sufficient to give a fair idea of his qualities or his career.

Born in 1812, M. Octave Feuillet began to be known toward the end of the first half of the century as one of the assistants and imitators of Alexandre Dumas the elder, then in the splendor of his most prodigal production. Just what share M. Feuillet may have had in any of the countless tales of his master it is impossible to say, nor how many bricks he may have made for the marvellous palace of Monte Cristo. With M. Paul Bocage, another of Dumas's disciples, M. Feuillet wrote a novel or two and several dramas. Among the plays are 'Échec et Mat' (1846), 'Palma, ou la Nuit du Vendredi Saint' (1847), and the 'Vieillesse de Richelieu' (1848). These pieces are rather ponderous dramas of the Dumas type, made on the model of 'Angèle,' 'Thérèse,' and 'Richard Darlington.' Although commonplace and conventional, they are not without a certain cleverness; but they made no mark, and they have nothing salient or individual about them, and so call for no comment here.

In these juvenile writings M. Feuillet was merely feeling his way; and, not finding success, he abruptly changed front, and, ceasing to follow Dumas, began to walk in the footsteps of Alfred de Musset. After the failure of one of his earliest plays, Musset had given up writing for the stage, while steadily putting forth pieces in dramatic form for the readers of the *Revue des Deux Mondes.* Without his knowledge, certain of these plays were acted at the French theatre in St. Petersburg; and, when the actress who had caused their performance returned from Russia to the Théâtre Français she brought Musset's comedies with her. And it happened that just about the time when M. Feuillet left off collaborating with M. Bocage, and began to look around for himself, Musset was having a series of unlooked-for successes on the stage. M. Feuillet came forward with comedies modelled on Musset's, but different from these in one important particular. Musset's heroes and heroines were a law unto themselves, as much as to say that their loves not seldom were lawless : now, M. Feuillet's pair of lovers had been duly married by the mayor.

Here occasion serves to remark on the meagreness of subject to be found in nearly all French fiction nowadays, — in the novel as well as in the drama. The inexhaustible fertility and ingenuity of the French literary workmen may hide for a while the thinness of the theme which they have wrought ; but sooner or later, in spite of all the variety of enamel, and all eccentricity of form by which the cunning artificers seek to distract attention, we detect the poverty and scantiness of the material which they are working. Just as most contemporary English fiction ends with the wedding-bells, so most contemporary French fiction rings the changes on the one tune, — lawless love. "Business," said Robert Macaire, "is other people's money." "Marriage," says most modern French fiction, "is other people's wives." To discuss why there is this tacit confession of a dearth of other subjects fit for fiction, would take me too long, and too far from the present text ; but that the scarcity exists, even in the plays of the best French dramatists of our time, is beyond doubt. Of the dozen dramas of M. Alexandre Dumas *fils*, all (with perhaps a single exception) turn on adultery or illegitimacy ; and one or the other of these subjects furnish forth half of M. Augier's plays, and perhaps two-thirds of M. Sardou's. It is not that these plays are all immoral : on the contrary, M. Dumas nowadays always writes with a conscious moral aim, though his morality has a queer twist of its own ; M. Augier's manly comedies have the morality inherent in all healthy works ; and even M. Sardou affronts the proprieties far less than one might suppose. Still the fact remains, that the majority of the dramas of these, the first three dramatists of our day, turn on the illicit relation of the sexes, as though that were the only theme capable of effective dramatic treatment, and worthy of it. Of course there are other themes. Pure love has its dramatic possibilities, as well as impure love. Love is only one of the passions ; and although popular will demands that it enter into every play, it may be made subordinate to the development of any one of the other passions. How few of Shakspere's plots spring from illicit love, or have any thing to do with it ! In the best English novels of this century we find absorbing interest and ample psychologic revelation with the slightest — perhaps even a too slight — attention to the theme which is the staple of corresponding French fiction. Scott and Thackeray, George Eliot and Hawthorne, have used unlawful passion, but in proportion only, and not to the neglect of the other motives which move mankind. French feeling differs from ours ; and perhaps the playwrights merely dwell to excess on a topic to which their countrymen in general give an exaggerated attention. There is a curious passage in one of the later writings of M. Dumas, in which he discusses marital misfortune, and tells us that every man thinks of it constantly, laughing at his neighbor, and fearing for himself. The American husband does not devote his days and nights to speculations about his wife's fidelity.

To the French public, thus familiar with the most high-flown and the least lawful passion, M. Feuillet gave a new thing : he offered it the old and ever welcome exhibition of amorous adventure, dexterously veiled by a pretence of morality. French morality is

at times rather humorsome; and in one of its freaks
it chose to accept M. Feuillet's pseudo-delicacy and
ultra-refinement, and to close its eyes to the falsity
of M. Feuillet's ethics. The public was tired of the
stormy souls in irregular situations seen in the stories
of Hugo, Dumas, George Sand, Merimée, and Musset;
and it was ready for a novelty. M. Feuillet took
Musset for his model, turning his morality inside out.
Musset's morality was easy, to say the least: and M.
Feuillet's was pretentiously paraded; his tender and
glowing interiors were certified to contain only a duly
married couple. Instead of the trio — husband, wife,
and lover — almost universal in French literature, there
was only a duo, in which the husband committed adultery with his own wife. It was an attempt to graft
the roses and raptures of vice on the lilies and lan-
guors of virtue. By giving conjugal endearments the
externals of criminal passion, M. Feuillet managed to
lower marriage to the level of vulgar gallantry, and to
make the reconciliation of husband and wife as interesting as the chance intrigues of a courtesan. In
these boudoir dramas he outraged the sacred secrecy
of wedded life; but so clever was his affectation of propriety, that many respectable people did not look beneath the surface, and took him at his own word. Then
there were those, who, having preached against the
wickedness of the world, could not denounce so ingen-
uous a writer when he declared himself their ally.
And yet another class was pleased by these new plays
— the pretentious prudes; for there are *précieuses ridicules* now as well as two hundred years ago, though
there is no Molière to put them in the pillory.

Fairness requires us to admit that perhaps the author

was more sincere then than we now judge from a study of his work ; and, if he believed in himself, why should not others believe in him ? Even those who detested him were not always sharp enough to see the underlying immodesty. One of these scoffingly nicknamed him the family Musset, — the "Musset des familles," a slanting allusion to an eminently proper periodical publication called the *Musée des Familles*. But he failed to blind so keen an observer as Sainte-Beuve, as any one may see who reads the perfidious compliments scattered through the study of M. Feuillet's work with which the great critic greeted ' Sibylle,' — a Roman-Catholic *Tendenz-Roman*, a "novel with a purpose," — written at the request of the devout and frivolous empress, and published in 1863.

M. Feuillet followed in Musset's footsteps, not only in the form of his new ventures, but also in the mode of putting them before the public. They appeared first in the *Revue des Deux Mondes*, and then in volumes called ' Scènes et Comédies ' and ' Scènes et Proverbes.' In Musset fashion again, it was some little time before the plays M. Feuillet had thus printed and published were brought out at a regular playhouse. Although there is everywhere in his work an odor of tuberoses, sweet and stifling, a few of these earlier little comedies are not open to the objection I have just urged ; and in such unpretentious and simple plays, as pretty as they are petty, M. Feuillet shows at his best. The ' Village ' is a touching little sketch of country life. The ' Fée ' is an amusing attempt to import some of the quaint mystery of fairy-folk lore into this matter-of-fact ninteenth century. The ' Urne ' is a lively reproduction or imitation — *pastiche* is the French word —

of the comedy of Marivaux and his fellows. M. Feuillet has a distinct sense of the comedy of situation, and
is not lacking in Gallic lightness; although his humor
has no depth, and his wit no edge. In all these little
plays he appears to advantage: he can handle two or
three characters in the compass of a single act without
overstraining his powers. Even the 'Cheveu blanc,' a
fine specimen of his new style of tickling the jaded
palate of Parisians by a highly-spiced dish served with
an insipid and enveloping moral sauce, is more tolerable,
because shorter, than his later and more ambitious attempts in the same vein. Elegant trifling, grace, ease,
and emptiness, and fine, unsubstantial talk about egotism and selfishness and honor, — these are the characteristics of the 'Scènes et Comédies;' and it is in these
that M. Feuillet excels.

The three more important plays of this period of M.
Feuillet's career are the 'Crise,' 'Dalila,' and 'Redemption,' all of which passed through the *Revue des Deux
Mondes* on their way to the stage; the 'Crise,' for
one, waiting from 1848, when it appeared in the magazine, until 1854, before it got itself acted in the theatre.
Seriously considered, 'Redemption' is an absurd play;
puerile, or at least boyish, in motive, and feeble even
in construction; for the prologue is useless, and the
scenes are disjointed. 'Dalila' is better and stronger
in itself; and, besides, it is free from the childish endeav-
or to grapple with tiny hands at the mighty problems
which vex men's souls. In Carnioli, too, there is a
character of force and freshness. Of these three plays,
however, the 'Crise' is first in interest, as it was in
point of time. It is the earliest of the dramas in which
M. Feuillet posed as the analyst of the feminine char

acter, and as one who had spied out all its secrets, and had a balm for all its wounds. The crisis from which the play takes its title is that eventful moment in life, when, according to our author, even the most honest and worthy woman, having aforetime led a reputable and humdrum life, all of a sudden has a mad desire to go to the devil headlong : it is an alleged culminating point of the feminine curiosity of knowledge of good and evil. There are plays which criticise themselves ; when the story is once told, no comment is called for : the 'Crise' is one of these.

In the four acts there are but three characters (save a servant or two) ; and these three characters are the eternal trio of French fiction, — husband, wife, and lover. For ten years the husband and the wife have lived happily together. To his oldest and best friend, who is also the family physician, the husband confides that of late his wife has changed : she could not be in better health physically ; but she is now, against her wont, at times restless, or irritable, or sentimental, or what-not, as the whim seizes her. The doctor explains that this is the crisis in her life, the epoch of maturity in woman, when she longs for a bite of forbidden fruit. The husband asks for a prescription. The doctor explains that the only cure for this strange taste is for the husband to find a devoted friend who will lead the wife to the brink of the abyss, but only to the brink ; and he vouches, that, when she shrinks back in horror, she will long no more for the apples on the other side of the chasm : it will be a radical cure. The husband instantly beseeches the doctor to try this experiment on his wife ; and the friend reluctantly but immediately consents to pretend to be the lover. Husband and lover then draw up a code, under which the lover is, if possible, to seduce the wife, — pausing before any damage is done, — so that the wife may be cured by an awful warning and a narrow escape. Time passes, and the lover makes headway. The husband finds his wife's private journal, and brings it to the lover ; and the two men read it together to see how the wife feels. In all this playing with fire, the lover and the wife kindle a flame in their own hearts. At last a guilty appointment is made. Morally, at least, the sin is committed. Just in time the husband intervenes, and, talking in parables, threatens to deprive the wife of her children, should she sin. This restless and sentimental woman, be it known, has two children. So effective are these parables of the husband's, that the new love fades out of the wife's heart, and she falls on her husband's neck ; and then the curtain falls also, leaving in doubt the fate of the unfortunate lover. Is not comment needless ?

In 1858 M. Feuillet turned his novel, the 'Romance of a Poor Young Man,' into a play ; and for sufficiently obvious reasons it is the most wholesome of his later dramas. The scene is skilfully chosen ; the characters are sharply contrasted ; and a dexterous use is made of our love for the heroic and self-sacrificing : so we see the play with pleasure in spite of its quick-tempered and disagreeable young woman, its high-toned and hot-headed young man, its absurd old pirate, and its atmosphere of effeminate sentimentality. Two years later it was followed by the 'Tentation,' the first comedy which M. Feuillet had written directly for acting, and not for reading ; and its simpler and closer structure shows the benefit of the experience gained in transfer ring its predecessors from the pages of a magazine to the boards of a theatre.   There is no need to dwell on the 'Tentation,' as it is as familiar to American audiences as the 'Romance of a Poor Young Man,' — Mr. Dion Boucicault having turned it into 'Led Astray.' Nothing better shows Mr. Boucicault's skill, and knowledge of the temper of our playgoing public, than the tact and taste with which he changed the relationship of the objectionable pair of foreign adventurers.   Mr. Boucicault's Irish soldier of fortune is a distinct character, with truly Irish wit and readiness; whereas M. Feuillet's foreigners were Frenchmen in disguise. Oddly enough, M. Feuillet is fond of using foreigners to give color and comic variety to his groups: we find them not only in this play, but also in 'Redemption,' 'Montjoye,' and the 'Sphinx.'   It is all the more odd that he should resort to this expedient for forcing a laugh, when he has a flow of easy comedy all his own, and nowhere shown to better advantage than in this very play.   There is brightsome humor and charming comedy in the courtship of the two young people; and, although the two old women are somewhat farcical, even they do their share in amusing.   But the main intrigue of the play is again husband and wife and lover; and again the heroine is a lady of passionate aspirations and valetudinarian virtue; and again, when every thing tends toward irretrievable mishap, the dramatist intervenes, and gives a sharp twist to plot and people; and after such a wrench the play cannot but end happily.

Any one of M. Feuillet's plays might be called 'On the Brink;' and in very few of them is there an actual fall over the precipice.   Here the author is lacking in intellectual seriousness: he is always ready to drop logic through a trap in his trick-table. "Consequences are unpitying," said George Eliot ; evidently M. Feuillet does not think so : however vicious any character may seem, we may be sure of his death-bed repentance, and that he will die in a state of grace and the odor of sanctity. Next to the uncleanness beneath the surface, this is M. Feuillet's worse defect ; and nowhere has it done him more harm than in 'Montjoye,' a comedy in five acts, brought out in 1863, three years after the 'Tentation.' Taken altogether, this is perhaps M. Feuillet's best play : it is the only one of his serious pieces in which he has not mistaken violence for strength. Montjoye himself is the central figure of the picture, and indeed the only one ; for all the others are merely accessory, and devised to set off the protagonist. Montjoye is a man of velvet manner and iron will, — a man who aims at success, and who believes that the end justifies the means, and who bends or breaks every thing to attain his end. He is a character boldly projected, although not sufficiently justified, and at the finish not self-consistent. He softens into sentiment, and so weakens the effect on the audience. In criticising M. Augier, M. Zola praises the final impenitence of Maître Guérin. This final impenitence is just what Montjoye lacks : in real life such a man would die game.

The fact is, M. Feuillet is no Frankenstein: he never creates any being he cannot control ; and he makes all his creatures do his bidding at the peril of their lives. He is rather a magician, who raises good and evil spirits at will. Or, to be more exact, he is a writer of fairy-tales. The stories he tells are not true, and they could not happen anywhere out of fairyland. In one of his 'Scènes et Comédies,' he ventured within the magic circle in that most mysterious little play called the 'Fée,' in which a benevolent and sprightly little fairy plays most charming and delightful pranks, — all of them, alas ! prosaically explained away before the curtain falls. Once granting that M. Feuillet is a writer of fairy-tales, and it is a matter of course to find the 'Belle au Bois dormant' in the list of his plays ; and it is perhaps characteristic that this 'Sleeping Beauty in the Wood' should be a drama rather than a comedy. The Sleeping Beauty is the last of a feudal line, declining into poverty, and representing the past. The young Prince is the head of a factory, rising in riches, and thus representing the future. The Beauty has an impractical and re-actionary brother ; and the Prince has a practical and progressive sister : thus is the play provided with two pair of lovers. So far is the fairy-tale followed, that when the young Prince gets into the castle, the author puts the Beauty to sleep off-hand, that the Prince may see her so. There is much cleverness in detail, as there is ingenuity in the main situation. Here, frankly face to face, is the conflict of old and new, past and future, — a conflict irrepressible and irreconcilable ; and there is no end to it.

And here, again, M. Feuillet shows his artistic weakness. His young Prince is no true man of the nineteenth century, having to do with men and machinery, and master of himself at all events. He is no true man at all : when he cannot get the woman he loves, he breaks down, and moons around, and weeps saltless tears. How much better this is handled in one of our own novels, as those will acknowledge who recall the same situation in the 'American' of Mr. Henry James, Jr. ! When Christopher Newman determines to marry the highborn French woman who has charmed him with her quiet grace, he hesitates at no obstacle, he is baffled by nothing, he works out his own work, he fights his own fight, and he bears every thing before him by sheer force of Yankee grit and Yankee wit, until at last the doors of a convent clang to, and the woman he seeks is shut up from him behind the walls of the church, — the one thing against which all Yankee energy, ingenuity, and perseverance are vain.

All this time M. Feuillet was slowly outgrowing the imitation of Musset. In the 'Romance of a Poor Young Man,' in the 'Tentation,' in 'Montjoye,' and especially in the 'Sleeping Beauty in the Wood,' it is easy to see traces of Musset's manner : taken altogether, however, these plays are truly M. Feuillet's own, and not fiefs for which he must needs do homage. As the recollection of Alfred de Musset was getting fainter, the influence of M. Alexandre Dumas *fils* was growing. Already in 'Dalila' one may see some sign of the 'Dame aux Camélias' and of 'Diane de Lys ;' and surely the 'Tentation' and 'Montjoye' would not have been what they are, had it not been for the 'Demi-Monde' and the 'Fils Naturel.' The influence of M. Dumas upon M. Feuillet is the influence of a man of marked individuality and vigor upon a man of feeble fibre ; and, as time passed, this influence became plainer and more emphatic. The author of the 'Crise' seemed to tire of the nickname the MM. de Goncourt had tagged to him, and refused any longer to be the "Musset des familles." Not content with charming, and drawing tears, he wished to thrill and to shock his audience ; and M. Dumas seemed to him the best model. But, in trying to vie with M. Dumas, M. Feuillet was going against his natural gifts. As M. Charles Bigot said in his admirable study of the author of 'Dalila,' "In reality, what the graceful talent of M. Feuillet lacks is strength, and, with strength, all the qualities which go with it, — logic, simplicity, frankness." Now, these are just the qualities which M. Dumas has most abundantly. So when M. Feuillet tries to be strong, he is only violent ; and, when he seeks to show his muscles, he lets us see that he has only nerves, to use the neat figure of M. Claretie.

'Julie,' a drama in three acts, which M. Feuillet brought out at the Théâtre Français in 1869, is plainly enough an attempt to repeat the effects of the 'Supplice d'une Femme,' of which M. Dumas is one of the authors, and the one to whom its success is due. But 'Julie' has none of the concentrated passion and remorseless logic which make the 'Supplice d'une Femme' so startling and successful ; and whereas the 'Supplice d'une Femme' seems dominated by a fate as inexorable as that which determined the destiny of the heroes of Greek drama, 'Julie' has all the weakness of any copy, in which reliance is placed on carefully-planned claptraps, rather than on the natural rush and expression of emotion. The 'Supplice d'une Femme,' although it is a high-strung play, easy to turn into ridicule, has the accent of sincerity. 'Julie' rings false. It was a play of a kind radically opposite to that which the author had hitherto produced ; and even so ingenious a writer as M. Feuillet cannot change his skin in the twinkling of an eye. In his treatment of woman M. Dumas is severe, and logical to the point of brutality : hitherto M. Feuillet had been petting, and illogical to the verge of mushiness ; and it was no wonder that the author of 'Julie' was greeted as a literary dandy who was affecting the intense. Of a truth, morality is not a garment which an author may don and doff at will : if it be good for any thing, his morality is in him, deep down in him, and cannot be torn thence.

Still more violent and feeble-forcible than 'Julie' is M. Feuillet's latest play, the 'Sphinx,' acted in 1874. It is hard to see in this ill-made and monstrous impossibility any trace of the neat workmanship and charming style of the family Musset. A vulgar and undigested drama like the 'Sphinx' forces us to remember that the author of the 'Romance of a Poor Young Man' and of the 'Sleeping Beauty in the Wood' was first of all the author of melodramatic crudities like 'Palma, ou la Nuit du Vendredi Saint.' Just how absurd the play is can best be seen by a rapid summary of the plot.

Blanche de Chelles is the wife of a naval officer absent on a cruise. She lives with her father-in-law, and near her friend Berthe de Savigny, whose husband, however, dislikes the intimacy, and seeks to break it off. It suddenly transpires that the cause of Blanche's wanton bravado of manner is her hitherto unsuspected love for M. de Savigny. As soon as M. de Savigny suspects this, he half responds, although he has hitherto disliked her. Then, with a revulsion of feeling, he pours forth his devotion to his wife. Blanche overhears this conjugal scene, and·instantly accepts the proposal of an impossible Scotch nobleman, Lord Astley, who has asked her to elope with him to Scotland. M. de Savigny forbids her running away, and she takes this as a confession of his affection for her. Now, Madame de Savigny has overheard M. de Savigny's avowals to Blanche, just as

Blanche had previously overheard his avowals to Berthe. (It is astonishing how everybody overhears every thing all through the play; and listeners, we know, never hear any good of themselves, and rarely of any one else.) Having discovered the guilty love of her husband and Blanche, Madame de Savigny says nothing, but suffers in silence, until the fourth act. Then she breaks out, and threatens Blanche with certain compromising letters she has found. (After putting people behind doors to listen, M. Feuillet makes use of compromising letters: surely these are children's toys, unworthy of a serious dramatist.) Blanche wears a mysterious ring with a hollow sphinx's head on it, containing a deadly poison. She opens the ring, and pours the poison into a glass of water, just as Berthe feels faint, and asks to drink. Here is the one dramatic scene of the piece, and one moment of suspense and uncertainty. Instead of giving the fatal draught to Berthe, Blanche drinks it off herself, and dies in horrible agony and with convulsive contortions.

Such success as the 'Sphinx' had was due to external accident. With M. Feuillet's usual ingenuity he had laid his weakest scene in one of the picturesque sites of which he is fond; and the moonlit marsh of the third act did nearly as much for the 'Sphinx' as the ruined tower, with its lissome coat of ivy, did for the 'Romance of a Poor Young Man.' And the author was fortunate in having Mlle. Croizette and Mlle. Sarah Bernhardt for his heroines. It was not the first time that the talent and authority of the actress had done much for the author, as those willingly bore witness who saw Mme. Favart in 'Julie,' and Mme. Fargueil in 'Dalila.' It was rumored at the time that M. Feuillet had not intended any such naturalistic display of toxicological phenomena as Mlle. Croizette exhibited, and that the author objected to the "sensational" devices of the actress. If so, he was ungenerous; for it was her last dying speech and confession which gave the play all the originality it could boast. As to the taste of such an exhibition, opinion may differ: in this case, certainly, it was quite in keeping with the tone of the play. "It is always difficult," wrote Lamb to Godwin, "to get rid of a woman at the end of a tragedy. *Men* may fight and die. A woman must either take poison, *which is a nasty trick;* or go mad, which is not fit to be shown; or retire, which is poor; only retiring is the most reputable."

'Julie' and the 'Sphinx,' however, are not really representative of M. Feuillet, save in minor detail; and they are artistically so inferior to his earlier plays, that they seem the result of some strange freak. The best group of his dramatic works is that which includes the pieces produced between 1858 and 1865, — the 'Romance of a Poor Young Man,' the 'Tentation, 'Montjoye,' and the 'Sleeping Beauty.' Although one can scarcely call these comedies strong plays, they are M. Feuillet's strongest, as they are his least offensive. They reveal his amiable talent in the most favorable light. Yet I am not sure whether some of his smaller plays, and in a painter's sense less "important," are not really better bits of work and of better workmanship. He lacks logic to construct your carefully-considered edifice in five acts; and he has no breadth of style. In the space of one act he does not exhaust himself or his spectator; and he has ample marge and room enough to show off his grace, his ease, his ingenuity, his charm of style, and his caressing and effeminate touch. There is some-thing feminine in the author of the 'Sleeping Beauty.' Sainte-Beuve remarked that M. Feuillet excelled in the women's diaries, of which he is fond: as who should say he had been a woman himself. Sustained effort is not to be expected from a writer of feminine qualities; and this is, perhaps, why certain of his little comedies are of greater worth than their bigger brothers. A humor-ous fantasy like the 'Fruit Defendu,' in which, too, the humor, though not robust, is not at all what a wo-man could have written; or a clear-cut intaglio from life, like the 'Village,' a little masterpiece, — these are worth, not only all the 'Julies' and 'Sphinxes,' but all the 'Romances of Poor Young Men' and 'Sleeping Beauties.' On the other hand, also in one act, are both the 'Cheveu Blanc' and 'Le Pour et le Contre,' the most disgusting of all his plays, in spite of their high polish and superficial decorum. To come across the 'Village' in the series of M. Feuillet's plays is like a vision of the country rising before you as you stand in the overladen air of a stifling ball-room. The 'Village' is one of the author's few incursions into real life. The most of his plays have their scenes laid in a world of his own, much pleasanter than this work-a-day world of ours. It is a world where youth and beauty, and wit and riches, and titles and idleness abound, and where there is nothing poor, or mean, or painful. Especially is there nothing like self-sacrifice. Every thing has a smooth surface and a fine finish. Everybody is happy, or will be before the curtain fall. What though the fair heroine suffer for a while for her fault? — in the end all will come right, as it always does in other fairy-tales.

The want of variety in the scene is to be detected also in the actions and characters of M. Feuillet's comedies, long and short. He has his favorite type of man and woman, and they re-appear again and again. His men all wear dress-coats of correct cut, and white ties beyond reproach : by preference they are men of the world, somewhat cynical, girding at society, but incapable of living out of the whirl and rush of passion : they are men

> "Who tread with jaded step the weary mill,
> Grind at the wheel, and call it 'Pleasure' still;
> Gay without mirth, fatigued without employ,
> Slaves to the joyless phantom of a joy."

This is his favorite hero ; and his favorite heroine is like unto him, save that he has greater skill in drawing women. His heroine is listless, excited, nay, feverish at times, sickly in body and soul, moved by a secret and nameless unrest born of idle luxury. She fancies herself abandoned and lonely. "Solitude," says Balzac, "is a vacuum ; and nature abhors a vacuum in morals as in physics." The wife in the 'Crise' is hysteria personified; the heroine of the 'Tentation' is no better : and there are a dozen like them. One feels like prescribing cold baths and out-door exercise for all of them. "Virtue, however solid you may think it, has need of some encouragement, and of some little support," says the heroine of 'Le Pour et le Contre.' Poor thing! and if her virtue is not propped and stayed, if there come a thunder-storm, or if any other of a hundred and one accidents happen, the fragile virtue gets a fall, and there is nobody to blame.

In discussing M. Victorien Sardou, the final word is that his work is clever; and, in considering M. Octave

Feuillet, the final word is that his works are unhealthy.
To my mind, the author of the 'Crise,' and of the
'Cheveu Blanc,' and of the 'Clé d'Or,' and of 'Le Pour
et le Contre,' is one of the most dangerous of modern
French writers of fiction.　His is an insidious immorality, parading itself in the livery of a militant virtue.
His is a false art, and false art is pretty surely immoral.
Summed up, his teaching is that you can touch pitch,
and not be defiled, so long as you wear ten-button kid
gloves ; that you can play with fire, and drop the torch
so soon as the flame begins to scorch your hands ; that
that you may handle edged tools, and get off scart-free;
and that you can rush headlong at the precipice, and
pull up somehow and safely right on the brink.　It
would be a wholesome pleasure to know how sturdy
and truly British Samuel Johnson, with his stalwart
morality, would have voiced his opinion of M. Feuillet's
ethics.　It happens that there is extant an American
equivalent for this British judgment.　I was re-reading
M. Feuillet's productions to write these pages, when
Mr. Stedman published his fine criticism of Walt Whitman ; and the tricksy humor, which is said to be an
American characteristic, made me ask myself if a
greater curiosity of literature could well be imagined
than a criticism of M. Octave Feuillet of the French
Academy, novelist and dramatist, by Walt Whitman,
American poet and essayist.　But a poet has the gift
of foreseeing our wants and of satisfying them before
we ask ; and so, when I took up 'Leaves of Grass' to
read it again through Mr. Stedman's spectacles, I found
that Whitman had expressed his opinion of Feuillet, or
what we may be sure would be his opinion, did he care
to consider the Frenchman.　It is in 'Chants Démo-
cratiques' (284), and it is as follows :—

> "They who piddle and patter here in collars and
> tailed coats — I am aware who they are —
> they are not worms or fleas."

If this seem a harsh judgment, remember that the
Frenchman has in excess the very qualities the American most detests in literature, — sweetness, feudalism,
the aristocratic atmosphere, a lady-like touch. If this
seem a harsh judgment, let us turn to Mr. Stedman, and
try M. Feuillet by the test and standard Mr. Stedman
sets up to gauge Whitman; and, though more courteously phrased, I doubt if the verdict will differ
greatly from the suppositions we quoted above from
'Leaves of Grass.' Here is what Mr. Stedman asks:
"How far does the effort of a workman relate to what
is fine and enduring? and how far does he succeed in
his effort?"

CHAPTER IX.

EUGÈNE LABICHE.

ONE of the most curious changes of opinion that is recorded anywhere in the history of literature took place in France during 1878 and 1879. For more than two-score years M. Eugène Labiche had been putting forth comic plays with unhesitating liberality. His humorous inventions had delighted two generations, and he was set down in the biographical dictionaries as one of the most amusing of French farce-writers. Attempting in rapid succession, and with almost unbroken success, every kind of comic play, from the keen and quick comedy of the Gymnase theatre to the broad buffoonery of the Palais Royal, for nearly forty years M. Labiche had been one of the most prolific and most popular of French playwrights. His work was seemingly unpretentious, and the author modestly made no higher claim than to be the exciting cause of laughter and gayety. Having made a fine fortune, he had watched for the first symptom of failing luck ; and, as soon as two or three plays were plainly not successes, he announced that he should write no more, and withdrew quietly to his large farm in Normandy.

The retiring of a mere comic writer was of no great moment, and few paid any attention to it. But it happened that M. Émile Augier was a friend of M. Labiche, and that one day he came to visit M. Labiche in his country retirement, and fell to reading the odd plays of

his host as he found them in his library. He was so
struck and so surprised with what he discovered, that
he prevailed on the author to gather together the best
of them into a series of volumes, promising to write an
introduction. In the spring of 1878 appeared the first
volume of the 'Théâtre Complet' of M. Eugène Labiche,
with a preface by M. Émile Augier, in which he pointed
out that the author of a hundred and fifty comic plays
was not a mere farce-writer, but a master of humor, for
whom he had the highest admiration. " Seek among
the highest works of our generation a comedy of more
profound observation than the 'Voyage de M. Perrichon,'
or of more philosophy than the 'Misanthrope et l'Auvergnat.' Well, Labiche has ten plays of this strength
in his repertory." The leading dramatic critics of Paris
— and in France dramatic criticism is still one of the
fine arts — fell into line, M. Francisque Sarcey first of
all. They read the volumes of M. Labiche's 'Théâtre
Complet' as they followed one another from the press ;
and with one accord almost all confessed their surprise
at the richness and fecundity of M. Labiche's humor.
Indeed, it seemed as though the critics had taken to
heart the repairing of their previous unwitting indifference, and were unduly lavish of admiration. So it came
to pass in the fall of 1879, when the tenth, and probably the final volume of the 'Théâtre Complet' appeared,
that, urged to overcome his modesty by his cordial
friends, M. Labiche became a candidate for a vacant
chair in the French Academy, seeking admittance among
the forty immortals chosen from the chiefs of literature,
science, and politics. Three years before, such a step
would have seemed a good joke ; but now no one laughed.
Certainly those did not laugh who opposed his election ;

and the staid *Revue des Deux Mondes,*—in an elaborate article written rather in the slashing style of the earlier *Edinburgh Review* than with the suave and academic urbanity we have been taught to expect in the pages of the French fortnightly, — the *Revue des Deux Mondes* argued seriously and severely against his election. But the tide had turned in his favor. He was elected ; and November, 1880, M. Eugène Labiche took his place in the Academy by the side of his fellow-dramatists, M. Victor Hugo, M. Émile Augier, M. Jules Sandeau, M. Octave Feuillet, M. Alexandre Dumas *fils*, and M. Victorien Sardou. A seat in the Academy, it may be remembered, was an honor refused to Jean Baptiste Poquelin de Molière, to Caron de Beaumarchais, to Alexandre Dumas, and to Honoré de Balzac.

It is said, but with how much truth I do not know, that what determined M. Labiche to stop writing for the stage was the recalling of an incident of Scribe's later years. One day, about 1860, M. Labiche had called on Jacques Offenbach, at his request, to see about the setting to music of a little play which had already been successful without it. While they were talking, a card was brought to Offenbach, who impatiently tore it up, and told the servant to say he was not at home. Then, turning to M. Labiche, the composer said that the visitor was Scribe, who had been bothering him to set one of his plays : "but I will not do it," added Offenbach roughly ; "for old Scribe is played out." M. Labiche at once resolved, that when he was old and rich, like Scribe, he would not lag superfluous on the stage. With the first intimations of failing power to please the fickle play-goers of Paris, he withdrew. For now nearly five years no new play from his pen has been brought out in Paris. He has written a trifle or two for the 'Théâtre de Campagne,' and for 'Saynètes et Monologues,' — two little collections of comedies for amateur acting; but for the paying public he has done nothing. It is to M. Émile Augier that the credit is due of bringing M. Labiche out of his retirement. The preface which M. Augier had been too lazy too write for his own collected plays he wrote for M. Labiche's; and it was this preface which first opened the eyes of the press and the public, and led to the frank acknowledgment of M. Labiche's very unusual merit. The theatrical managers are now only too eager for new pieces from him; and, in default of these, they have revived right and left some of the most mirthful of his plays. The 'Grammaire' at the Palais Royal, the 'Trente Millions de Gladiateur' at the Nouveautés, and, above all, the 'Voyage de M. Perrichon' at the Odéon, were received with great cordiality and appreciation.

To most Americans, I fancy, the name of M. Labiche is utterly unknown; and one may well ask, What manner of plays are these, that they could remain so long misunderstood? The question is easier to ask than to answer. The most of them are apparently farces, in one, two, three, four, or even five acts, — farces somewhat of the Madison Morton type. Mr. Morton borrowed his 'Box and Cox' from one of them; the late Charles Mathews took his 'Little Toddlekins' from another; from a third came the equally well-known 'Phenomenon in a Smock-frock.' These are all one-act plays. Of his larger work, a version of the 'Voyage de M. Perrichon' has been done at the Boston Museum as 'Papa Perrichon;' and Mr. W. S. Gilbert has used the plot, and tried to catch something of the spirit, of the 'Chapeau de paille d'Italie' in his 'Wedding March.' In many of M. Labiche's plays, perhaps in all but the best of them, the first impression one gets is that of extravagant buffoonery: the phrase is scarcely too strong. But soon one sees that this is no grinning through a horse-collar; that it has its roots in truth; and that, although unduly exuberant, it is in essence truly humorous. To the very best of M. Labiche's plays, the half-dozen or so comedies which entitle their author to take rank as a master, reference will be made later. In all his work, in the weakest as well as in the best, the dominant note is gayety: they are filled full of frank, hearty, joyous laughter. In reading his plays, as in seeing them on the stage, you have rarely that quiet smile of intellectual appreciation which is called forth by Sheridan in English, and by Beaumarchais, and M. Augier, and M. Dumas, in French. The wit is not subtle and quiet, excepting now and again in the half-dozen chosen comedies. There is rather the rush of broad and tumultuous humor than the thrust of wit, and the clash of repartee. It is not that the dialogue has not its felicities, and its not always felicitous quibblings and quips: it is because the laughter is evoked by a humorous situation, from which, with great knowledge of comic effect, and with unfailing ingenuity, the author extracts all the fun possible. A comedy ought to stand the test of the library, — how few modern comedies there are in English which will stand it!— but a farce, making no pretensions to be literature, may well be excused if it does not read as well as it acts. Yet M. Labiche's plays, frankly farces as the most of them are, and devised to lend themselves to the whim and exaggeration of comic actors, will still repay perusal. I have just finished the reading of the ten volumes of his 'Théâtre Complet;' and I confess to real enjoyment in the course of it. The fundamental idea of each piece is in general so humorous, and the individual scenes are so comic, that I paid my tribute of laughter in my chair by myself almost as freely as I should have done in my seat at the theatre. Even in the plays where the fun seems forced, as though the author were out of spirits when he wrote, at worst there is nearly always one scene as mirthful as any one could wish. This quality of humor, which does not rely upon any merely verbal cleverness, is difficult to set before a reader. An epigram of Sheridan's, or of the younger Dumas's, can be selected for quotation, which shall be typical of the writer's whole work. It would be only by long paraphrases of entire plays, or at least of the main plots, that any fair idea could be given of M. Labiche's merits, so closely, as a rule, is his humor the result of his comic situation. But the attempt must be made, however inadequately. In the 'Trente Millions de Gladiateur,' one of the poorest of M. Labiche's plays, is a scene which M. Francisque Sarcey thus spoke of when the piece was last given in Paris : —

"The scene of the slaps is now legendary. I do not know any thing more unexpected, or more laughable. A druggist, very much in love with a young lady, has by accident, one night, thinking to strike another, given his future father-in-law a resounding slap. The father of the lady declares that he will never consent to the marriage until he has returned the blow. But the druggist is a man of dignity, and he has been a commander in the national guard: still, after many a hesitation he submits. He presents himself to be slapped, and holds forth his cheek. But he has no sooner received the blow, than, carried away by an irresistible impulse, he returns it, crying with disgust, 'That does not count. We must begin again.' Finally, at the very end of the piece, when she whom he loves is, unknown to him, promised to another, love brings him again to the father, and again he holds out his cheek for the blow. The father rolls up his sleeve, gives him the slap, and then at once points to the other suitor, and says, 'Allow me to present my future son-in-law.'"

Another scene as characteristic is to be found in the 'Vivacités du Capitaine Tic.' The captain is a very quick-tempered man. His cousin Lucile, whom he loves, says she will have nothing to do with him if he forgets himself in future as he has done in the past. An irritating old man, who wishes to marry Lucile to his nephew, determines to provoke the captain into an outbreak. Lucile promises to warn her cousin, when he begins to get heated, by tapping a hand-bell. The old man is intentionally irritating; and the young officer warms up at once, to be checked by a tap of the bell. As Lucile puts the bell down, the old man unconsciously takes it up, and goes on with his insulting remarks. Again the captain boils over, and is about to throw the insulter out of the window, when Lucile shakes the old man's arm, and so rings the bell. The officer laughs; and after that he has no difficulty in keeping his temper, in spite of the strength of the old man's provocation, which indeed goes so far as to call Lucile to her feet to defend her cousin with warmth, not to say heat. Then the captain, leaning coolly against the fireplace, taps a bell there, and calls his cousin to order. Both of the young people break into a hearty laugh, and ring their bells once again under the nose of the disappointed old man, who goes out saying that the captain "has no blood in his veins."

All this may sound simple enough, and perhaps dull enough, in a bald paraphrase; but no one would call the scene dull when it is read in full as M. Labiche has written it, with manifold clever little turns in the action, and neat little touches in the dialogue. Both of the plays from which these scenes are taken have stood the severest of tests, — the ordeal by fire : they have been tried in the glare of the foot-lights. It is no easy task to bring a smile on the faces of a thousand people assembled together ; it is no light endeavor to force the smile into a hearty laugh ; and nowhere is a public more experienced and more exacting than in Paris. But most of M. Labiche's plays have received due meed of merriment. The laughter is not always evoked, it must be confessed, by devices as simple as those just set forth. There is sometimes a descent into the broadly fantastic, both of situation and of dialogue. The effort to be funny is at times apparent, and the means adopted are now and then far-fetched.

M. Labiche's plays divide themselves readily into three classes : first, the farcical comedies of broad and generous fun ; second, the plays in which the fun has run away with itself, and become extravagance, — still founded on a humorous idea, it is true, but none the less extravagant ; and, third, the plays in which the humor has crystallized around a thread of philosophy, — the plays in which the fun rises from the region of farce into the domain of true comedy of a high quality. Most

of the fifty-seven plays in the ten volumes of the 'Théâ
tre Complet' take their places at once in the first division.
They are comic dramas, neither falling into wild farce,
nor rising into real comedy. They are comedies of large
and hearty laughter, with no Rabelaisian breadth of
beam, but with not a little of Molièrian swiftness. The
linking thus of M. Labiche's name with that of the
great humorist who wrote the 'Misanthrope,' is not
as incongruous as it might seem. Along with other
and nobler qualities for which we revere him, Molière
had comic force, the *vis comica*, in its highest expression, to a degree, indeed, equalled only by Shakspere
and Aristophanes. And this is a quality which M. Labiche has, as we have seen, in a very full measure. In
a few other particulars it might be possible to trace
something of a likeness. M. Labiche, in his most fanciful inventions, could scarcely surpass the exuberant
fancies of Molière : the author of the 'Bourgeois Gentilhomme' and the 'Malade Imaginaire' does not hesitate to be exuberant, and extravagant also, when he needs
must make the pit laugh. And now and again, in M.
Labiche's very best work, there are strokes which the
author of the 'School for Wives' would not despise.

If M. Labiche were always as strong as his strongest
work, just as a bridge is as weak as its weakest point,
he would hold high rank among the heirs of Molière.
His 'Théâtre Complet' is not really complete ; indeed,
it contains barely a third of his dramatic writing : but
it would give the reader a higher opinion of his powers,
if it were but a third of what it is ; if instead of ten
volumes, we had only three or four ; and of these, one,
or at most two, would suffice to hold the few plays which
raise the author above most, if not all, of the other
French stage-humorists of our time.

This best work of M. Labiche's, this third division of his plays, includes a half-dozen comedies, each of which is devoted to illustrating a philosophic truth. They may be called dramatizations of La Rochefoucauld-like maxims. In 'Célimare le Bien-Aimé' the truth illustrated is seemingly the homely one, that our pleasant vices are chickens, which will surely come home to roost. In the 'Voyage de M. Perrichon' it is the more ducal axiom, that we like better those whom we have bene-fited than those who have benefited us. The history of this last play, if current report may be credited, affords an instance of the rather roundabout, not to say half-accidental, way in which M. Labiche has made his masterpieces. He started out with the well-worn plan of getting fun out of the misadventures of a Parisian shopkeeper in Switzerland; but just as Dickens soon abandoned the sporting exploits of Mr. Winkle, which were at first intended to form the staple of the 'Pickwick Papers,' so M. Labiche, when the play was half written, coming to a scene in which Perrichon was rescued from mortal peril by the suitor for his daughter's hand, saw at once that this scene ought to have its counterpart, in which Perrichon should pose as the relieving hero. This suggested the axiom, that we like better those whom we have benefited than those who have bene-fited us; and the author thereupon rewrote the play, taking this maxim as the Q. E. D. Perrichon's daughter now has two suitors, one of whom, acting up to the axiom, coolly calculates that to have been foolish enough to get into danger will not be a pleasant recol-lection, while to have saved another's life will be most gratifying to recall. So he pretends to be in danger, and lets Perrichon get him out of it, and calls him a preserver, and has the rescue elaborately noticed in the newspaper. The simple and conceited shopkeeper avoids the man who saved him, and seeks the man he saved; and so the play goes on. Whenever one suitor really serves Perrichon, the other devises a fresh occasion for Perrichon apparently to benefit him. In the end, of course, all is exposed and explained, — in a less skilful manner than is usual with M. Labiche, — and the really brave and deserving young man gets the fair daughter. Here, again, all paraphrase is bald and bleak when contrasted with the fertile luxuriance of the humorous original; but I trust the subject has been shown plainly enough for the reader to see that it lends itself readily to comic treatment. I trust, too, that the reader may be induced to examine for himself (and also for herself) the play as it is in the second volume of M. Labiche's 'Théâtre Complet,' where it is accompanied by the 'Grammaire,' a bright and lively little play in one act; by the 'Petits Oiseaux;' by the 'Vivacités du Capitaine Tic,' already referred to; and by the 'Poudre aux Yeux,' an almost equally amusing though short comedy in two acts, perhaps better known in America than any other of its author's work, as it forms part of the excellent college series of French plays edited by Professor Bôcher of Harvard. These five plays are all entertaining, characteristic of the author, and free from all taint of impropriety.

A certificate of good moral character cannot be given to all of M. Labiche's plays. The 'Plus Heureux des Trois' and 'Célimare le Bien-Aimé,' two of his best works, had better be avoided by those who have not been broken in to French ways of looking at life. But two other plays very nearly as good, the 'Cagnotte'

and 'Moi,' are without any Frenchiness or Parisianism.
These four plays, with the 'Voyage de M. Perrichon,'
represent M. Labiche at his best. The first query
which the reader of the rest of his works puts to himself is, Why does not M. Labiche write always at this
level? Why does he let wit so lively, and humor so
true, waste themselves on the wildness of farce? The
answer is not far to seek. It is to be found in the
insultingly modest way he spoke to M. Augier about his
own writings. It is because he really did not know
how good his best work was. He apparently ranked
all his plays together : he had aimed only at fun, at
amusement in making them ; and, although some had
paid better and been more praised than others, he did
not see that now and again one of them rose right up
from the low level of farce to the broad table-land of
true comedy. This, of course, suggests the further
question, Why did he not see his own merits? And
that is not so easy to answer. Perhaps it is owing to
his writing generally for farce theatres, where the comic
company so overlaid his work with the freaks of individual fantasy that he could not see the higher qualities
of what was best, any more than did the professional
critics, whose duty it surely was to sound a note of
warning, and prevent such pure comic force from wast-
ing itself. Perhaps it is due to some want of self-
reliance, — of which one may possibly see proof in the
fact that there are fifty-seven plays in the ten volumes
of 'Théâtre Complet,' containing in all one hundred
and twelve acts, and that four acts only are the work
of M. Labiche alone, and unaided by a collaborator.

Literary partnerships are the fashion in France nowadays, — a fashion which tends to the general improve-

ment of play-making, but which has hampered M.
Labiche, and kept him from doing his best. In one
way his reluctance to rely on himself is freely shown
when we come to examine the result of his collaborating. First of all, we see, that although at least a
dozen different writers at different times, some of them
again and again, worked in partnership with him, yet
the fifty-seven plays are all alike stamped with his
trade-mark. M. Augier and M. Legouvé and M. Gondinet are authors of positive force and distinct characteristics; yet the plays they have written with M.
Labiche are like his other plays, and unlike their other
plays. In the development of the comic theme, in
expressing all possible fun from the situation, in giving
the action unexpected turns to bring it back again for
a fresh squeeze, — in all this M. Labiche is unexcelled,
in all this the plays are beyond peradventure his doing.
But in the technical construction, in the sequence of
scenes, in the mere stage-craft, which differs in different
pieces, and is indifferent in many of them, there is nothing of M. Labiche's own : in all probability, intent upon
his higher task, he slighted this, and left it in great
measure to his coadjutors. M. Augier points out the
generic likeness of all the plays which M. Labiche has
signed, and suggests that it is because he writes all
these plays alone. In M. Augier's case, repeated con-
versations between him and M. Labiche enabled them
to make out a very elaborate *scenario :* this was their
joint work; and, this done, M. Labiche requested permission to write the piece himself, which M. Augier gen-
erously granted, revising the completed play in a few
minor points only. It may be remarked parenthetically
that this piece, the ' Prix Martin,' is not a good specimen of the handiwork of either author.

Although in general the technical construction of the play seems to be the work of his collaborator of the moment, yet even in the construction we can now and again detect traces of M. Labiche's individual cleverness. No one of the contemporary comic dramatists of France can so neatly and so simply get out of a seemingly inextricable entanglement. A single sentence, a solitary word sometimes, a slight turn given to the dialogue, and the knot is cut, and nothing remains but "Bless you, my children," and the fall of the curtain. An instance of this dramaturgical cleverness can be seen in the 'Deux Timides,' one of the most amusing of his one-act plays.[1]

The critic in the *Revue des Deux Mondes*, pleading specially against M. Labiche's candidature for a seat among the forty, pointed out that he has not hesitated to use the same idea twice ; that, for instance, the 'Vivacités du Capitaine Tic' is erected on the same foundation as the shorter and slighter 'Un Monsieur qui prend la Mouche,' both being based on the identical hot-headedness of the hero. He might have instanced also, that, instead of repeating the situation, M. Labiche sometimes reverses it ; that the 'Plus Heureux des Trois' is, in part, the turning inside out of the idea of 'Célimare le Bien-Aimé.' In spite of discoveries like these, one of the first things which strikes the reader of M. Labiche's plays is his almost inexhaustible variety of comic incident. Any one of his plays is a series of freshly humorous situations. What little old material may here and there be detected is wholly

[1] An admirable adaptation of this amusing little piece, by Mr. Julian Magnus, has been printed in 'Comedies for Amateur Acting.' (New York: D. Appleton & Co., 1879.)

cast in the shadow by the brilliant fun of the original incidents. But, strange to say, the sterility of character is almost as quickly remarked as the fertility of situation; and this shows at once that he cannot, no matter at what interval, be put even in the same class with Molière, who sought for humor in the human heart, and not in the external circumstances of life.

This repetition of characters is but added evidence in proof of M. Labiche's lack of ambition, and want of belief in his best powers; for in 'Moi,' written for the Comédie-Française, he has shown a capacity for the searching investigation of characters invented with almost as much freshness as he had in other plays contrived comic incidents. There are lines in 'Moi' worthy of the highest comedy. And in more than one other play his characters deserve, indeed demand, study. But in general they are merely the Punch-and-Judy puppets required by the plot. There is scarcely a female figure in all his plays which the memory can grasp: all are slight, intangible, shadowy, merely the projections needed by the story. M. Sarcey tells us that M. Labiche does not pretend to "do" girls or women: he says that they are not funny.

None of his men are as weak as his women. Some of his peasants are drawn with great and amusing accuracy. Most of his minor characters are vigorously outlined, and well contrasted one with another; and one character, repeated with but little alteration as the central figure in perhaps two dozen plays, is drawn with a marvellous insight into the inner nature of the *bourgeois* of Paris. Although grotesque almost in its humor, the caricature is vital; for it is a personification of the exact facts of *bourgeois* life. M. Perrichon and Célimare and Champbourcy (in the 'Cagnotte'), and their fellows in many another play, are not unlike Mr. Matthew Arnold's *homme sensuel moyen;* and with a master hand M. Labiche lays bare the selfish foibles and petty vanity of the average sensual man.

One cannot help wondering what Mr. Matthew Arnold's opinion of M. Labiche's 'Théâtre Complet' would be, if it were of high or of equal enough merit to deserve his study. Mr. Arnold would surely be confirmed in his belief that it is for the average sensual man that the French dramatist of our day writes. Not that there is any pandering to sensuality in M. Labiche's plays: on the contrary, the ultimate moral of his work is always wholesome. As the sharp critic of the *Revue des Deux Mondes* confessed, his pleasantry is not either heavy and gross as in the old vaudeville, or licentious as in the new opera-bouffe. "Generally it is gay, witty, and, what is not without value, at bottom always honest." And as M. John Lemoinne told M. Labiche in his answer to his reception-speech at the French Academy, "Your comedy is perhaps light, nay, even risky: but there is always something which keeps it from being immoral; it is never sentimental."

This is no more than the exact truth. Perilously risky as some of M. Labiche's plays are, none of them have any trace or taint of sentimentality; and when they are acquitted of that deadly sin, they cannot be fundamentally immoral. In fact, M. Labiche is too healthy to take kindly to vice; but like other hearty natures, like Rabelais and like Molière, he is not always free from a fancy for breadth rather than length. He has the old French *sel gaulois* rather than Attic salt.

If, dropping morality, we consult Mr. Arnold as to

M. Labiche's right to a seat in the Academy, we shall
have no difficulty in getting an answer. In the essay
on the 'Literary Influence of Academies,' Mr. Arnold
gives us Richelieu's words in founding the French Academy : its "principal function shall be to work with all
the care and all the diligence possible at giving sure
rules to our language." It was to be a literary tribunal.
"To give the law, the tone, to literature, and that tone
a high one, is its business." Sainte-Beuve said that
Richelieu meant it to be a *haut jury,* — "a sovereign
organ of opinion." And M. Renan tells us that "all
ages have had their inferior literature ; but the great
danger of our time is, that this inferior literature tends
more and more to get the upper place. No one has the
same advantages as the Academy for fighting against
this mischief." To make these quotations is to quash
M. Labiche's title to a seat among the forty jurists.
But, if the Academy exists for such high aims, why is
it not true to them ? How many of the dramatists who
now have seats there are entitled to them ? M. Victor
Hugo of course is ; and equally, of course, is M. Émile
Augier, for he is a master, writing in the grand style.
And perhaps M. Jules Sandeau may justly claim a place
for his 'Mademoiselle de la Seiglière,' and also for his
share in the ever-admirable 'Gendre de M. Poirier.'
But by what right is M. Octave Feuillet there ? The
empress used to like his novels. And is M. Alexandre
Dumas, or M. Victorien Sardou, a writer who can speak
with "the authority of a recognized master in matters
of tone and taste"? M. Dumas is strong and brilliant ;
and M. Sardou is very clever. If these have each a seat
among the forty, why not M. Labiche also ? He is
surely not more out of place than they. Their election

was the reward of skill and ability and success : his would mean no more and no less. If the Academy is what Richelieu meant it to be, M. Labiche belongs outside. If its duty is to reward success, — as the election of M. Feuillet, M. Dumas, and M. Sardou apparently asserts, — then M. Labiche also deserved his election ; for, as M. Émile Augier tells us in the preface from which quotation has been made before, M. Labiche is a master ; "and without hyperbole, since there are as many degrees of mastership as there are regions in art, the important thing is to be a master, not a schoolboy. It is in a matter like this that Cæsar's phrase is so true : ' Better to be the first in a village than the second at Rome.' I prefer Teniers to Giulio Romano, and Labiche to the elder Crébillon. It is not the hazard of the sentence which brings together under my pen the names of Labiche and of Teniers. There are striking analogies between these two masters. There is at first the same aspect of caricature : there is, on looking closer, the same fineness of tone, the same justness of expression, the same vivacity of movement." And here follows a remark, already cited, but repeated now because it is the ultimate expression of M. Labiche's ability : "The foundation of all these *joyeusetés à toute outrance* is truth. Look among the highest works of our generation, seek for a comedy of more profound observation than the ' Voyage de M. Perrichon,' or of more philosophy than the ' Misanthrope et l'Auvergnat.' Well, Labiche has ten plays of this strength in his repertory."

The adverse criticism of the *Revue des Deux Mondes* has been cited : in due course of time the *Nouvelle Revue* bore witness in his favor. A long essay in the younger magazine praised M. Labiche very highly, and suggested that we are to see in him the comic underside of the realistic movement of which M. Augier and M. Dumas offer the more serious examples. The same writer calls him half a Gaul and half a Parisian, and then draws a close parallel between M. Labiche and LaFontaine, the spoilt child of French literature. Here we have M. Labiche's name linked with M. Augier's and M. Dumas's. What M. Augier thinks of him has already been quoted. What M. Dumas thinks of him is equally worthy of quotation. In a brief consideration of the present state of the French stage,[1] M. Dumas takes occasion to say that he is " one of those who laughs and is glad to laugh . . . at ' Célimare le Bien-Aimé ' and the ' Voyage de M. Perrichon,' and at two or three other of the plays of Labiche, who, in parenthesis, is one of the finest and frankest of the comic poets who have existed since Plautus, — the only one, perhaps, who can be compared to him."

Here is high praise, and enough. Likened by the *Nouvelle Revue* to Jean LaFontaine, by M. Augier to Teniers, and by M. Dumas to Plautus, surely M. Labiche is a writer of no common quality, and well worth the study of all who seek to discover the secrets of the stage.

[1] Entr'actes, iii. 336. (Paris : C. Lévy, 1878.)

CHAPTER X.

HENRI MEILHAC AND LUDOVIC HALÉVY.

No doubt it may surprise some theatre-goers who are not special students of the stage to be told that the authors of 'Froufrou' are the authors also of the 'Grand Duchess of Gérolstein,' and of the 'Belle Hélène,' of 'Carmen,' and of the 'Petit Duc.' There are a few, I know, who think that 'Froufrou' was written by M. Victorien Sardou, and who, without thinking, credit Jacques Offenbach with the composition of the words as well as the music of the 'Grand Duchess;' and, as for 'Carmen,' is it not an *Italian* opera? and is not the book, like the music, the work of some Italian? As a matter of fact, all these plays, unlike as they are to each other, and not only these, but many more, — not a few of them fairly well known to the American play-goer, — are due to the collaboration of M. Henri Meilhac and M. Ludovic Halévy.

Born in 1832, M. Henri Meilhac, like M. Émile Zola, dealt in books before he began to make them. He soon gave up trade for journalism, and contributed with pen and pencil to the comic *Journal pour Rire.* He began as a dramatist in 1855, with a two-act play, at the Palais Royal theatre. Like the first pieces of Scribe and of M. Sardou, and of so many more who have afterward abundantly succeeded on the stage, this play of M. Meilhac's was a failure; and so also was his next, likewise in two acts. But in 1856 the 'Sarabande du Cardinal,' a delightful little comedy in one act, met with favor at the Gymnase. It was followed by two or three other comediettas equally clever. In 1859 M. Meilhac made his first attempt at a comedy in five acts ; but the 'Petit-fils de Mascarille' had not the good fortune of his ancestor, whose godfather Molière was.

In 1860, for the first time, M. Meilhac was assisted by M. Ludovic Halévy ; and in the twenty years since then their names have been linked together on the title-pages of twoscore or more plays of all kinds, — drama, comedy, farce, opera, operetta, and ballet. M. Meilhac's new partner was the nephew of the Halévy who is best known out of France as the composer of the 'Jewess ;' and he was the son of M. Léon Halévy, poet, philosopher, and playwright. Two years younger than M. Henri Meilhac, M. Ludovic Halévy held a place in the French civil service until 1858, when he resigned to devote his whole time, instead of his spare time, to the theatre. As the son of a dramatist and the nephew of a popular composer, he had easy access to the stage. He began as the librettist-in-ordinary to Offenbach, for whom he wrote 'Bata-clan' in 1855, and later the 'Chanson de Fortunio,' the 'Pont des Soupirs,' and 'Orphée aux Enfers.' The first very successful play which MM. Meilhac and Halévy wrote together was the book of an operetta for Offenbach ; and it was possibly the good fortune of this first venture which finally affirmed the partnership. Before the triumph of the 'Belle Hélène,' in 1864, the collaboration had been tentative, as it were : after that, it was as though the articles had been definitely ratified ; not that either of the parties has not now and then indulged in outside speculations, trying a play alone, or with an outsider, but this is without prejudice to the permanent partnership.

This kind of literary union, the long-continued conjunction of two kindred spirits, is better understood amongst us than the indiscriminate collaboration which marks the dramatic career of M. Eugène Labiche, for instance. Both kinds were usual enough on our stage in the days of Elizabeth; but we can recall the ever-memorable example of Beaumont and Fletcher, while we forget the chance associations of Marston, Dekker, Chapman, and Ben Jonson. And in contemporary literature we have before us the French tales of MM. Erckmann-Chatrian, and the English novels of Messrs. Besant and Rice. The fact that such a union endures is proof enough that it is advantageous. A long-lasting collaboration like this of MM. Meilhac and Halévy must needs be the result of a strong sympathy and a sharp contrast of character, as well as of the possession by one of literary qualities which supplement those of the other.

One of the first things noticed by an American student of French dramatic literature is that the chief Parisian critics generally refer to the joint work of these two writers as the plays of M. Meilhac, leaving M. Halévy altogether in the shade. At first this seems a curious injustice; but the reason is not far to seek. It is not that M. Halévy is some two years the junior of M. Meilhac: it lies rather in the quality of their respective abilities. M. Meilhac has the more masculine style; and so the literary progeny of the couple bear rather his name than his associate's. M. Meilhac has the strength of marked individuality, he has a style of his own, one can tell his touch; while M. Halévy is merely a clever French dramatist of the more conventional pattern. This we detect by considering the plays which each has put forth alone, and unaided by the other. Pausing before one of M. Meilhac's works, we are in no doubt as to the maker; and there is no need to seek in a corner for the *Meilhac inv^t et del^t;* while M. Halévy's clever pictures of Parisian society, less distinct in their individuality, might be perhaps passed over as belonging simply to the "Modern French School."

Before finally joining with M. Halévy, M. Meilhac wrote two comedies in five acts, of high aim and skilful execution; and two other five-act pieces have been written by MM. Meilhac and Halévy together. The 'Vertu de Célimène' and the 'Petit-fils de Mascarille' are by the elder partner: 'Fanny Lear' and 'Froufrou' are the work of the firm. Yet in these last two it is difficult to see any trace of M. Halévy's handiwork. Allowing for the growth of M. Meilhac's intellect during the eight or ten years which intervened between the work alone and the work with his associate, and allowing for the improvement in the mechanism of play-making, I see no reason why M. Meilhac might not have written 'Fanny Lear' and 'Froufrou' substantially as they are, had he never met M. Halévy; but it is inconceivable that M. Halévy alone could have attained so high an elevation, or have gained so full a comic force. Perhaps, however, M. Halévy deserves credit for the better technical construction of the later plays: merely in their mechanism, the first three acts of 'Froufrou' are marvellously skilful. And perhaps, also, his is a certain softening humor, which is the

cause that the two later plays, written by both partners, are not so hard in their brilliance as the two earlier comedies, the work of M. Meilhac alone.

It may seem something like a discussion of infinitesi-
mals ; but I think M. Halévy's co-operation has given
M. Heilhac's plays a fuller ethical richness. To the
younger writer is due a simple but direct irony, as well
as a lightsome and laughing desire to point a moral when
occasion serves. It happens that M. Halévy has put
forth two volumes of sketches and stories, — 'Monsieur
et Madame Cardinal' and the 'Petites Cardinal,' in
which the chief characters are two sisters in the ballet
of the opéra, and their parents, — as disreputable an old
couple as you could find anywhere in Paris. The gar-
rulity, and, so to speak, *bonhomie*, of the old wife, and
the highly humorous linking of dignity and depravity
in the husband, recall the somewhat similar figures of
M. and Mme. Pipelet in Sue's 'Mysteries of Paris.'
(Here occasion offers to note that it was as the princi-
pality of the marvellous young man who plays the part
of Providence in Sue's book that the Grand Duchy of
Gérolstein made its first appearance in fiction.) M. Halévy's touch is lighter than Sue's, and his humor is less
oily. He succeeds in giving M. and Mme. Cardinal more
color, and less monotony, than Sue endowed his M. and
Mme. Pipelet with. The type is common enough, I
fancy, in Paris, where the porter's lodge is the stepping-
stone to the stage-box ; and a comparison of the studies of it, made in 1840 with those made in 1870 and
1880, is not uninstructive. I have mentioned M. Halévy's two volumes here, because they are his only considerable publications apart from M. Meilhac's, and
because also I think I can detect in them an ironical

morality not to be discovered in M. Meilhac's work.
Most of these little sketches were written for the *Vie
Parisienne*, and this is to say that they are not intended *virginibus puerisque;* but the attitude of the author
is that of a half-pitying, half-contemptuous moralist.
Whenever the same ironical morality is to be detected
in the plays written by both authors together, it seems
to me fair to give M. Halévy the greater share of the
credit; and even in stories written for the *Vie Parisienne*, and in plays written for the Palais Royal theatre,
the discovery may be made far more often than the
chance reader might suppose.

Certainly I shall not hold up a play written to please
the public of the Palais Royal, or even of the Gymnase,
as a model of all the virtues. Nor need it be, on the
other hand, an embodiment of all the cardinal sins.
The frequenters of the Palais Royal theatre are not
babes. Young people of either sex are not taken
there; only the emancipated gain admittance; and to
the seasoned sinners who haunt theatres of this type
these plays by MM. Meilhac and Halévy are harmless.
Indeed, I do not recall any play of theirs which could
hurt any one capable of understanding it. Most of
their plays are not to be recommended to ignorant
innocence or to fragile virtue. They are not meant for
young men and maidens. They are not wholly free
from the taint which is to be detected in nearly all
French fiction. The mark of the beast is set on not a
little of the work done by the strongest men in France.
M. Meilhac is too clean and too clever ever to delve in
indecency from mere wantonness. He has no liking for
vice: but his virtue sits easily on him; and, though he
is sound on the main question, he looks upon the vaga-

ries of others with a gentle eye. M. Halévy, it seems to
me, is made of somewhat sterner stuff. He raises a
warning voice now and then, — in 'Fanny Lear,' for
instance, the moral is pointed explicitly ; and, even
where there is no moral tagged to the fable, he who has
eyes to see, and ears to hear, can find " a terrible example" in almost any of these plays, even the lightest.
Considered aright, there is a moral lesson in 'Froufrou ;'
and, as M. Claretie said of the authors when it was first
acted, " Their work is like a red-hot iron dipped in rice-
powder : it smells good, but it cauterizes too."   For
the congregation to which it was delivered, there is a
sermon in 'Toto chez Tata,' perhaps the piece in which,
above all others, the muse seems Gallic and *égrillarde*.
That is a touch of real truth, and so of a true morality,
where Tata, the fashionable courtesan, leaning over her
stairs as Toto the schoolboy bears off her elderly lover,
and laughing at him, cries out, " You, my little fellow,
I'll catch you again in four or five years ! "   And a cold
and cutting stroke it is a little earlier in the same little
comedy, where Toto, left alone in Tata's parlor, negli-
gently turns over her basket of visiting-cards, and sees
"names which he knew because he had learnt them by
heart in his history of France."   Still, in spite of this
truth and morality, I do not advice the reading of 'Toto
chez Tata' in young ladies' seminaries.   Young ladies
in Paris do not go to hear Madame Chaumont, for whom
'Toto' was written ; nor is the Variétés, where it was
played, a place where a girl can take her mother.

  It was at the Variétés in December, 1864, that the
'Belle Hélène' was produced : this was the first of half
a score of plays, written by MM. Meilhac and Halévy, for
which Jacques Offenbach composed the music.   Chief

among these are 'Barbe-bleue,' the 'Grand Duchess of Gérolstein,' the 'Brigands,' and 'Périchole.' When we recall the fact that these five operas are the most widely known, the most popular, and by far the best, of M. Offenbach's works, there is no need to dwell on his indebtedness to MM. Meilhac and Halévy, or to point out how important a thing the quality of the opera-book is to the composer of the score. When we recall that the 'Grand Duchess' and 'Belle Hélène' are the typical *opéras-bouffes*, and that other *opéras-bouffes* are mostly attempts to imitate them or emulate them, there is no need to dwell on the fact that *opéra-bouffe* as we now know it owes as much to MM. Meilhac and Halévy as it does to Jacques Offenbach. So long as MM. Meilhac and Halévy furnished Offenbach's books for him, the resultant was always a work of art, with the restraint which art demands. So soon as he went to other librettists, the product of the conjunction became violent, vulgar, and inartistic; above all, the "moral game-flavor" which Ambros and Mr. Apthorp find in Offenbach's work was intensified beyond endurance by decent people. What MM. Meilhac and Halévy kept subordinate, and at best suggested, was by their copyists paraded and emphasized. In short, it is not unjust to say that the credit of *opéra-bouffe* belongs to MM. Meilhac and Halévy, and the discredit of it belongs to the feebler and louder librettists who tried hard to give a double meaning to words without any.

The earlier librettos which MM. Meilhac and Halévy wrote for Offenbach were admirably made: they are models of what a comic-opera book should be. I cannot well imagine a better bit of work of its kind than the 'Belle Hélène,' or the 'Grand Duchess.' Plot and dialogue and characters, — all are admirable, and nowhere are they wanting. Since MM. Meilhac and Halévy have ceased writing for Offenbach, they have done several books for M. Charles Lecocq: among them are the 'Petit Duc' and the 'Grande Demoiselle.' These are rather light comic operas than true *opéras-bouffes*. But, if there is an elevation in the style of the music' there is an emphatic falling-off in the quality of the words. From the 'Grand Duchess' to the 'Petit Duc' is a great descent. The former was a genuine play, complete and self-contained: the latter is a careless trifle, a mere outline sketch for the composer to fill up. The story, akin in subject to Mr. Tom Taylor's fine historical drama, 'Clancarty,' is pretty; but there is no trace of the true poetry which made the farewell letter of 'Périchole' so touching, or of the true comic force which projected Général Boum. 'Carmen,' which, like 'Périchole,' owes the suggestion of its plot and characters to Prosper Mérimée, is little more than the task-work of the two well-trained playmakers. It was sufficient for its purpose, no more and no less.

Of all the opera-books of MM. Meilhac and Halévy, that one is easily first and foremost which has for its heroine the Helen of Troy, whom Marlowe's Faustus declared, —

> " Fairer than the evening air,
> Clad in the beauty of a thousand stars."

In the 'Belle Hélène' we see the higher wit of M. Meilhac. M. Halévy had been at the same college with him, and they had pored together over the same legends of old time. But, working without M. Meilhac on 'Orphée aux Enfers,' M. Halévy showed his inferiority;

for 'Orphée' is the old-fashioned anachronistic skit on antiquity, — funny, if you will, but with a fun often labored, not to say forced, — the fun of physical incongruity and exaggeration. When, however, M. Halévy wrote his next play of Greek life, M. Meilhac's finer insight prevailed; and in the 'Belle Hélène' the fun, easy and flowing, is of a very high quality, and it has root in mental, not physical incongruity. Here, indeed, is the humorous touchstone of a whole system of government and of theology. And allowing for the variations made with comic intent, it is altogether Greek in spirit, — so Greek, in fact, that I doubt whether any one who has not given his days and nights to the study of Homer and of the tragedians, and who has not thus taken in by the pores the subtle essence of Hellenic life and literature, can truly appreciate this French farce. Of its kind the 'Belle Hélène' seems to me a great work : the kind, of a truth, is not great ; but it is great in its kind. Planché's 'Golden Fleece' is in the same vein, but the ore is not so rich. Frere's 'Loves of the Triangles,' and some of his Anti-Jacobin writing, are perhaps as good in quality ; but the subjects are inferior and temporary. Scarron's vulgar burlesques and the cheap parodies of many contemporary English play-makers are not to be mentioned in the same breath with this scholarly fooling. There is something in the French genius akin to the Greek ; and here was a Gallic wit who could turn a Hellenic love-tale inside out, and wring the uttermost drop of fun from it, without recourse to the devices of the booth at the fair, — the false nose or the simulation of needless ugliness. The French play, comic as it was, did not suggest hysteria or epilepsy ; and it was not so lacking in grace that we could not recall the original story without a shudder. There is no shattering of an ideal ; and one cannot reproach the authors of the 'Belle Hélène' with what Theophrastus Such calls " debasing the moral currency, lowering the value of every inspiring fact and tradition." They have not, to use the quotation from La Bruyère which Mr. Such takes as the text of the essay from which I have just borrowed, — they have not seen the ridiculous where it was not, to the spoiling of their own taste and that of others ; but they have seen what *was* ridiculous in the old Hellenic legend, and they have set it forth with grace, and in a manner which pleases. (As to the "instruction" which La Bruyère also requires, I will say nought. We must not ask too much from one of Offenbach's opera-books.) To the ridiculous from the sublime is but a hair's breadth ; and who shall say on which side of the line Menelaus stands, this epic husband? And Helen herself, if half the tales about her were true, is not a lady who would be received in society nowadays, except perhaps in princely circles. I cannot but think that after all, MM. Meilhac and Halévy may have given us a better portrait of the lovely daughter of Leda and the swan, than hangs in any gallery of historical paintings. What a living, loving bit of flesh and blood their fair Helen is ! — Greek to the back-bone, but a Greek who had read the dramas of M. Victor Hugo. With her "fatality," she is a true heroine of the Romanticists. And Paris, as Homer shows him to us, — has he not something of the comic-opera tenor ? And Achilles, as thick-witted, no doubt, as he was thin-skinned, — he must have been very much the sort of a bore he appears to us in M. Meilhac's play. But above all these figments of antiquity, conceived as they are

with high comic richness and strength, towers the busi-
ness-like priest Calchas, the Augur we cannot meet
without laughter, the quintessence of classical mythol-
ogy, an unforgettable figure of the fullest comic force.

Surpassed only by the 'Belle Hélène' is the 'Grand
Duchess of Gérolstein.' It is more than fifteen years
since all the world went to Paris to see an Exposition
Universelle, and to gaze at the "sabre of my sire;" and
since a Russian emperor, going to hear the operetta
said to have been suggested by the freak of a Russian
empress, sat incognito in one stage-box of the little
Variétés theatre, and, glancing up, saw a Russian grand
duke in the other. It is fifteen years now since the
tiny army of her Grand-ducal Highness took New
York by storm, and since the American play-goer
hummed his love for the military, and walked from the
French Theatre along Fourteenth Street to Delmonico's to supper, sabring the waiters there with the vene-
rated weapon of her sire. The French Theatre is no
more; and Delmonico's is no longer at that Fourteenth-
street corner; and her Highness Mlle. Tostée is dead,
and so is Offenbach himself; and his sprightly tunes
have had the fate of all over-popular airs, and are forgotten now. *Où sont les neiges d'antan?*

It has been said that the authors regretted having
written the 'Grand Duchess,' because the irony of
history soon made a joke on Teutonic powers and prin-
cipalities seem like unpatriotic satire. Certainly they
had no reason to be ashamed of the literary quality of
their work: in its class it yields only to its predecessor. There is no single figure as fine as Calchas. Général Boum is a coarser outline; but how humorous and
how firm is the drawing of Prince Paul and Baron

Grog! and her Highness herself may be thought a cleverer sketch of youthful femininity than even the Hellenic Helen. It is hard to judge the play now. Custom has worn its freshness, and made it too familiar : we know it too well to criticise it clearly. Besides, the actors have now overlaid the action with overmuch "business." In spite of all these difficulties, the merits of the piece are sufficiently obvious. Its constructive skill can be remarked : the first act, for example, is one of the best bits of exposition on the modern French stage.

Besides these plays for music, and besides the more important five-act comedies to be considered later, MM. Meilhac and Halévy are the authors of thirty or forty comic dramas, — as they would be called on the English stage, — or farce-comedies in one, two, three, four, and even five acts, ranging in aim from the gentle satire of sentimentality in the 'Veuve' to the outspoken farce of the 'Réveillon.' Among the best of the longer of these comic plays are 'Tricoche et Cacolet' and the 'Boule.' Both were written for the Palais Royal ; and they are models of the new dramatic species which came into existence at that theatre about twenty years ago, as M. Francisque Sarcey recently reminded us in his interesting article on the Palais Royal in the *Nineteenth Century*. This new style of comic play may be termed realistic farce, — realistic, because it starts from every-day life and the most matter-of-fact conditions ; and farce, because it uses its exact facts only to further its fantasy and extravagance. Consider the 'Boule.' Its first act is a model of accurate observation : it is a transcript from life ; it is an inside view of a common-place French household which incompatibility of temper has made unsupportable. And then take the following acts, and see how, on this foundation of fact, and screened by an outward semblance of realism, there is erected the most laughable superstructure of fantastic farce. I remember hearing one of the two great comedians of the Théâtre Français, M. Coquelin, praise a comic actor of the Variétés whom we had lately seen in a rather cheap and flimsy farce, because he combined "la vérité la plus absolue avec la fantaisie la plus pure." [1] And this is the merit of the 'Boule:' its most humorous inventions have their roots in the truth.

Better even than the 'Boule' is 'Tricoche et Cacolet,' which is the name of a firm of private detectives whose exploits and devices surpass those imagined by Poe in America, by Mr. Wilkie Collins in England, and by Gaboriau in France. The manifold disguises and impersonations of the two partners when seeking to outwit each other are as well-motived, and as fertile in comic effect, as any of the attempts of Crispin, or of some other of Regnard's interchangeable valets. Is not even the 'Légataire Universel,' Regnard's masterpiece, overrated? To me it is neither higher comedy, nor more provocative of laughter, than either the 'Boule,' or 'Tricoche et Cacolet;' and the modern plays, as I have said, are based on a study of life as it is; while the figures of the older comedies are frankly conventional. Nowhere in Regnard is there a situation equal in comic power to that in the final act of the 'Réveillon,' — a situation Molière would have been glad to treat.

Especially to be commended in 'Tricoche et Cacolet' is the satire of the hysterical sentimentality and of the

---

[1] "The most absolute truth with the purest fantasy."

forced emotions born of luxury and idleness. Just as the Belle Hélène herself is a heroine of Hugo or the elder Dumas, so the Bernardine of this play is a heroine of M. Octave Feuillet. The parody of the amorous intrigue which is the staple of so many French plays is as wholesome as it is exhilarating. Absurdity is a deadly shower-bath to sentimentalism. The method of Meilhac and Halévy in sketching this couple is not unlike that employed by Mr. W. S. Gilbert in ' H. M. S. Pinafore' and the 'Pirates of Penzance.' Especially to be noted is the same perfectly serious pushing of the dramatic commonplaces to an absurd conclusion. There is the same kind of humor too, and the same girding at the stock-tricks of stage-craft, in ' H. M. S. Pinafore' at the swopping of children in the cradle, and in ' Tricoche et Cacolet' at the "portrait of my mother," which has drawn so many tears in modern melodrama. Even the exaggerated sense of duty which bound the 'prentice to the pirates also holds firmly the conscience of Bernardine. But MM. Meilhac and Halévy, having made one success, did not further attempt the same kind of pleasantry, — wiser in this than Mr. Gilbert, who seems to find it hard to write any thing else.

As in the 'Château à Toto' MM. Meilhac and Halévy had made a modern perversion of the 'Dame Blanche,' so in the 'Cigale' did they dress up afresh the story of the 'Fille du Régiment.' As the poet asks, —

> " Ah, World of ours, are you so gray,
>   And weary, World, of spinning,
>   That you repeat the tales to-day
>   You told at the beginning?
>   For lo ! the same old myths that made
>   The early stage-successes,
>   Still hold the boards, and still are played
>   With new effects and dresses."

I have cited the 'Cigale,' not because it is a very good play, for it is not, but because it shows the present carelessness of French dramatists in regard to dramatic construction. The 'Cigale' is a very clever bit of work: but it has the slightest of plots, and this made out of old cloth; and the situations, in so far as there are any, follow each other as best they may. It is not really a play: it is a mere sketch touched up with Parisianisms, "local hits," and the wit of the moment. This substitution of an off-hand sketch for a full-sized picture can better be borne in a little one-act play than in a more ambitious work in three or four acts.

And of one-act plays Meilhac and Halévy have written a score or more, — delightful little *genre* pictures like the 'Été de Saint-Martin,' simple pastels like 'Toto chez Tata,' and vigorous caricatures like the 'Photographe' or the 'Brésilien.' The Frenchman invented the rûffle, says Emerson : the Englishman added the shirt. These little dramatic trifles are French ruffles. In the beginning of his theatrical career M. Meilhac did little comedies like the 'Sarabande' and the 'Autographe,' in the Scribe formula, — dramatized anecdotes, but fresher in wit, and livelier in fancy, than Scribe's. This early work was far more regular than we find in some of his latest, bright as these are. The 'Petit Hôtel,' for instance, and 'Lolotte,' are etchings, as it were, instantaneous photographs of certain aspects of life in the city by the Seine, or stray paragraphs of the latest news from Paris.

It is perhaps not too much to say that Meilhac and Halévy are seen at their best in these one-act plays. They hit better with a single-barrel than with a re-volver. In their five-act plays, whether serious like

'Fanny Lear,' or comic like the 'Vie Parisienne,' the interest is scattered, and we have a series of episodes rather than a single story. Just as the egg of the jelly-fish is girt by circles which tighten slowly until the ovoid form is cut into disks of independent life, so, if the four intermissions of some of Meilhac and Halévy's full-sized plays were but a little longer and wider and deeper, they would divide the piece into five separate plays, any one of which could fairly hope for success by itself. I have heard that the 'Roi Candaule' was originally an act of the 'Boule;' and the 'Photographe' seems as though it had dropped from the 'Vie Parisienne' by mistake. In M. Meilhac's earlier five-act plays, the 'Vertu de Célimène' and the 'Petit-fils de Mascarille,' there is great power of conception, a real grip on character; but the main action is clogged with tardy incidents, and so the momentum is lost. A rifle-ball hits the bull's eye more surely than a charge of buckshot: only when they made 'Froufrou' had they any use for a rifle. In both these early comedies of M. Meilhac there is, as their titles show, an intention of modelling on Molière, and of carrying on his work after a lapse of two centuries. In the 'Petit-fils de Mascarille' there are touches not unworthy of the original inventor of Mascarille: one scene in particular, between Clavarot and the impudent valet Jean, would have been appreciated not a little by the author of the 'Bourgeois Gentilhomme.'

In both of these earlier comedies of M. Meilhac's, and especially in the 'Vertu de Célimène,' besides the influence of Molière, and even more potent than that, is to be seen the influence of the new school of M. Alexandre Dumas *fils*. And the inclination toward the strong, not to say violent emotions which Dumas and Augier had imported into comedy is still more evident in 'Fanny Lear,' the first five-act comedy which MM. Meilhac and Halévy wrote together, and which was brought out in 1868. The final situation is one of truth and immense effectiveness, and there is great vigor in the creation of character. The decrepit old rake, the Marquis de Noriolis, feeble in his folly, and wandering in his helplessness, and yet irresistible when aroused,—this is a striking figure; and still more striking is the portrait of his wife, now the Marquise de Noriolis, but once Fanny Lear, the adventuress,—a woman who has youth, beauty, wealth, every thing before her, if it were not for the shame which is behind her. Gay and witty, and even good-humored, she is inflexible when she is determined : hers is a velvet manner and an iron will. The name of Fanny Lear may sound familiar to some readers because it was given to an American adventuress in Russia by a grand-ducal admirer.

After 'Fanny Lear' came 'Froufrou,' the lineal successor of the 'Stranger,' as the current masterpiece of the lachrymatory drama. Nothing so tear-compelling as the final act of 'Froufrou' had been seen on the stage for half a century or more. The death of Froufrou was a watery sight, and for any chance to weep we are many of us grateful. And yet it was a German, born in the land of Charlotte and Werther, it was Heine, who remarked on the oddity of praising the "dramatic poet who possesses the art of drawing tears,—a talent which he has in common with the meanest onion." It is noteworthy that it was by way of Germany that English tragedy exerted its singular influence on French come-

dy. Attracted by the homely power of pieces like the
'Gamester' and 'Jane Shore,' Diderot in France, and
Lessing in Germany, attempted the *tragédie bourgeoise;*
but the right of the "tradesmen's tragedies," as Goldsmith called them, to exist at all, was questioned, until
Kotzebue's pathetic power and theatrical skill captured
nearly every stage in Europe. In France the bastard
offspring of English tragedy and German drama gave
birth to an equally illegitimate *comédie larmoyante.*
And so it happens that while comedy in English literature, resulting from the clash of character, is always on
the brink of farce, comedy in French literature may be
tinged with passion until it almost turns to tragedy. In
France the word "comedy" is elastic, and covers a
multitude of sins : it includes the laughing 'Boule' and
the tearful 'Froufrou :' in fact, the French Melpomene
is a sort of *Jeanne qui pleure et Jeanne qui rit.*

So it happens that 'Froufrou' is a comedy. And indeed the first three acts are comedy of a very high order,
full of wit, and rich in character. I mentioned the
'Stranger' a few lines back ; and the contrast of the
two plays shows how much lighter and more delicate
French art is. The humor to be found in the 'Stranger'
is, to say the least, Teutonic ; and German humor is
like the simple Italian wines, — it will not stand export.
And in the 'Stranger' there is really no character, no
insight into human nature. 'Misanthropy and Repentance,' as Kotzebue called his play (the 'Stranger' was
Sheridan's title for the English translation he revised
for his own theatre), are loud-sounding words when we
capitalize them ; but they do not deceive us now : we
see that the play itself is mostly stalking sententious-
ness, mawkishly overladen with gush. Now, in 'Frou

frou' there is wit of the latest Parisian kind, and there
are characters, — people whom we might meet, and
whom we may remember.   Brigard, for one, the repro-
bate old gentleman, living even in his old age in that
Bohemia which has Paris for its capital, and dyeing his
few locks because he feels himself unworthy to wear
gray hair, — Brigard is a portrait from life.   The Baron
de Cambri is less individual; and I confess I cannot
quite stomach a gentleman who is willing to discuss the
problem of his wife's virtue with a chance adorer.   But
the cold Baroness herself is no commonplace person.
And Louise, the elder sister of Froufrou, the one who
had chosen the better part, and had kept it by much
self-sacrifice, — she is a true woman.   Best (better even
than Brigard) is Gilberte, nicknamed "Froufrou" from
the rustling of her silks as she skips and scampers
airily around.   Froufrou, when all is said, is a real creation, a revelation of Parisian femininity, a living thing,
breathing the breath of life, and tripping along lightly
on her own little feet.   Marrying a reserved yet deeply-
devoted husband because her sister bid her; taking into
her home that sister who had sacrificed her own love
for the husband ; seeing this sister straighten the household which she in her heedless seeking for idle amusement had not governed ; then beginning to feel herself
in danger, and aware of a growing jealousy — senseless
though it be — of the sister who has so innocently sup-
planted her by her hearth and even with her child ;
making one effort to regain her place, and failing, as
was inevitable, — poor Froufrou takes the fatal plunge
which will at once and forever separate her from what
was hers before.   What a fine scene is that at the end
of the third act, in which Froufrou has worked herself

almost to a frenzy, and, hopeless in her jealousy, gives up all to her sister, and rushes from the house to the lover she scarcely cares for! And how admirably does all that has gone before lead up to it! These first three acts are a wonder of constructive art. Of the rest of the play it is hard to speak so highly. The change is rather sudden from the study of character in the first part to the demand in the last, that if you have tears, you must prepare to shed them now. The brightness is quenched in gloom and despair. Of a verity, frivolity may be fatal, and death may follow a liking for private theatricals and the other empty amusements of fashion; but is it worth while to break a butterfly on the wheel, and to put a humming-bird to the question? To say what fate shall be meted out to the woman taken in adultery is always a hard task for a dramatist. Here the erring and erratic heroine comes home to be for-given, to kiss the child she abandoned, and to die, like Pope's Narcissa, to the very end thinking of fine linen and a change of raiment; and so, after the fresh and unforced painting of modern Parisian life, we have a finish full of conventional pathos. Well, death redeems all; and, as Pascal says, "the last act is always tragedy, whatever fine comedy there may have been in the rest of life. We must all die alone."

CHAPTER XI.

IN his admirable essay on the genius of Calderon, Archbishop Trench has pointed out that thrice, and thrice only, has there been a really great and popular drama, and that "the conditions of a people which make a grand outburst of the drama possible make it also inevitable that this will utter itself, not by a single voice, but by many." In a note, the archbishop shows us that each of these dramatic outbursts has been comprised in the space of a century, or but little more: thus Æschylus was born B.C. 525, and Euripides died B.C. 406; Lope de Vega was born in 1562, and Calderon died in 1681; and Marlowe was born in 1565, and Shirley died in 1666. Now, although in France there has been no grand outburst of the drama as the one voice through which the nation was uttering itself, and spake to foreign countries and posterity, there have been two occasions, when, beyond all cavil, the drama was the first and most important form of literature. The earlier and by far the greater of these two epochs, when the supremacy of the drama in French literature is indisputable, was the space of a little less than a hundred years, which elapsed between the birth of Corneille in 1606, and the death of Racine in 1699, — a scant century, which saw the making of all the masterpieces of Molière, and which displays a dramatic literature inferior only to that of Greece and of England, and it may be, of Spain. The second and secondary occasion when the drama became the most important form in French literature is in our own time, in the half-century extending from 1830 to 1880. Just what will be the future estimate of this drama, we cannot now do more than guess at, nor what it is to become in the immediate future. But it is possible to recapitulate briefly the course of the drama in France, from the beginning of this century, and to see whether we cannot discover in what direction lie its present tendencies.

"The theatre is, of all the countries of the world, the one most subject to revolutions," says M. Edmond About: "it renews itself and gets younger every day, like the society of which it is the image. . . . The stage is a magnifying mirror, in which are reflected the passions, the vices, the follies, of each epoch. Now, the vices of yesterday are no longer those of to-day: fashion governs passion, and we change our follies as we do our hats. Molière did not know the stockbroker: we have lost the courtier. The shopkeeper turned gentleman is played out; but we have the gentleman turned shopkeeper, selling wine and flour, and putting the family arms on his labels. We must not be too greatly astonished, if, after thirty or forty years, plays, like women, begin to age, — excepting only a few masterpieces, whose style preserves them. We may say of a comedy, as of a duchess, that she was beautiful in 1720. We may say of a drama, what the Spaniards say of a soldier, 'He was brave such-and-such a day.'"

French drama has had two such revolutions in this century: it has got younger twice; and even now it may be on the edge of a third rejuvenescence. At the opening of the century, the theatre in France was op pressed by the rigidity of the imperial rule, fettered by a blind obedience to the so-called unities, and shackled by a superstitious regard for dignity and propriety. After Beaumarchais abandoned the stage, the drama was lifeless, except in the minor theatres, where melo-dramas of the German type drew throngs. In 1817 Eugène Scribe began to renovate the national vaude-ville, and in his hands it gained value and variety. In 1827 a young French poet, Victor Hugo, published a play called 'Cromwell,' to which he prefixed a declara-tion of dramatic principles; and the revolt of the Ro-manticists against the Classicists was proclaimed. In 1829 'Henri III.,' a drama by a young quadroon called Alexandre Dumas, took everybody by surprise. The next year was acted Victor Hugo's 'Hernani;' and, as Señor Castelar puts it picturesquely, it "was wondered at like a comet, and announced in the heavens a war in the realm of poetry." In their revolt against the formality and severity of the old school, the Romanti-cists went to the other extreme. They slighted accu-racy and even common sense: they sought to astound and to stupefy the spectator into silent acquiescence. Not a few of the most brilliant of French dramas saw the light of the lamps at this time. Historical plays especially found favor in the eyes of French theatre-goers, and a fantastic semblance of history filled the stage. And so, at last, a movement which promised much accomplished little. The rubbish of Classicism was cleared away, and that was all. "The great point," said Goethe, "is not to pull down, but to build up; and in this humanity finds pure joy." The Romanticists pulled down, but the power of united action in build-ing up failed them. A few fine works by the great

writers who led the movement still survive, but toward
the foundation of a distinct and enduring school Romanticism did little or nothing. It was Maurice de
Guérin who characterized Romanticism as "that youthful literature which has put forth all its blossom prematurely, and has left itself a helpless prey to the returning frost."

It is important to remember that the romantic drama
in France, although seemingly a fresh creation, was in
great measure an evolution from the melodrama of the
minor theatres. Before Hugo and Dumas were Victor
Ducange and Pixérécourt; and 'Henri III.' and 'Hernani,' although immensely superior to 'Thirty Years
of a Gambler's Life,' differed from it in degree rather
than in kind. The poets of the Romanticist movement
robed in royal verse plots not greatly above those which
the humbler playwright clothed in common prose.
Even during the height of the movement, Bouchardy
drew the multitude to see 'Lazare le Pâtre.' When the
poets gave up the stage, successors to Ducange and
Pixérécourt and Bouchardy were not wanting. M.
Dennery and his fellows began the long list of modern
melodramas, of which the best specimens are 'Don
César de Bazan' (suggested by a scene or two of
Hugo's 'Ruy Blas') and the 'Two Orphans.' Lacking in elevation, their plays were constructed with
the utmost technical skill. Nothing was neglected to
heighten the effect on the play-goer, and every thing
was sacrificed to it.

In this making of melodramas, the influence of the
Romanticists was very obvious, and indeed unmistakable. There was one form of drama on which the
movement led by Hugo and Dumas had had no effect

whatever. After having made over the vaudeville to his own satisfaction, Eugène Scribe invented the comédie-vaudeville; and from this to comedy in three or five acts was but a step. To the writing of comedy, Scribe brought the unexampled skill acquired in the writing of a hundred minor plays. His knowledge of the stage, and of what could be done there, and of how to do it, has never been equalled, and probably never will be. The present world-wide acceptance of French drama is owing to the perfection of Scribe's methods, — methods which he used in vaudeville and comedy, and which M. Dennery and his associates imitated in the making of melodramas. What Scribe on the one hand, and the melodramatic playwrights on the other, devoted themselves to, was the construction of a self-acting plot; and, when once constructed, this plot could be dressed up just as well in English, or German, or Icelandic, as in the original French. But after we have once admired the pretty trickeries of mere ingenuity, we tire of them and crave something better, something more substantial. The melodramatists and the Romanticists still in active practice met this demand by extravagance and by the accumulation of horrors. Time was ripe for another transformation.

In 1843, perhaps fifteen years after the beginning of the Romantic movement, a young poet named Ponsard brought out a tragedy called 'Lucrèce,' and was at once hailed as the founder of a new school, — the School of Common Sense, a compromise, as it were, between the coldness of Classicism and the fire of Romanticism. It is useless to be hailed as the founder of a school, if you have no scholars; and Ponsard had none. It is true that when a friend of his produced a delightful little poetic comedy of antique life, its author, M. Émile Augier, was declared to be of the School of Common Sense. But M. Augier never set himself down as a disciple of Ponsard's; and, when the real transformation of the drama did come at last, it was seen, not only that M. Augier did not belong to the School of Common Sense, but that the school itself had never had any substantial existence. It sprang up quickly; but it had no root, and it withered away as quickly. Further: when the new movement began it was not poetic, but prosaic. Nothing more clearly declares that the present is not a time for a great outburst of the drama than the fact that there is nowadays an almost universal divorce between the poet and the playwright. In the three great epochs of Greece, Spain, and England, and even in the French literature under Louis XIV., the dramatist was perforce a poet. Now, not only in France, but everywhere, the playwright is very rarely a poet, and the stage is correspondingly prosaic. Even Hugo is not a true dramatic poet: he is a curious combination of a playwright and a lyric poet. Alfred de Musset was a poet first, and a dramatist by accident only. Ponsard was a respectable poet; and M. Émile Augier can write fine verse; but the mass of contemporary French drama has but little touch of poetry. Now and again a comedy in verse, or an old-fashioned tragedy in five acts, gets before the footlights; but, although the form is relished by the inner circle of literary epicures, it is out of fashion with the throng which alone can fill a theatre. Beautiful as some of these poetic plays are, — and I know nothing more beautiful in the modern drama than M. Théodore de Banville's 'Gringoire' (which, although written in prose, is instinct with the truest poetry), or than M. François Coppée's 'Luthier de Crémone,' both written for the acting of that admirable comedian, M. Coquelin of the Comédie-Française, — they remain individual efforts only, and are insufficient in either number or importance to be considered as a school. The accidental success of M. Henri de Bornier's declamatory tragedy, the 'Fille de Roland,' is not evidence of a popular revival of interest in an obsolete formula : it is to be explained easily enough, as the chance result of the appropriateness of the patriotic speeches, in which the piece abounds, to the feelings of the French at the time it was acted.

About the middle of the century, there was a sharp re-action against the violence of the melodramatists, and against the childishness of the machine-made plays, against M. Dennery and his fellows, and against Scribe. Fact began to take the place of fantasy. Dramatists invented less, and observed more. A photograph of modern life was offered in place of a pretentious historical painting, the maker of which had relied on his fancy for all details. Romanticism was followed by Realism. Hugo and Alexandre Dumas were succeeded by M. Émile Augier and M. Alexandre Dumas *fils ;* just as, in pictorial art, the large manner of Decamps and Delacroix gave way to the *genre* painting of MM. Meissonier and Gérôme. The dramatist sought to be probable, to give an exact transcript of life as he saw it around him, to do for the stage what Balzac was doing for prose fiction. In 1852 M. Dumas *fils* brought out his 'Dame aux Camélias,' and two or three years later began the series of social studies which includes the 'Demi-Monde,' the 'Fils Naturel,' and 'M. Alphonse.' M. Émile Augier, whose hand had hitherto hesitated, saw at once where his real strength lay, and, abandoning verse, gave us the stirring and sturdy satires of which the 'Fils de Giboyer' is the best, and the long list of high and keen comedies, chief among which is the 'Gendre de M. Poirier.' In the footsteps of M. Dumas and M. Augier have walked Théodore Barrière, M. Victorien Sardou, and MM. Meilhac and Halévy. The effect of their example was felt even by the melo-dramatists who left the middle ages and sought for subjects and excitement in the crimes of the present.

When the 'Dame aux Camélias' was first acted, Théophile Gautier hailed it as a protest against the cheap complications of the Scribe school, and the dark, deep plots of the Dennery melodramatists. "What does most honor to the author," he wrote, "is that there is not the slightest intrigue, surprise, or compli-cation in all these five acts, despite their intense inter-est." Any one who glances through the volumes of Théophile Gautier's collected dramatic criticisms can-not but note how often he flings out against the machine-made plays of his day, in which one part fitted so per-fectly into another, that there was no room for any life or nature, and all that the spectator was called upon to admire was a sort of Chinese-puzzle ingenuity. Scribe's formula, for instance, was to take a simple situation, to present it frankly, and then to carry it out to a care-fully-considered conclusion by means of a series of amusing scenes, which, while showing various phases of the idea, seemed to delay the determined end, while in reality they were skilfully made to serve in its prepa-ration. There was, in short, an essential unity of plot, carried on by a well-balanced and intricately-complicated intrigue, in the course of which poor human nature was wofully twisted to suit the exigencies of an end arbitrarily agreed on. This principle of construction is right enough, if not pushed to extremes; but the temptation to which Scribe and his disciples succumbed was to invent difficulties from mere delight in their own dexterity in surmounting them. With the coming of Realism, and the consequent demand for a closer resemblance to actual existence, the machine-made play went out of fashion. Unfortunately, the pendulum swung as far one way as it had the other, and plays are now as ill made as they were then too well made. I have read somewhere, that Scribe wondered why his later plays did not hit the popular taste, declaring that his pieces were as well made as ever. No doubt; but the French play-goer had ceased to care for a well-made piece, or rather, he wanted something more in a piece than clever joinery. Exactly the same change has taken place in the making of French plays within a quarter of a century which has taken place in the making of English novels within half a century. As Mr. Richard Grant White reminded us a year ago, the modern novel — Mr. Anthony Trollope's, for instance — slights plot, and is slovenly in structure when we compare it with one of Scott's, in which we cannot but be struck by the neatness of the workmanship and the dexterity with which the story is shaped. In France, Scribe has gone out of fashion, and his formula with him. Just as Gautier protested against the well-made play, so now M. Francisque Sarcey has to protest constantly against the neglect of constructive principles which characterizes nearly all the French drama of our day.

Even the farces and comic dramas, which in Scribe's

hand were as carefully finished as plays of more importance, now rely on the wit of their dialogue and
the jests liberally sprinkled through them, and only
a little on the humor of the situation.   Instead of a
comic plot, which could be used in any language, we
have only an anecdote in dialogue, purely Parisian in
its abundant allusions, and full of a local wit which loses
its color ten miles from the capital.   Many of the comic
plays of M. Gondinet and of MM. Meilhac and Halévy,
delightful as they are to those who can appreciate their
Parisianism, do not bear exportation : they are like the
fairies who cannot cross running water.   The pieces of
inferior artists are indeed *articles de Paris:* they are
like the cheap French bronzes, — glittering and hollow
and brassy, and they do not wear well.   Even in more
important comedies the same defect is to be detected.
Clever as are the later comedies of M. Gondinet, —for
instance, the charming play called the 'Grands Enfants,'
— we find in them no unity of plot, no sequence of
situations, scarcely, indeed, any situations at all : instead, we have a pell-mell medley of pictures of different phases of the fundamental idea, huddling one after
another with no apparent order, and lit up by a rapid
running fire of very good jokes.   A play of this kind,
pleasant as it may be, presents no unity of impression,
and fades out of memory far more easily than a play
of inferior material so constructed that there is something salient for the mind to cling to.   As I said, M.
Gondinet is not alone in this failing : he serves however as an admirable example, for no play of his has
ever been adapted for the American stage, no doubt, because of this very deficiency.

Romanticism dates from 1827 ; Realism, from 1852.

Another quarter of a century has elapsed, and what new force is now making itself felt on the French stage in the stead of the Realism which has spent itself? If we pay attention only to the noise a new doctrine and its disciples are wont to make, there is no need of hesitation : the coming power is Naturalism, and M. Zola is its prophet. M. Émile Zola is a robust young man who has roughly shouldered his way into literature. In this country he has rather an unsavory reputation, from the dirt which encumbers the corners of his ignoble but powerful novels. Dirt has been defined to be matter in the wrong place; and in Zola's novels it is in the wrong place, for it hides their strength, and keeps many men from reading them, who would keenly appreciate their force, were it not for their indecency. Although indecent, they are not immoral, any more than a clinic or a dissection is immoral ; and it is as the operator at a clinic that M. Zola poses. The system of an artist always takes color from his personality : Naturalism is no exception ; it has been warped to fit the nature of M. Zola. So it is well first to consider what manner of man he is, before discussing his literary code.

The first impression we get from his works is one of main strength, often perversely misapplied, and never corrected by good taste. M. Zola seems to delight in describing the unspeakable. In his eye every thing is unclean, sordid, and despicable. He has a gloomy dissatisfaction with life, and is, indeed, as disgusted with it as most readers are with the degradation laid bare in his novels : Schopenhauer himself could scarcely be more pessimistic. This explains his dislike of sympathetic characters : he simply does not believe in them ; in his eyes, Colonel Newcome would be an idiot or an impossibility. To him there are no good men, though some men are not so bad as others. Health is as scarce as virtue : so he studies the diseases of his characters, and details their sufferings. It is hard for him to meet the accusation that the Naturalists are artists who refuse to paint your portrait unless you are pitted by the small-pox. M. Zola has none of the saving grace of humor. In fact, he has a most un-French lack of *esprit* and a corresponding hatred of it. His chance attempts at jocoseness are painful : when he trees a poor little joke he brings it down mercilessly, and nails up its skin as a warning. No writer ever stood more in need of the sense of humor than M. Zola; and he has it not. It takes a strong stomach to read through certain of his books without qualms, and a hearty laugh would do much toward clearing the atmosphere of its foulness. His grossness may be matched in Rabelais perhaps; but M. Zola's work is without the broad breeze of humor which blows across the pages of Rabelais, setting the reader in such a gale of laughter that he has no need to hold his nose. He is as devoid of humor as a graven image. His substitute for it is a chill and bitter irony, with which he is not scantily supplied.

Turning from the man to the system, we may define Naturalism as the application to novels and plays of the principles of what, in history and criticism, is known as the "historical method." It is easy to trace the growth of this idea to its present maturity as we look back through M. Zola's writings. Fifteen years ago he declared, "I must find a man in every work, or it leaves me cold. I frankly sacrifice humanity to the artist. If I were to formulate my definition of a work of art, it would be, 'A work of art is a corner of creation seen through a temperament.' And what matters to me all else? I am an artist, and I give you my flesh and my blood, my heart and my thought. . . . Have you, then, not understood that art is the free expression of a heart and of an intelligence, and that it is the greater the more personal it is?" A year later the idea had grown: "I am for no school, because I am for human truth, which excludes all sects and all system. The word *art* displeases me: it contains I do not know what ideas of necessary arrangement, of absolute ideal. To make art (*faire de l'art*), is it not to make something which is outside of man and of nature? I wish that you should make *life:* I wish that you should be alive, that you should create afresh, outside of all things, according to your own eyes and your own temperament. What I seek first of all in a picture is a man, and not a picture."

A platform like this needed but one more plank to let M. Zola take a purely scientific view of literature, excluding art utterly. This plank was soon added. M. Zola's advanced doctrine has been most succinctly formulated in his essay on 'Naturalism in the Theatre.' He defines Naturalism as "the return to nature: it is what scientific men did when they first thought of beginning with the study of bodies and phenomena, of basing themselves on experience, of working by analysis. Naturalism in literature is also the return to nature and to man, direct observation, exact anatomy, the frank acceptance and depicting of the thing as it is." M. Zola claims Homer as a Naturalist, which is rather damaging to the assertion that Naturalism is a new thing. From Homer it is a far cry to Diderot; but M. Zola clears the distance at a single stride.

Diderot, as we all know, begat Balzac; and Stendhal and Balzac bring us down to Flaubert, and to the brothers de Goncourt, and to M. Zola himself. In its perfected form as it is to be in the future, — for perhaps all present Naturalists are too tainted with the conventionalities of contemporary art ever to rise to the height which their followers may easily attain, — the Naturalistic novel or drama is to be "simply an inquest on nature, beings, and things;" and its interest is to be sought "no longer in the ingenuity of a fable well invented and developed according to certain rules. Imagination is no longer needed, plot is of little consequence." What the coming Naturalist must stand and deliver is facts, documents on humanity. "Instead of imagining an adventure, complicating it, preparing stage surprises, which from scene to scene will bring it to a final conclusion, one simply takes from life the history of a being, or of a group of beings, whose acts one faithfully registers." The work has no other merit than "exact observation, the penetration more or less profound of the analysis, the logical linking of events." In short, the theatre is to be made "the study and painting of life," and not "a mere amusement of the intellect, an art of balance and symmetry, ruled according to a certain code."

Like most reformers, M. Zola breaks too many images : his zeal runs away with him. The drama, like all other arts, exists only through certain conventions which are absolutely necessary to its existence. Other conventions there are, not absolutely necessary, and changing from time to time : these M. Zola may attack with impunity and credit; but all struggle against the former is futile. On the stage the absolute reproduction of nature is neither possible nor desirable. There are scores of every-day situations which cannot be shown in the theatre. As M. Dumas reminded us in his preface to the 'Étrangère' (intended as an answer to M. Zola's essay), no matter how closely we seek to copy nature, there is always a point at which exact imitation must stop, and convention take its place. "An artist," says M. Dumas concisely and conclusively, "a true artist, has a higher and more difficult mission than the mere reproduction of what is : he has to discover and to reveal to us that which we do not see in things we look at every day, — that which he alone has the faculty of perceiving in what is apparently patent to all of us." No less apt is Lowell's remark, that Wordsworth, who also proclaimed a new gospel in literature, sometimes confounded fact, which chokes the Muse, with truth, which is the breath of her nostrils.

Then, again, the inborn eagerness we all have for story-telling, is this to be satisfied by coldly-scientific statements of ascertained facts ? Bare facts are poor food for the fancy. The imagination which stirs us while yet in the cradle is not to be shut out at M. Zola's bidding : indeed, he cannot even shut it out of his own work. When we examine his novels, we find his practice better than his precepts. He is often an artist in spite of himself, as in the 'Faute de l'Abbé Mouret,' for instance ; and again he falls below his doctrine to the other extreme, and gives us in 'Nana' a tale as conventional and cheap as it is dull and obscene. It is but fair to add, that these two stories are units in a series to contain twenty tales, and called collectively the 'Rougon-Macquart, Natural and Social History of a Family under the Second Empire,' laid out on strictly

scientific lines, and having for its backbone the principle of heredity. To prove how the character of each
child is the result of its parentage, he prefixed to one of
his novels a family tree of his double set of personages.
It might surprise M. Zola to be told that Lowell has
shown us how Shakspere had applied the principle of
heredity, making no parade about it, and that in Hamlet
we see the blending of the characteristics of the Queen
and the Ghost. This identity of view between Shakspere and himself may not interest M. Zola; for it
happens that he has a poor opinion of Hamlet, preferring his own Coupeau, the drunkard, whose death from
delirium-tremens gives relief to his novel the 'Assommoir' and to the play taken from it. In the preface to
this play M. Zola says, "I laugh at Hamlet (*je me
moque parfaitement d'Hamlet*), who no longer comes
within my ken, who remains an enigma, a subject for
dissertations; while I am ardently interested at the sight
of Coupeau, whom I can hold fast, and on whom I can
try all sorts of interesting experiments."

A proof of the importance of the drama in France
nowadays, and of the fact that there, at least, it is still
the highest form of literature, can be found in M. Zola's
anxiety for the success of his principles on the stage.
The Naturalists of to-day, like the Romanticists of half
a century ago, look upon the theatre as the final battle-
ground on which their theories must conquer or perish.
With those who have possession of the stage now, M.
Zola is thoroughly dissatisfied. He brushes Hugo aside
impatiently, and sweeps away Scribe. The three chief
Realists of the contemporary drama fare a little better
at his hands. M. Sardou is a prestidigitator who plays
with marionettes, and his "human documents" are

commonplace and second-hand. M. Dumas is a Naturalist at times, and his "human documents" are fresher;
but he is too witty and too clever, and he "uses truth
as a spring-board to jump into space," — to repeat a
quotation I have made before. M. Augier is nearly
always a Naturalist; but his plays are too well made,
and some of his characters are too good to live.

Just what kind of a play M. Zola wants, it would be
hard to say. No play yet acted exactly meets his
views. Three times he has himself come forward as
a dramatist, and the pieces have been damned out of
hand. A dramatization of his novel, the 'Assommoir,'
made by two hack playwrights, was successful; but
M. Zola distinctly disavowed its paternity. A dramatization of 'Nana,' also successful, was made by one
of these playwrights, apparently aided by M. Zola
himself; but neither of these plays has any literary
value. No one of his own three plays fits into his
formula. Two of them are rough and coarse farces,
suggested, one by Ben Jonson's 'Volpone,' the other by
one of Balzac's 'Contes Drôlatiques.' M. Zola's hand
is too heavy for fun, even of the lugubrious kind here
attempted; and such gayety as he can command is
stolid and sodden. The third play, 'Thérèse Raquin,'
is a grim and ghastly drama, full of main strength and
directness, and having the simplicity of genius. It
failed in Paris, but has since had better luck in Italy.
The figure of the paralyzed Madame Raquin, ever present between the two murderers of her son, like a pal-
pable and implacable ghost, gazing at them with eyes
of fire, and gloating motionless over their misery, is a
projection of unmistakable power. If M. Zola had
written nothing but this one play, it would be impossible to contest his ability.

After the Romanticists had declared their principles,
they proceeded at once to put them in practice, and in
'Henri III.' and 'Hernani' exhibited concrete specimens of their theories. The same obligation rests on
the Naturalists; and so far, at least, it has not been
met. For ten years or more, M. Zola has been crying
aloud from the housetop, that reform is necessary in
the drama; but he has not yet proved his case by
showing an example of the improved play. The only
visible effect of his exhortation has been to accentuate
the tendency to the more exact imitation of reality in
the scenery, costumes, and accessories of the stage.
There is a general desire now in the playhouse, wherever it is possible, to substitute the real thing for the
imitation of it, which has hitherto contented both stage-
folk and spectators. Within limits, this taste for exactness is unobjectionable; but it may readily be carried
to excess, and at best it tends to divert attention from
more important parts of the performance, — from the
play and from the playing. It is well to remember that
when there is a real interest in the drama as such, there
is always great indifference to dresses, scenes, and prop-
erties. The play, the play's the thing: all else is of
small account. In two, at least, of the three great outbursts of the drama, in England in Shakspere's time,
and in Spain in Lope de Vega's and Calderon's, when
the drama was the chief expression of the national life,
the mounting of the plays was simple and even shabby.

That the drama at large is to be made over to fit M.
Zola's theories may be doubted; as yet, at any rate,
there are no signs of it: but that they will have a distinct influence on French dramatic art in the immediate
future seems to me indisputable. This influence will

be good in so far as it may make the coming dramatist a more attentive student of life, a closer investigator of human nature, a more diligent seeker after truth, which has to be sought long and earnestly before it yields itself. In so far, however, as it may tend to exclude poetry and imagination, and to limit fiction to the transcript of the bare realities of life, we may unhesitatingly declare it to be doomed to sterility. In so far also as it seeks to decry the technical skill of the trained playwright, it is misleading, and sure of contradiction by the event. It is the abuse, not the use, of technical experience, which is to be decried : it is the production of plays by writers who have no other qualification for the work than their familiarity with the boards. The true dramatist cannot ignore the exigencies of the stage : he ought, indeed, to have so thoroughly mastered all the tricks of the trade, that he can use them unconsciously. In a word, the dramatist should know the grammar of construction so well, that he need give it no more thought than the trained speaker gives to the grammar of language. Shakspere and Molière owed no small share of their success to their complete mastery over the tools of their trade : besides being the hack dramatist of his company, each was actor and manager, and had a share in the takings at the door.

The century begins to draw to a close ; and on the French stage Romanticism and Realism have come forward in turn, and played their parts. It is full twenty years now since M. Victorien Sardou, the youngest of the three chief Realists, made his first appearance. It is time for a new doctrine and for a new man. It may be that Naturalism will be the new doctrine, and M. Zola the new man ; but, for the reasons given in the pre-

ceding pages, I doubt it. That he himself is a potent
force must be admitted ; but that his principles are des-
tined to triumph, I do not believe. To my mind, the
outlook indicates a return, sooner or later, to the well-
made play, to be written by those as deeply imbued
with the desire for physiologic and psychologic accuracy
as M. Zola himself. It will be a union of the school of
the past with what M. Zola proclaims as the school
of the future, blending the best features of both, and so
obliterating the weakness of either. It will, in short,
be that commonplace thing, a compromise. With a
simple and most skilful symmetry of plot, the playwright will have to unite the most vigorous exactness
of character ; and so shall we have a new drama, compounded of the theories of the past and the present.
We may rest content with the prediction of M. Dumas, who declares that whenever there shall come a
writer knowing man like Balzac, and knowing the stage
like Scribe, he will be the great dramatist of the future.

We may be sure, too, that morality will find full expression, consciously or unconsciously, in the plays
of this dramatist of the future, in spite of M. Zola's
precept and practice. We may be sure, also, that the
imagination will not be left out of the compound altogether, if indeed it be not a more potent ingredient
than it is now. And, if we may judge what is to come
by what was gone before, we may fairly expect to find
that the French drama of the few remaining years of
the nineteenth century will not reach deep down into
the depths of humanity, or rise far up in flights of poetry, but that it will cultivate the level table-land of
modern life with extraordinary dexterity and success.
Above all, we may safely prophesy, that for the most

part and in general its note will be the note of comedy, since that is the department of the drama in which the French have always and especially excelled. Molière is greater than Corneille or Racine; Beaumarchais lives while the tragic authors of his time are clean forgotten; and of the ten dramatists whose plays have been considered in the preceding pages, only two, the first and the last, Victor Hugo and Émile Zola, are wanting in the gift of comedy: all the rest — the two Dumas, Augier, Scribe, Sardou, Feuillet, Labiche, Meilhac and Halévy — have found in comedy their best expression. Tragedy calls for a largeness and a freedom foreign to the nature of the Frenchman, readily ruled in all things. Comedy paints the manners of society, and seeks its models there; and nowhere has the art of society been carried to more nearly complete perfection than in France. And comedy affords most scope for that dexterous commingling of gentle sentiment and lively wit which the French excel in, and which an American poet has set forth in four lines : —

> " Black Tragedy lets slip her grim disguise,
>   And shows you laughing lips and roguish eyes;
>   But when, unmasked, gay Comedy appears,
>   'Tis ten to one you find the girl in tears."

CHAPTER XII.

TEN years do not fill a broad space in the lifetime of a nation or in the history of a literature, especially when they are as uneventful as the decade which has slipped past since the earlier chapters of this book were first published. But ten years are ten years after all; and they afford a perspective even though it be contracted. The end of a decade gives a good chance to take stock and to audit our accounts, deciding what must finally be charged off to profit and loss. The development of an art is often as sluggish as the progression of a glacier; yet if three stones be laid on the ice in a straight line, one in the centre and one near either shore, the stone in the middle will be moved forward in ten years' time, and by it we may make a guess at the rate of advance.

Certainly there are some things which can be seen more plainly now than ten years ago. One of these is that Romanticism has run its course. Since the death of Victor Hugo not a few who had kept silent out of deference to him have spoken out boldly. Romanticism had served its purpose when it killed Classicism, falsely so called ; but when it tried to substitute its own cast-iron creed for that which it destroyed, it had a hard fight, and finally it failed. All but the best of the works of the Romanticists seem now almost as old-fashioned and out-worn as the works of the Classicists whom they superseded. It is not threescore years and ten since Victor Hugo raised the standard of revolt, but already the victories he won seem empty and the conquests he made now acknowledge other masters. "In art and poetry," M. Weiss remarks in his suggestive volume of essays on 'Le Théâtre et les Mœurs,' "as in politics and philosophy, there are but a very few truths — always the same : true invention and wholesome originality do not consist in adding to them, but in modernizing their explanation and their practice." The Romanticists sought to substitute for the Greeks, Romans, and Antiquity, Italy, Spain, and the Middle Ages ; but this was not a true modernization, and the inconsequence of their reform and its insubstantiality are now sufficiently obvious. No one of the many dramas of the elder Dumas is alive now, not 'Henri III.,' not the 'Tour de Nesle,' not 'Antony' ; and of Hugo's plays only 'Ruy Blas' and 'Hernani' survive on the stage to this day.

The success of the Romanticists was for a season only ; but it was indisputable while it lasted in every form of art, — sculpture, painting, poetry, music, and the drama. The great movement which followed Romanticism, and for which the Romanticists unwittingly made the path straight, was Naturalism. Looking down the vista of the decade, another thing is quite as obvious as the disappearance of Romanticism ; and this is that the Naturalists, despite their utmost effort, have not yet taken the theatre by storm, — and the theatre was almost the first stronghold of the enemy captured by the Romanticists. Strive as diligently as it can, Naturalism has not yet found its dramatic formula. And here, perhaps, is the character of the past ten years ; they are a period of fumbling in the dark, of feeling toward the light, of unsatisfactory graspings, and of unrewarded endeavor. It may be doubted whether any appreciable progress has been made during the decade. But, perhaps, all inquiry into the existing tendencies of the French drama had best be postponed until after a consideration of the actual work French dramatists have accomplished in the years 1881–1891.

When Hugo died, in 1885, he had brought out in the theatre no new play since the failure of the 'Burgraves' in 1843; and such pieces of his as have been published posthumously, or in the last years of his life, reveal nothing new. They are exactly what one might expect — little more than sketches and fragments left over from the earlier days of dramatic enthusiasm. Eugène Labiche died in 1888, and Emile Augier in 1889; and neither of them had written anything for the stage for more than ten years before his death. The best comedies of both continue to be revived; and while Augier holds his own stanchly, Labiche is probably more highly esteemed now than he was when he gave up work, perhaps because it is only his better plays which are now familiar, while the memory of his unconsidered trifles is fast fading away. Of Augier's strong, nervous, honest comedies, the 'Gendre de M. Poirier,' and the 'Aventurière,' and the 'Fourchambault' seem likely to continue foremost in popular favor.

Yet another of the eleven dramatists considered in detail in the earlier chapters of this book has closed his career recently, — Octave Feuillet; and of the dead he was the only one criticised in these pages with harshness or severity. Sympathy is the germ of fertile criticism; and for Feuillet's novels and comedies, for his theory of life, and for his methods in art, I must still confess a plentiful lack of sympathy. Nor have I found anything to change my opinion in either of the two pieces produced by him since 1881. Neither 'A Parisian Romance' nor 'Chamillac' is to my mind a good play or a wholesome spectacle. The sudden death of a dissipated atheist at the supper-table just when he is proposing a toast to Matter strikes me as tricky, cheap, childish; as Dr. Klesmer, in 'Daniel Deronda,' said of an aria of Bellini's, it indicates "a puerile state of culture — no sense of the universal." And a sense of the universal is just what is wanting in 'Chamillac,' the hero of which is a person of the most strangely contorted and high-strung morality, in whose sayings and doings the audience takes singularly little interest, possibly because the author wilfully chose to keep a secret till the last act, leaving the spectators so far in the dark that they could not see whither the action tended or the motives of the characters. In the drama obscurity is a fatal defect, and a transparent clearness is an absolute necessity, if those who sit in judgment are to follow the story with interest. I had liefer praise Feuillet than not, for he was a gentleman and he wrote with profound respect for himself and for art; but most of his more serious writings seems to me essentially false and insidiously demoralizing. But although I do not like his unreal fictions, it would perhaps be unfair not to suggest that many accomplished critics have admired Feuillet: one of M. Jules Lemaitre's cleverest essays is devoted to the author of 'M. de Camors.' Even M. Lemaitre, however, is moved to complain that the

rarefied "high-life" atmosphere of Feuillet almost makes
him long for the barnyard odors of Zola.

MM. Meilhac and Halévy are now both of them
members of the French Academy, but they are no
longer in partnership. The firm was dissolved nearly
fifteen years ago, and M. Halévy has not since written
for the theatre. Even when the vogue of his charming novel, 'Abbé Constantin,' moved a manager to
ask for a dramatization, M. Halévy left this labor to
other hands. M. Meilhac has not been idle, and no
twelve months pass without the production of a play
from his pen. He writes alone or with chance collaborators ; and his comedies have always wit, grace,
fantasy, and observation ; and they are nearly always
wanting in the unswerving directness of subject which
the stage demands. He is fond of chasing two hares
at once, and while he enjoys the exercise, his guests
often go without their game-pie. His pieces delight the
delicate, but they rarely attract the broader public, which
prefers stronger fare. Yet no man who can appreciate
the play of a subtle intelligence and the exercise of a
brightsome humor has any right to be disappointed at
' Gotte ' or ' Décoré ' or ' Ma Cousine.' No one of
these has any rash American manager ever ventured
to adapt ; and Voltaire declares that "there are no
really good works except those which go to foreign
nations, which are studied there, and translated."
This is a hard saying of Voltaire's, and were it unerr-
ingly applicable, it would bear severely on Augier as
well as on M. Meilhac.

' Le Monde où l'on s'ennuie ' was brought out in
1881, and since then M. Pailleron has produced only one
comedy, the ' Souris,' a scanty showing due, it may be, to

the timidity which is prone to seize a man of letters on the morrow of a triumphant success, just as Sheridan was said to be afraid of the author of the 'School for Scandal.' M. Pailleron is witty, but inclined to be precious and tortured in style. His spontaneity is the result of taking thought, and his effects are often far-fetched. Clever he is, no doubt, but the vogue of 'Le Monde où l'on s'ennuie' seemed accidental and inordinate. The 'Souris' suffered from the comparison, and its chilly reception can be measured by the gibe of a fellow-dramatist to the effect that M. Pailleron was a lucky fellow since he had two of his plays at the Théâtre Français at the same time, — the 'Souris' on the stage and *le monde où l'on s'ennuie* in the house.

Edmond Gondinet, who died only two or three years ago, was a dramatist of ampler gifts than M. Pailleron and of a wider experience. Though his hand was uncertain, and though he left behind him few pieces which show him at his best, his gifts for the stage were indisputable. He had originality, deftness, and the literary touch; but much of his time was wasted in fruitless collaborations, despite the obvious fact that his best work was done alone — excepting always the 'Plus Heureux des Trois,' in the writing of which he had Labiche for his partner. The 'Parisien' was the last comedy of Gondinet's to be acted at Théâtre Français ; it was a bright but inconclusive piece, with just a hint of sentiment. After the play written in partnership with Labiche, probably the most characteristic of Gondinet's pieces were the 'Panache' and the highly amusing 'Gavaut, Minard et Cie.'

Perhaps it is not fair to M. Bisson to compare him with Gondinet, whose successor in some sort he seems to be. Gondinet was a humorous dramatist; M. Bisson is merely a comic playwright; and the difference is fundamental. Yet M. Bisson's 'Député de Bombignac' was acted for many a night by the Comédie-Française with M. Coquelin as the hero; and the 'Surprises du Divorce' would make a Vermont deacon laugh out in meeting. The last play Sir Roger de Coverley had been at was the 'Committee,' "which I should not have gone to, neither," the worthy knight explained, "had I not been told beforehand that it was a good Church of England comedy." Perhaps it would be an exaggeration to liken the 'Surprises du Divorce' to the 'Committee,' but the French farce, despite its title and a stray note or two of bad taste, is innocent enough. Farce stands to comedy, I take it, in a relation like that borne by melodrama to tragedy, in that action predominates over thought, plot is more prominent than character, what is done has a far greater importance than what is said or felt; but although farce and melodrama are doubtless inferior, they are quite as legitimate forms of the drama as comedy and tragedy. A really good farce is almost as great a rarity as a good comedy; and there is no need to despair of French dramatists as long as they are capable of a farce as unfailingly and persistently funny as the 'Surprises,' a marvel of constructive skill, without hurry or hesitation, and with the utmost tribute of laughter adroitly expressed from every situation. Even the master-magician of the modern stage, M. Sardou, could not have extracted more fun out of the theme, although there would have been some tincture of literature in the play had he written it.

Of all the French dramatists to whom the earlier chapters of this volume have been devoted, M. Sardou is the only one who has retained his productivity. In the past ten years he has produced ten plays. Of these, 'Georgette,' 'Marquise,' and the 'Crocodile' were flat failures; 'Odette' and 'Cléopâtre' were little better; 'Belle-Maman,' 'Théodora,' and 'La Tosca' met with a fair measure of success; 'Thermidor' was suppressed by the government because its pictures of the Revolution gave rise to rioting; and 'Fédora' is the only play of the ten the popularity of which rivalled that of the better pieces of M. Sardou's earlier career. The most of these plays were careless in workmanship, hasty in construction, slovenly in their writing. Voltaire says that a man always talks ill when he has nothing to say, so it is easy to account for the ill-writing in most of these later plays. French critics did not hesitate to accuse M. Sardou of working for the export trade — of thinking more of the possible receipts of the performances in London, New York, San Francisco, and Melbourne, than of the artistic presentation of his subject to the Parisian public.

Four of these ten plays were written for Mme. Sarah Bernhardt, as clever and as careless in her art as is M. Sardou in his, and equally wanting in respect for her audiences. There is a certain fitness in their conjunction, and they seem made for each other, the actress for the author and the author for the actress, both being possessed of surpassing cleverness and both having a taint of charlatanry; but none the less did the alliance prove disastrous to both parties and together both deteriorated. 'Fédora' is the first play of the four and by far the best; 'Théodora,' the second, is inferior; 'La Tosca,' the third, is weaker yet; and 'Cléopâtre,' the last, is the least of all. And the strongest of them,

'Fédora,' is a brutal play, holding the spectator breathless, with a violent physical oppression, as though he was held down by a nightmare he was powerless to throw off. But it is a masterpiece of technic; the joinery is most artful; and the fitting together of the various parts is as clever as can be. Mr. James was right when he called M. Sardou a "supremely skilful contriver and arranger." In its way and of its kind nothing better than 'Fédora' has ever been seen on the stage; but the kind is one that the stage could spare without serious loss.

"The man of talents possesses them like so many tools, does his job with them, and there an end," Mr. Lowell tells us; "but the man of genius is possessed by it, and it makes him into a book or a life according to its whim. Talent takes the existing moulds, and makes its castings, better or worse, of richer or baser metal, according to knack and opportunity; but genius is always shaping new ones and runs the man in them, so that there is always that human feel in its results which gives us a kindred thrill." M. Sardou is a man of talents, beyond all question, but may one venture to term M. Alexandre Dumas *fils* a man of genius? When I contrast his later plays with M. Sardou's, I am inclined to risk the phrase, for the difference between the two dramatists grows apace; and it strikes me now as wider and more radical than ever before.

And yet I doubt if either of the two plays which M. Dumas has produced during this decade has raised my opinion of him. Neither 'Denise' nor 'Francillon,' pathetic as is the first, and brilliant as is the second, and interesting as they both are, is a work of the calibre and range of the 'Demi-Monde.' But in both can be seen a power beyond M. Sardou's, because

M. Dumas has so sure a knowledge of the tricks of the trade that he can dispense with them and move us without their aid. There are men and women now and again in the plays of M. Dumas, while in M. Sardou's later pieces we soon discover that all the dolls are stuffed with sawdust. Of M. Dumas's sincerity I may still have my doubts, although I incline more and more to the opinion that M. Dumas at least believes in himself. But of his ability, of his intellectual force, of his gift for propounding social puzzles and so setting people thinking, and above all, of his dramaturgic skill and of his sense of form, there cannot be two opinions. Both 'Denise' and 'Francillon' have a solid simplicity of structure worthy of all praise.

In both plays M. Dumas has a subject other than his mere story, — a theme which the incidents of his drama are intended to demonstrate. In 'Denise,' he raises again the question he first put forth in 'Idées de Madame Aubray,' — Is a single lapse from virtue sufficient to bar a girl from marriage to a man who knows her history and who loves her and respects her in spite of it? In 'Francillon,' the inquiry is, Whether there is an equal obligation on both parties to a marriage contract to be faithful to each other, or whether the infidelity of the husband justifies that of the wife? In 'Denise' M. Dumas decides as he decided in the 'Idées de Madame Aubray'; and as is his wont, he has a personal mouthpiece in his own play, a condensation of the multiplex Greek Chorus into a single personality, charged with the duty of delivering a most Parisian parabasis. In 'Denise,' the name of this *deus ex machina* in a dress-coat is Thouvenin; and even the skill of M. Dumas is tasked to the utmost to get our

attention to the preachments of this obtruding character.
In 'Francillon,' with far better art, the events as they
succeed swiftly set forth their own moral; and there
needs no lecturer to explain the figures. But 'Francillon' lacks the final sincerity of 'Denise,' where the
author poses his problem and forces us to accept his
solution. In the latter comedy M. Dumas dodges —
there is no other word for it. He plays a trick on us,
a practical joke of the most dazzling description, but
still a practical joke only. If Francillon is innocent,
if she has told a lie when she confesses her fault, then
the comedy is but a *vaudeville à la Scribe*, not to be
taken seriously; and we need not make believe that it
ever happened. M. Dumas has been playing the game
for its own sake, and not for the possible profit. In
mere dramaturgic art, in the technic of the playwright,
nothing can be swifter, bolder, better, than 'Francillon';
it is a marvel and a despair to all other makers of plays.
And it is written with sustained brilliancy, — and of the
best kind, — since the wit is struck out by the situations
and by the characters and loses its effect when detached.

It is to be noted that M. Dumas did not dramatize his
novel, the 'Affaire Clémenceau,' just as M. Halévy left
the adaptation of the 'Abbé Constantin' to other hands.
Having been dramatists before they were novelists,
M. Dumas and M. Halévy knew the impossibility of
making satisfactory plays out of their stories, so they
put off on others the responsibility of the attempt. The
one playwright who has pushed to the front in the past
ten years is a story-teller, also, all of whose dramas are
presented to the public as novels first; this is M.
Georges Ohnet, the author of 'Serge Panine,' the
'Maître de Forges,' the 'Comtesse Sarah,' and the

'Grande Marnière,' — works which have had an enormous sale in the bookstores (and some of them a success almost as overwhelming on the stage), and which either in the library or in the theatre stand wholly outside of literature. The *pièces Ohnettes*, as the small wits of the boulevard call them, make even the hastiest play of M. Sardou's seem literary. M. Ohnet's methods are the acme of the commonplace, the conventional, and the cut-and-dried ; and in his pieces we know every character almost before he opens his mouth, we foresee every situation at the first word of preparation, and we recognize as an old friend almost every phrase of the dialogue. "All copyists are contemptible," Mr. Ruskin has said ; "but the copyist of himself is the most so, for he has the worst original."

This summary, imperfect though it must needs be, of the theatrical output in Paris during the decade, shows that no new French dramatist of high rank has come forward within this period. It is significant of the changing condition of literature in France that in the past ten years three novelists of unusual endowment have made themselves known to us, — M. Guy de Maupassant, M. Paul Bourget, and "Pierre Loti," as he calls himself. Nowadays the young man of high literary expectations finds his account rather in prose fiction than in writing for the stage. At last the novel is almost as profitable as the play ; and of course the story pays even better than the play if it is set upon the stage after it has conquered success in the bookstores.

Literary tendencies may be likened to the currents of the air ; we can see the clouds moving above us, but we know that the winds are changeable and capricious, blowing by fits and starts, and often two ways at once.

and it is not always easy to tell which of the two struggling breezes is the stronger and will bring the final
storm. The weather-wise, nevertheless, hardly doubt
that to-day in France, as in Spain and in America,
there is an overmastering tendency toward Naturalism.
It is a fact that four or five of the foremost French
novelists are now adherents of the Naturalistic school.
Slowly these writers, M. Zola and M. Daudet at the
head of them, have made their way to the forefront of
French fiction, and now they are seeking for success in
the theatre also. At first they allowed more practised
playwrights to shape their stories for the stage; M. Bus-
nach lent M. Zola his experience in dramatizing 'Germinal,' and M. Belot aided M. Daudet in making a play
out of 'Froment jeune et Risler ainé.' With increas-
ing experience, the novelists are gaining self-reliance;
M. Zola himself modified 'La Curée' into 'Renée';
M. Daudet dramatized 'Sapho' without assistance; and
M. de Goncourt was solely responsible for the stage versions of 'Germinie Lacerteux' and of the 'Fille Élisa.'

That no one of these dramatizations was wholly
satisfactory is due chiefly to the fact that the novels
of the Naturalists lend themselves with difficulty to the
dramatizer, as they are far less fit for the purpose of
the theatre than the stories of the old Romanticists,
and they suffer far more in the transfer. A liberal share
of M. Zola's powers abandon him when his fictions are
produced in the theatre without the aid of his sturdy
and strenuous faculty of description. Rank strength
is perhaps his chief characteristic; and on the stage he
is shaven and shorn perforce. 'Germinal,' for example,
one might call the strongest story of the past ten years;
there was in it not a little of the splendid sweep of a

great epic; it had the irresistible and inevitable movement of a solemn tragedy; but taken from the pages of
a book and put on the boards of a theatre, nearly all
this evaporated, and there was little left but a rather
vulgar panorama of violence and suffering.

In like manner the essential element of M. Daudet's
'Sapho' was dissipated when she was presented to us in
the person of Mme. Jane Hading, and in only five acts—
a division quite insufficient to show adequately the flux
and reflux of contending duty and desire, and yet quite
enough to lay bare the apparent monotony of the incidents.   Perhaps it was the perception of this which has
led M. Daudet to come forward as an original dramatist.
His last two plays, the 'Lutte pour la Vie' and the
'Obstacle,' are not adapted novels like 'Sapho' and
'Numa Roumestan'; nor is either elaborated from a
short story like the 'Arlésienne.'   They were written
for the stage in the first instance, and they are therefore most interesting experiments, tentative no doubt,
but indisputably promising.   They have manifest signs
of inexperience, but they indicate that M. Daudet is
feeling the way, and that he is determined to "know the
ropes" before he gives up.

Mr. Brownell has told us that "of every problem
which the French artist attacks, he knows in advance
various authoritative and accepted solutions," and that
"irresistibly he is impelled to take advantage of these."
In no art is this truer than in the dramaturgic, and as
a result there is no art more bound by convention.   In
no other form of literary endeavor is it as difficult to
get free from the shackles of tradition.   So it happens
that while the technic of many French plays is absolutely impeccable, they have the smooth perfection of

machine-work. As Mr. Brownell's Italian fellow-traveller said to him, the French " charge you more for potatoes *au naturel* than for potatoes served in any other way." M. Daudet is one of those who are discovering by personal experience that it is more difficult for a Frenchman to serve potatoes *au naturel* than *sautées* or *soufflées,* as his countrymen have been accustomed to see potatoes served.

M. Henri Becque is another. M. Becque is unlike his fellow-Naturalists in that he is a dramatist primarily, and not at all a novelist. He is the author of the 'Corbeaux' and of the 'Parisienne,' plays of a hard originality both of them, of a dark vigor and of an uncompromising directness. Both of them have been acted by the Comédie-Française ; and neither met with popular approval, notwithstanding its remarkable qualities. M. Becque is a leader in the search for a new theatrical formula. He declares that the existing dramatic moulds are hopelessly worn out. He hates the "patent buffer-and-coupler" play quite as much as Mr. Howells, and with a far deeper understanding of the principles which underlie the art of play-making. Yet M. Becque in his distaste for the conventional is on the verge of denouncing all convention, forgetting that convention is the foundation of every art. In the drama, for example, it is a condition of the existence of the art, that the fourth side shall be taken off the room so that the spectators can see what is going on within. It is a condition also that the actors shall so raise their voices above the ordinary and so face the footlights, that the audience can hear them. The comedian must allow for the perspective of the stage, and therefore he cannot act as he would really in life, but with just sufficient exaggeration or emphasis that he may appear to be absolutely natural when seen from afar. So also the dramatist must simplify, explain, make clear, condense, and heighten his story, that it may be presented completely within two or three hours, so that a thousand men and women of average intelligence can apprehend its movement and its meaning. I have no desire to defend the "patent buffer-and-coupler" play — far from it; but if I am going a journey unto a far country, I know that a proper buffer-and-coupler will spare me many a jolt.

The Naturalists, like all reformers, are inclined to be intolerant. They are prone also to claim all the virtue for their own party. But it was a professional playwright, a master of every secret of the dramaturgic art, M. Alexandre Dumas *fils*, who broke the bonds of the Scribe formulas forty years ago and let a flood of fresh air into the theatre. M. Meilhac, in collaboration with M. Halévy, and with other of his chance assistants, and alone, has repeatedly served a most appetizing dish of potatoes *au naturel.* So did Gondinet, now and again. So once, in a way, did two hardened veterans of the theatre, MM. Blum and Toché, in 'Paris Fin-de-Siècle,' a play as plotless and as amusing as any one could wish, a satirically humorous collection of scenes from real life, strung together anyhow. Here occasion serves to say that it is only an experienced cook who can prepare a simple dish, and that the "picture of real life" is most likely to be painted by the men who best understand all the devices of the studio; neither Mr. Harrigan nor the author of the 'Old Homestead' is a novice.

It is a strange truth also — and it is one that helps to explain the lack of success the Naturalists have met with in the plays they have produced as yet — that while a man may be a pessimist alone, in a multitude he is inclined to be an optimist. By himself, at his own fireside, he may be eager to gaze on a picture of total depravity, and to exalt ' Barry Lyndon ' over ' Henry Esmond ' as the more enjoyable work of art ; yet in company with his fellows, in the seats of a theatre, he likes a suggestion of heroism or self-sacrifice, and he is moved to resent M. Zola's habit of holding an inquest on humanity in the presence of the corpse. So far the Naturalists have found it very difficult to overcome the desire for idealization which seems to exist among the body of play-goers, although this very mass is composed of individuals who are ready enough to read ' Sapho ' and ' Germinal ' at home. And the plain speaking also which a man will stand when it is a whisper in his private ear, shocks him into protest when he touches elbows with some hundreds of his fellow-men.

A consciousness of this curious fact has been the cause of the most peculiar development in the French stage during the past ten years. This is the founding of the Théâtre Libre. M. Antoine, an enthusiast for the drama and an extremist in his application of the doctrines of Naturalism, has given a series of subscription performances in Paris during the past five or six winters, at which he has produced plays of the new school such as had no hope of acceptance by the managers of the regular theatres. Among the pieces he has brought out for two or three performances only are Tolstoï's ' Powers of Darkness ' and Ibsen's ' Ghosts.' Another is M. Hennique's matter-of-fact tragic sketch, ' La Mort du Duc d'Enghien.' Yet another is M. de Goncourt's

'Fille Élisa.' All of these are experiments most curious to witness. And all of them have had the advantage of the undeniably effective stage-management of
M. Antoine, who has taught a trick or two to his
predecessors. But many of the plays he has produced
have been both dirty and dull; and most of them have
been hard, cold, unfeeling, laboriously unconventional,
wholly devoid of inspiration. The Théâtre Libre has
been little more than a dramatic dissecting-room for
the dreary exhibition of offensive subjects. That it
exists, however, that it is sustained year after year,
that its performances excite ardent discussion, — these
are all signs of the vitality of the drama in France,
even if they have no further significance.

To sum up the ten years, 1881–1891, and to declare
their total value is not yet possible, although it is easy
to see that the decade has been a time of transition —
like every other decade of the world's history. No new
dramatist has taken his place by the side of Augier,
M. Dumas, and M. Sardou. No new formula has won
acceptance. There is an irrepressible conflict between
the new school and the old, but the result of the struggle is likely to be a slow evolution rather than a sudden
revolution. And so best, no doubt; for the Jacobin
and the Jacobite are as dangerous, one as the other.
It is to be remembered also that the most diverse colors
in the spectrum of art, if we may so call it, as we gaze
at it through the prism of history, range themselves in
regular order and melt one into the other by insensible
gradations. In the present condition of the French
drama the extreme Naturalists are at one end, and the
extreme Idealists at the other, — and, as usual, safety
is in the centre.

CHAPTER XIII.

AT THE END OF THE CENTURY.

In his essay on Gray, Lowell said: "Let us admit that the eighteenth century was, on the whole, prosaic, yet it may have been a pretty fair one as centuries go," and he added, with characteristic shrewdness, "every age is as good as the people who live in it choose to make it, and if good enough for them, perhaps we, who had no hand in the making of it, can complain of it only so far as it had a hand in the making of us." Now as the nineteenth century is leaving us for ever, let us admit that it has been a pretty fair century on the whole, — not prosaic like its predecessor, which had a hand in the making of it, but essentially poetic, as perhaps no earlier century can have been, in so far as vast vistas of speculation have been suddenly disclosed to the mind of man. A practical century, it has been, no doubt; but then every other century must also have been practical, since the day's work had always to be done. Never before has man been less bound down to mere journeyman labor; never before has life been so strangely interesting, with so constant a succession of surprises, due to our conquest of nature and to our expansion of knowledge.

It may be that the twentieth century — which the nineteenth has had a hand in making — will be prosaic again, that it will settle down and seek to set in order what its predecessor has poured out lavishly, that it will be content to live in the past rather than in the future, that it will be critical rather than creative. Should this come to pass, the critics and the commentators will find ready for their investigation and evaluation a certain number of movements, more or less complete, in the hundred years that followed 1800, — movements of less importance, indeed, than the Renascence or the Reformation, or the Decline and Fall, but none the less well worthy of inquiry and analysis. For example, the rise of Transcendentalism in the United States and its effect on American character, — here is a theme to be handled satisfactorily only after a due interval of time. As M. Jules Lemaître has assured us, "criticism of the works of yesterday is not criticism; it is conversation," — a harsh saying this to come from the author of the 'Contemporains.' Again, the final weighing of each of the remarkable group of British writers whom we are wont to call the Victorian poets and the investigation of the true relation of each of them to the others — here we have a subject likely to task the best critical faculty of the twentieth century. And a third theme, as rich as either of the others, I think, and as tempting, can be discerned in the development of the drama in France during the half-century that stretches from 1830 to 1880.

All that took place in the playhouses of Paris before the first performance of 'Hernani' may be regarded as but the preparation and the prelude of that startling event; and all that has happened there since the first performance of 'Le Monde où l'on s'ennuie' cannot be considered as of primary importance in itself, for no one of the plays of the final twenty years of the century is epoch-making, — no one of them has more than a secondary importance, as it either continues the tradi-

tion of the 1830–1880 period, or more or less obviously
protests against that tradition. The Romantic movement made smooth a path for the Realistic movement
that followed it inevitably; and Hugo and the elder
Dumas lived to see their formulas and their philosophy
disestablished by Augier and the younger Dumas. But
in the final decades of the century it was seen that
Realism had spent its force, and yet no new movement
had swept forward to renew the drama again. No new
man has come boldly to the front to declare a fresh set
of principles, and to impose his formulas and his philosophy upon his more impressionable contemporaries.
The last twenty years of the century are not so blank
as were the first thirty, — from which little or nothing
now survives; but they supply us with scanty indication
of the lines along which the drama is likely to modify
itself in the immediate future.

The year 1830 is still a date to be remembered, and
the battle of 'Hernani' remains a picturesque episode
in literary history; and yet, as we look down on the
struggle now from the height of the threescore years
and ten that have elapsed, — the span of a man's life
already, — the conflict seems petty and the result inconclusive. The Classicists were feeble folk, all of them,
and they had no strength to withstand the first onslaught; there was no life in them or in the theories
which they thought they were defending; they were
dead, even if they did not know it. What vitality can
there be in a criticism which asserts that tragedy must
fulfil twenty-six conditions, while comedy need fulfil
only twenty-two, and the epic only twenty-three, — and
which is ready with a list of the twenty-six conditions,
the twenty-two, and the twenty-three? What real glory

is to be gained by overcoming antagonists as pettily pedantic as these?

The Romanticists began bravely, but they did not persist. They routed the Classicists readily enough, but, when their foes were overthrown, they did not press on to other victories. They were content to rest on their laurels; and very early did keen critics discover the inherent weakness of their attitude. Maurice de Guérin, for example, said that Romanticism had "put forth all its blossom prematurely, and had left itself a helpless prey to the returning frost." The real reason for this sterility was that the core of Romanticism was revolt. In so far as it was destructive, it was successful; and it did not really set out to be constructive. As M. Souriau points out in his acute and scholarly edition of the preface of 'Cromwell,' Romanticism "is rather a reaction than a renascence"; and he quotes from the elder Dumas to the effect that in those days the ardent young fellows were in doubt as to what they wanted, but they were in no doubt as to what they did not want.

Not only were their literary doctrines negative rather than affirmative, but they strove to throw off all restraint and to denounce all rule. As a typical hero they were prone to present an outlaw, who added to acts that were illegal a birth that was illegitimate and loves that were illicit. Hernani is a bandit and Antony is a bastard. To the men of 1830, the most complex problem of all times was simple; they saw no difficulty in the relation of man to society, and in the proper restraint of the right of the individual to assert himself, when his self-assertion may be harmful to the community. They proclaimed the complete liberty of the individual; and they never declared the duty of every man to sacrifice himself, if need be, for the good of all the rest. Carried to their logical conclusion, their principles led straight to anarchy, with every man a law unto himself. As Thiers said in 1871, when the French republic was fighting for its life, "The Romanticists — that's the Commune!"

Much high-flown eulogy of the famous books of the past is as unimpressive now as the perfunctory flattery of an epitaph in which manifold and contradictory virtues are imperishably inscribed. The praise is all very well in its way, but the real question is, does the famous book keep on being read? The proof of the play is the acting. After two centuries, the one or two masterpieces of Corneille and the two or three masterpieces of Racine still hold the attention of French playgoers. But of all the plays of the elder Dumas none keeps the stage to-day, except possibly one or another of his lighter comedies in which the Romanticism has been reduced to the vanishing point. Of all Hugo's dramas in prose and verse only 'Hernani' and 'Ruy Blas' survive in the theatre. Here the selection of time seems as satisfactory as it always must. These are the two plays in which Hugo's merits are most abundantly displayed, and in which his demerits are diminished. They, in their turn, are beginning to be considered as classics. It was Goethe who declared that the important point for a work of art is that it should be "thoroughly good, and then it is sure to be classical. I call the classic healthy, the romantic sickly." Perhaps it is a little difficult to assert that 'Hernani' and 'Ruy Blas' are really healthy in tone; but there is no doubt that they are the least sickly of all Hugo's plays.

One may wonder what Goethe would have thought of

the Realistic movement that followed the Romanticist. Would he have relished Balzac? Would he have found 'Madame Bovary' healthy? How would he have enjoyed the 'Demi-Monde' of the younger Dumas and the 'Gendre de M. Poirier' of Augier and Sandeau? Recalling Goethe's profound delight in Molière, we may guess that the 'Gendre de M. Poirier' would have pleased him. But while the 'Demi-Monde' would have interested him indubitably, we cannot be sure just how the author of 'Elective Affinities' would have taken it. Of this thing, however, we may be certain: Goethe would have seen and acknowledged the dramaturgic skill of Augier and the younger Dumas, for he had the craftsman's liking for technic.

Less gaudy than Romanticism, but richer as a topic for investigation, is the history of the so-called "well-made play," *la pièce bien faite.* As it happens, we can trace almost every step in the career of this formula, — its beginning, its rise, its development, its modification, and its decadence at last. Suggested, perhaps, by Beaumarchais, the form was carried to the highest point of mechanical complexity by Scribe; then it was simplified by the younger Dumas and accepted by Augier, having Sarcey for its press-agent; until, in the end, it wore out its welcome and was rejected of the Théâtre Libre, which refused to be bound by any formula whatsoever.

What is the formula of the well-made play? When Regnard, who followed in Molière's footsteps more faithfully than he knew, imitated the master also in writing a critique on one of his comedies that had been attacked, he tried to show that the first act of his play "exposes the subject; the second ties the knot; in the third the action begins; it is continued in the following acts; everything concurs in the event; the complication grows until the final scene; the *dénoûment* is drawn from the heart of the subject." Here Regnard comes very near to giving us the definition we seek. A well-made play is a piece having a beginning, a middle, and an end (as every work of art ought to have), and containing nothing that does not help in the movement of the plot. In a perfect play of this type, every scene is carefully prepared for, and led up to, and so is every character; every situation inherent in the theme is treated in its proper place and in its due proportion; there are no digressions, however alluring the opportunity; and nothing is allowed to interfere with the more or less intricate convolutions of the plot. Such a play is the 'Bataille de Dames,' of Scribe and Legouvé, or the 'Pattes de Mouche' of M. Sardou. Such a play at its best is likely to be a marvel of ingenuity in invention and construction. Such a play, when its writer was not a master mechanic or was not at his best, is likely to be hard and dry, empty and unsatisfactory.

It was Scribe who had perfected this mechanism, and who applied the formula most rigorously. The best of Scribe's plays are masterpieces of dramaturgy; but the breath of life is not in them. He delighted in dexterity for its own sake; and, in his eyes, the playwright was a rival to the juggler who keeps three brass balls in the air with one hand, while with the other he spins a bowl on the end of a rod. Mere craftsmanship can go no further; but while he was playing his tricks, the drama was getting divorced from literature. Yet the influence of Scribe was so potent toward the middle of the century, and he had so completely succeeded in imposing his standards upon the playgoing public, that even authors of marked individuality, men who looked at life with their own eyes, Augier and the younger Dumas, could not help following in his footsteps, even when they were resolved to go their several ways. A certain artificiality, a certain theatricalness, a certain complacency in adroitness, which we discover now and again even in their best plays, may be set down as the result of the overwhelming vogue of Scribe in the days when Augier and Dumas began their careers as dramatists.

Although a humorist, like Labiche, and a pair of wits, like Meilhac and Halévy, chose to learn the formula of the well-made play, and could apply it when they saw fit, they rebelled against its restrictions, which irked their vagabond fantasy. In some of their more frolicsome pieces they refused to be bound by it. They reverted to more primitive and easier formulas, like that which Molière had been content to employ in one or another of his earlier pieces, — the 'Étourdi,' for example, and the 'Facheux,' — before he had learned how to achieve the solid structure of 'Tartuffe.' They did not develop their theme with narrow and inexorable logic; rather did they play with it, showing now this aspect of it, and now that. The 'Chapeau de paille d'Italie' of Labiche and the 'Boule' of Meilhac and Halévy are each of them a sequence of comic scenes, having about as much unity as a string of sausages. They are humorous panoramas of life rather than organic comedies. Their plots are so loosely knit that almost any act might be omitted without being missed. And no doubt not a little of the freshness and the frank fun of these pieces is to be credited to the refusal of their authors to accept the limitations of the well-made play.

The partnership of Meilhac and Halévy had been dissolved when the century had nearly a quarter of its course to run, and at the very moment when the full effect of the plays they had produced was beginning to be visible. As it happened, the realist novel was just then entering on its period of vogue; and under the lead of Daudet and M. Zola, not a few of the younger story-tellers came to believe that the background was quite as important and as interesting as the grouping of the characters themselves. This could not but have its echo on the stage also. Yet it is chiefly to the influence of Meilhac and Halévy that we must ascribe the fragmentary construction which is to be observed in many of the pieces performed during the final years of the century. But whereas the authors of 'Froufrou' had known from their youth up what the well-made play was, and what were the principles of its construction, even though they often preferred to depart from the formula, their later followers, M. Henri Lavedan, for instance, and M. Maurice Donnay, have not mastered the art of play-making in the same severe school. These younger men, clever as they are, and witty and observant, have to be contented with a casual structure because they do not know any better. Their works are therefore a little too sketchy; they are a little too lavish of minor details; they are frequently overneglectful of the main subject, and overwilling to sacrifice the essential scene for the accidental effect. They have not gone quite so far as the even more ignorant enthusiasts of the Théâtre Libre who took the final step, and at one fell swoop cast aside all the accepted principles of the dramatic art as well as all the ordinary decencies of life, and whose plays are many of them to be described as unactable, unreadable, unspeakable.

Underlying the formula of the well-made play was a sound principle which the dramatist can disregard only at his peril. This principle is as old as Aristotle, who tells us that the plot "must have for its object a single action, whole and complete, with a beginning, a middle, and an end, that, like a single living organism, it may produce its appropriate pleasure." What Scribe and his disciples did was to cramp the drama by applying this principle too narrowly. The principle itself is one which every great dramatist has accepted and obeyed, — Sophocles in 'Œdipus the King,' and Shakspere in 'Othello,' no less than Molière in the 'Femmes Savantes,' and Ibsen in 'Ghosts.'

As Aristotle was the critic and theorist of the Greek drama, so the late Francisque Sarcey was the critic and theorist of the French drama of the nineteenth century. Toward the end of his career, it is true that his mind lost a little of its former flexibility ; but this is only what often happens to old men. He was the most philosophic of all critics of the acted drama since Lessing. His code of maxims was not made up out of his own head arbitrarily, or taken over second-hand from the books of his library ; it was derived, like Aristotle's and like Lessing's also, from a long-continued, very careful, and most conscientious study of the theatre of his own time. He had the equipment of a scholar and the insight of a true critic. He was extremely expert in disentangling the real point at issue, and in applying to it the decisive principle. More than one of the commonplaces of current French dramatic criticism was an original discovery of Sarcey's.

For example, a favorite phrase of his was to the effect that in a given play the author had or had not shirked the scene he ought to have treated, the *scène à faire*, the scene that must be in the play. Here Sarcey condensed into three words an inviolable principle of dramatic construction, that the essential situation of the story must be shown on the stage in action. If the subject calls for a meeting of two characters at the crisis of the piece, this meeting must take place in sight of the audience. It cannot pass behind closed doors or between the acts; it cannot be told by a messenger; it must be seen and heard directly by the spectators, who are expecting it, although, of course, they do not know just what it is they do expect. If it is not presented to them, they will be disappointed; they will feel vaguely that they have been balked of a pleasure somehow, and they will be dissatisfied. Perhaps one reason why Sarcey esteemed the well-made play so highly is that it is always certain to contain the one or more *scènes à faire* implicit in its theme. The scene in which Iago distils the poison of jealousy into the ear of the unsuspicious Othello, the scene in which Tartuffe makes love to Elmire while Orgon is hidden under the table, the scene in which Lady Teazle tells the truth to Sir Peter after the screen has fallen, — all these are *scènes à faire*. In the final analysis, what we seek in the theatre is the pleasure the art of acting can bestow; and it is the earmark of a genuine *scène à faire* that it always gives the actors their best chance.

The success of the 'Étourdi' and of the 'Chapeau de paille d'Italie' shows that the comic dramatist need not always follow the formula of the well-made play; but in the final years of the nineteenth century in Paris,

the failure of many a comedy brisk with incident and
character and bristling with witty speeches is proof
that a comic dramatist can disregard the *scène à faire*
only at his peril.   Of course, plot-making can be overdone, as Scribe exemplified; but it can be underdone
also, as only too many recent French plays make
evident.   The proper protest against the undue insist-
ence upon mere mechanical ingenuity has led to a
loose slovenliness of form, which in its turn is bringing
about a reaction.   The French, after all, are very Latin
in their likings; they joy in beholding the orderly
framework of a play put together in due obedience to
the traditions of the craft.   They may tolerate a laxity
of structure sometimes, but they do not really admire it.
The reaction against the happy-go-lucky method of play-
making is likely also to be aided greatly by the strong
impression which Ibsen's social dramas have made
upon the Parisian public, and the high esteem in which
the Scandinavian dramatist is held by the more serious
of the French critics.

No modern literature has been less swerved aside by
foreign example than the French; and none has gone
on its own way with less hesitation; and yet in the
course of history French literature has received a succession of vivifying shocks from one foreign source or
another.   In the Renaissance it was Italy that gave
this stimulus; to Corneille it came from Spain, and to
Rousseau from England; the share of Germany in
bringing to pass the Romanticist revolt is large enough,
although perhaps not to be declared with precision.
The latest irritants come from still further North, —
from Russia and from Scandinavia.   Just what effect
the example of Tolstoy will have on the French drama

no one can even venture to guess now; as the Russian is known chiefly as a novelist and scarcely at all as a dramatist, his influence on the writers of plays is likely to be somewhat indirect, — although to say this is not to say that it may not in time prove to be powerful. Yet I doubt if it will be very potent, except in so far as his broad toleration, his immense sympathy, his abundant compassion, may be contagious and may help to soften the hardness and the contempt which are marked characteristics of the writings of Flaubert and of his school. On the whole, Tolstoy's ideal is too remote from that of the French themselves, for them to be able to cherish it and to adopt it.

But Ibsen is a dramatist; so far as mere dramaturgic skill goes, he is one of the greatest of all dramatists. Almost every one of his social dramas has been performed in Paris; and even though some of them have been acted but two or three times, still they have been seen on the stage, — the only true proving-ground of a genuine dramatist's work. Few of these plays really pleased the Parisians, — and why should they? Ibsen is not Gallic, but very Scandinavian; he is not at all gay, indeed he is austere. But after they had seen a certain number of these Scandinavian austerities, they came away dissatisfied with the ordinary Parisian play. However inacceptable their ethical code may seem sometimes to us Anglo-Saxons, the French are moralists to the marrow; and what they seek on the stage is "a picture of life, — which is also a judgment." They may not have recognized the picture of life to which Ibsen called their attention, and they may have refused to accept his judgment on the case presented; but they could not but see where Ibsen had set a higher stand-

ard, ethically and esthetically, than their own later
dramatists.

The symbolism, the vagueness, the mysticism —
which to many of us are the least interesting phase of
Ibsen's later works — puzzled the Parisians repeatedly.
Many of the characters he had projected into life were
far too bold and reckless in asserting their right to live
out their own lives in their own way, to please a people
governed by the social instinct as the French are. The
occasional morbidness, the lack of wholesome material
sometimes, the merely Scandinavian problem presented
once or twice in place of one of the eternal and universal puzzles of human existence, — all these things tended
to disconcert the French playgoing public. But no
people could more heartily appreciate Ibsen's merciless
logic and his severity of form.

It may be fanciful in me, but I have always wondered
whether or not the social dramas of Ibsen are what
they are, because the militant comedies of the younger
Dumas preceded them, — just as these comedies in
their turn are what they are because they had for fore-
runners Scribe's ingenious plays. Scribe had a complexity of plot, and, so far as may be, no moral whatsoever.
Dumas did away with the half of Scribe's machinery;
and he insisted on pointing the moral, getting up himself to declare it, if occasion served. Now Ibsen has
gone a step farther, profiting by the labors both of
Scribe and Dumas, and having studied their works
diligently. He is now able to make the plots of his
plays seem perfectly simple, although, as a matter of
fact, they are often very elaborate; and the moral
which is explicit in Dumas, Ibsen has intensified by
keeping it implicit. His craftsmanship is so masterly

that the French are glad to claim it; Sarcey called the 'Doll's House' a French play,—except in the arbitrary departure of Nora in the final act.

This mastery of dramatic form is another quality of Ibsen's which the next generation of French playwrights will probably seek to acquire. Already has M. Paul Hervieu, in the 'Loi de l'homme,' and in other pieces, succeeded in attaining a certain plain simplicity, not unlike Ibsen's. Perhaps also the directness of one or two of M. Jules Lemaître's plays may be ascribed likewise to Ibsen's severe example. But it is hard for M. Lemaître to lay aside his irony; and irony—not the tragic irony of Sophocles, but the disintegrating comic irony of Renan—is fatal to the success of a dramatist. No audience is willing to be laughed at; it has not paid its money to serve as a butt. That Ibsen is somewhat deficient in humor is probably to his advantage. Certainly no taint of comic irony ever mars the force of his straightforward sincerity.

Perhaps the French do not find a complete satisfaction in the solutions that M. Hervieu and M. Lemaître propose for the problems they have propounded. But Ibsen has not always solved those he has presented, as Mr. Howells reminds us:—"It is not by the solution of problems that the moralist teaches, but by the question that his handling of them suggests to us respecting ourselves. Artistically he is bound, Ibsen as a dramatist is bound to give an esthetic completeness to his works, and I do not find that he ever fails to do this; to my thinking they have a high beauty and propriety; but ethically he is bound not to be final; for if he forces himself to be final in things that do not and can not end here, he becomes dishonest, he becomes a Nordau.

What he can and must do ethically is to make us take thought of ourselves, and look to it whether we have in us the making of this or that wrong; whether we are hypocrites, tyrants, pretenders, shams, conscious or unconscious; whether our most unselfish motives are not really secret shapes of egotism; whether our convictions are not mere brute acceptances; whether we believe what we profess; whether, when we force good to a logical end, we are not doing evil."

The most popular play of the final decade of the century presents no problem whatsoever and avoids any criticism of life. Apparently, its author has never heard of Ibsen, and never seen any play by the younger Dumas. He has not taken his stand on firm reality, but has preferred to build an airy fantasy, as unsubstantial as it is charming. His aim has not been to enlighten, but merely to entertain; and he has accomplished his purpose superabundantly. Since 'Hernani,' no play has been so enthusiastically acclaimed at its first performances as the 'Cyrano de Bergerac' of M. de Rostand, its humorously poetic hero being acted with incomparable variety by the most accomplished of contemporary comedians, M. Coquelin. This play, which pleased many thousands of spectators, not only in France, but also in Germany, in Italy, and in America, was joyfully hailed by certain Parisian critics as the harbinger of a new springtime for the French poetic drama. M. Rostand was welcomed as a reviver of the best traditions, and he was eulogized as one who — like Corneille with the 'Cid,' and like Hugo with 'Hernani' — had set a new model which later dramatists might vainly strive to surpass.

It may be bad manners to look Pegasus in the mouth

or to smile at the cooing murmurs of delight that run round the Porte Saint Martin at the exquisite delivery of a mellifluous couplet; and there is no disputing that 'Cyrano de Bergerac' is very clever and very adroit, that it has color and vivacity, that if it lacks passion, it has at least sentiment, that if it wants real action, it has abundant movement, and, above all, that it makes an extraordinarily wide appeal — to those who like love-making and romance, to those who relish easy wit and lively humor, and to those who revel in combats and in the peril of life and death. But it cannot fairly be called an epoch-making novelty. It is, instead, an old thing done in a new way. The plot is put together by a playwright who has absorbed every device of the elder Dumas, and the verse is written by a lyrist who has learned every trick of the Parnassians. It is, in short, an old-fashioned piece, — but with all the modern improvements.

An adverse critic might suggest that M. Rostand had used his story to display his verbal virtuosity. He has a very pretty lyric gift, — always a rare endowment among the French. He can touch wit with sentiment, and he can thrust a hint of pathos into an extravagant simile. He combines clearness and elegance, and his verse is both facile and finished. The quality of his poetry is almost exactly that of the *vers de société*, — the verse in lighter vein of Prior and Mr. Austin Dobson, of Locker and Dr. Holmes. M. Rostand is brilliant and buoyant as Praed is, for example; and Cyrano's description of a kiss may be compared curiously with the stanza in the 'Chaunt of the Brazen Head,' in which the lyrist liltingly tells us what he thinks of love.

'Cyrano de Bergerac,' for all its bravery of epithet and all its briskness of motion, is at bottom too slight a thing to serve as the corner-stone of a new school. It contains no promise of future development, nor do the author's other plays, less coruscating than 'Cyrano,' but possessing the same qualities. And even in 'Cyrano' itself, there is no character of real originality or of genuine verity; it is peopled only by the masks of the stage. The play itself lacks depth and breadth; it is without ultimate sincerity; it has as its basis an unworthy trick, and it holds up before us as a hero whom we are to honor with our approval and with whom we are expected to sympathize, a man engaged in deceiving a woman into a marriage certain to bring her misery so soon as she discovers, though too late, the dulness of the man she has wedded. M. de Rostand's play is clean externally, but it is essentially immoral, — in so far as it erects a false standard and parades a self-sacrifice which, to use Mr. Howells's apt phrase, is "a secret shape of egotism."

Whatever the real value of 'Cyrano de Bergerac,' it is not to be denied that it was the last play of the nineteenth century to achieve a triumph at once immediate and widespread. Yet there is no dispute about the fact that it stands frankly outside the line along which the French drama has been developing in the past fifty years. M. Rostand's piece is not "a picture of life, which is also a judgment"; and unless it is this, no play is likely long to satisfy the French. That is what we find in the 'Tartuffe' of Molière, in the 'Mariage de Figaro' of Beaumarchais, in the 'Demi-Monde' of Dumas *fils*, and the 'Gendre de M. Poirier' of Augier and Sandeau. It is what we find in the plays of M. Paul

Hervieu, on the one hand, and, on the other, in those of M. Henri Lavedan.

If we may guess at the future from our knowledge of the past, we must expect that the masterpiece of the French theatre in the twentieth century will be like those of the nineteenth century and of the eighteenth century and of the seventeenth. It will be a comedy almost on the verge of stiffening into the serious drama. It will deal gravely and resolutely with life, but it will also be charged with satire and relieved by wit. Perhaps it will not be robustly comic; — but is 'Tartuffe' really so very laughter-provoking? Its subject will be logically thought out and symmetrically presented, — for the dramatic anarchists of the Théâtre Libre are already routed and dispersed. Its craftsmanship will be sure; and it will have the prime merits of simplicity, of straightforwardness, and of sincerity.